AN INTRODUCTION TO POLICING AND POLICE POWERS

Cavendish
Publishing
Limited

London • Sydney

AN INTRODUCTION TO POLICING AND POLICE POWERS

Leonard Jason-Lloyd
Senior Lecturer in Law, Coventry University

Cavendish
Publishing
Limited

London • Sydney

First published in Great Britain 2000 by Cavendish Publishing Limited,
The Glass House, Wharton Street, London WC1X 9PX, United Kingdom
Telephone: +44 (0) 20 7278 8000   Facsimile: +44 (0) 20 7278 8080
E-mail: info@cavendishpublishing.com
Visit our Home Page on http://www.cavendishpublishing.com

British Library Cataloguing in Publication Data

Jason-Lloyd, Leonard
An introduction to policing and police powers
1 Police – Great Britain 2 Police power – Great Britain
I Title
345.4'1'052

ISBN 1 85941 554 7

Printed and bound in Great Britain

PREFACE

In recent years, general interest in the study of policing and the application of police powers has increased substantially. As far as academic activity is concerned, the study of police powers and certain aspects of the nature of policing have formed part of constitutional law courses for many years and, more recently, as a major component in the study of civil liberties. The most recent development has been their inclusion within criminal justice studies.

This book has been written with the newcomer in mind, including those with little or no legal knowledge who need to understand policing and police powers as part of wider study. It is not intended to provide an exhaustive treatise on this subject, since this service is provided for in other works which are cited in the appropriate footnotes and constitute recommended further reading on particular topics. This publication is therefore focused on the key issues affecting the exercise of police powers which are most likely to be of interest to students.

This book is designed for complete beginners as well as those with some knowledge of policing and police powers, in an endeavour to help bring them as close to degree level on the subject as they are able to reach. It is also intended that this book will be of use to practitioners, whether in the legal profession or otherwise, who need a quick, but comprehensive, grasp of some of the most important aspects of this subject. The principal aim of this work is to make this study as accessible as possible to a wide range of students and practitioners, and to act as a stepping stone to further in-depth study, particularly to higher degree level. A further aim is to provide an up to date textbook on the most widely used police powers, which has become necessary in view of extensive changes in the law since the mid-1990s.

In order to facilitate a better understanding of the subject and the way that it has evolved, the relevant statutory and other provisions have been reproduced at the appropriate stages where their wording is self-explanatory, as well as case law applicable to the points in question. However, it is not intended to submerge the reader in too many cases, but rather to cite the most important and relevant case law applicable to the key areas of the subject. Charts and diagrams have also been included in order to facilitate better understanding of the more complex issues arising from this study.

My thanks go to Jo Reddy, Managing Editor at Cavendish Publishing, for her help and support, and to Steve Foster at Coventry University for his appraisal of the initial draft of the final chapter of this book. Special thanks are extended to my wife, Usha, for her unfailing patience and support which is always prominently displayed whenever I embark upon any major project. I have endeavoured to state the law as at 31 March 2000, although several recent legal developments have been added at the proof-reading stage.

Crown copyright is reproduced with the permission of the Controller of Her Majesty's Stationery Office.

Leonard Jason-Lloyd
August 2000

CONTENTS

Contents

TABLE OF CASES

TABLE OF STATUTES

TABLE OF STATUTORY INSTRUMENTS

TABLE OF CONVENTIONS

INTRODUCTION

One of the main reasons why so much interest has been generated in the study of police powers in modern times is that increasing numbers of the wider populace are beginning to question the exercise of such authority. Indeed, some go further and actually challenge the legitimacy of such powers and the way they are exercised. This was done in a particularly violent manner during the 1980s, when it became evident, through a spate of serious disorder in this country, that certain sections of the public were seriously questioning the manner and form in which some police powers were being employed. However, concerns regarding policing in general have not, by any means, been confined to public protest alone. For instance, in 1978, the Royal Commission on Criminal Procedure[1] was convened to examine the exercise of police powers, with particular reference to the investigation of crime and the rights of suspects. This body consisted of 15 members, which included its chairman, Sir Cyril Philips, and also a judge, two police officers, a Queen's Counsel, a stipendiary magistrate, a defence lawyer and several lay magistrates, as well as other laypersons.[2] Three years later, the Commission published its findings, which not only concerned the subject of police powers, but also addressed the issue of an independent system for conducting criminal prosecutions. In short, the former resulted in the passing of the Police and Criminal Evidence Act 1984 and the latter resulted in the Prosecution of Offences Act 1985 being enacted, which, *inter alia*, led to the institution of the Crown Prosecution Service.

Largely in response to concerns regarding a spate of miscarriage of justice cases in previous years, another Royal Commission was instituted. In 1991, under the leadership of Lord Runciman, the Royal Commission on Criminal Justice[3] began to examine this issue, as well addressing wider concerns regarding the effectiveness of the criminal justice system in convicting the guilty and acquitting the innocent. Its findings were reported two years later and a number of the Commission's recommendations were later enacted in the Criminal Justice and Public Order Act 1994 and the Criminal Procedure and Investigations Act 1996. But these are certainly not the only statutes which have more recently affected police powers. For example, in 1996, two further Acts were passed which significantly affected the police service. The first was the Prevention of Terrorism (Additional Powers) Act 1996 (see Chapters 2 and 4) and the second was the Offensive Weapons Act 1996 (see Chapter 4). In 1997, the Knives Act was passed, and this was followed later in the same year by the passing of the Confiscation of Alcohol (Young Persons) Act 1997 (see Chapter 5). The powers available to the police have been further augmented by a number of provisions under the Crime and Disorder Act 1998 (see

---

1 Otherwise known as the Philips Royal Commission.
2 Zander, M, *The Police and Criminal Evidence Act 1984*, 3rd edn, 1995, London: Sweet & Maxwell.
3 Cm 2263, 1993, London: HMSO.

Chapter 3) and all this is indicative of the rate at which police powers have been increased in recent years. It is partly because of this flood of recent enactments, together with a build up of relevant case law, that the publication of this book has been necessitated.

It should be mentioned that, whilst the relevant Royal Commissions have endeavoured to address wider and longer term concerns regarding policing in this country, specific incidents have also been the subject of judicial inquiries into the police, such as that conducted by Lord Scarman in the early 1980s in respect of the Brixton disorders. In addition, other inquiries and investigations have been commissioned, arising from concerns stemming from a number of other issues. For example, an investigation by the Avon and Somerset Police during the mid-1980s into the conduct of the Greater Manchester Police during a demonstration outside Manchester University Students' Union. Also, in 1979, Sir Patrick McNee, who was then Commissioner of the Metropolitan Police, commissioned a study of his force by the Policy Studies Institute, with particular reference to community relations.[4] Whilst many of these inquiries and investigations have impacted mainly on internal rules governing police conduct, some have motivated law reform to a certain extent. The most recent example is the Macpherson Report, published in 1999, regarding the murder of Stephen Lawrence which, *inter alia*, has led to the Law Commission proposing reform of the double jeopardy rule, which could enable criminal cases to be re-tried as a result of significant new evidence becoming available.

The most significant law reform, as far as substantive police powers are concerned, was the Police and Criminal Evidence Act 1984, which accounts for the bulk of this book. As mentioned above, this was primarily the result of recommendations made by the Royal Commission on Criminal Procedure, necessitated by ongoing concerns regarding certain police powers and the way they were exercised. Much of this criticism ultimately stemmed from the lack of codification of such powers and the generally outdated mode in which they existed:

> Before 1 January 1986, when the Police and Criminal Evidence Act 1984 came into effect, the law governing police powers for the investigation of crime was unclear and antiquated. It had developed piecemeal since the establishment of professional police forces in the 19th century. Parliament had added fitfully to the few common law principles, but there was no clear statement of police powers. This varied and scant law was supplemented by:
>
> (a) rules of guidance as to the admissibility of confessions provided by the Lord Chief Justice (the Judges' Rules);
>
> (b) national administrative guidance in the form of Home Office Circulars (notably that attached to the Judges' Rules); and
>
> (c) local administrative guidance, in the shape of standing orders issued within each police force.

---

4   Emsley, C, *The English Police: A Political and Social History*, 2nd edn, 1996, London: Longman.

The result was patchy legal obligations and powers for the police and local variations in powers (for example, some police forces had wide stop and search powers, whereas others were tied to a few narrow national powers). New and heavier pressures on the police and more critical public opinion demanded that the powers of the police be placed on a modern statutory footing.[5]

On analysis, perhaps a fundamental cause of this state of affairs was that the modern police service at that time was based, to a significant extent, on certain laws, practices and procedures that were often rooted in the Victorian origins of this law enforcement body. During a debate on this issue during the 1980s, one media commentator referred to the police service as 'The Bow Street Runners with cars and radios', which possibly encapsulates this argument in those few words.

How did the modern police service develop? What is the current structure of the police service in modern times? What is the general legal and constitutional status of a police officer? These questions will be addressed in the following chapter.

---

5   Lidstone, K and Palmer, C, *Bevan and Lidstone's The Investigation of Crime: A Guide to Police Powers*, 2nd edn, 1996, London: Butterworths.

CHAPTER 1

THE DEVELOPMENT AND FOUNDATIONS OF MODERN POLICING

INTRODUCTION

I ... of ... do solemnly and sincerely declare and affirm that I will well and truly serve our Sovereign Lady the Queen in the office of constable, without favour or affection, malice or ill will; and that I will, to the best of my power, cause the peace to be kept and preserved, and prevent all offences against the persons and properties of Her Majesty's subjects and that while I continue to hold the said office, I will, to the best of my skill and knowledge, discharge all the duties thereof faithfully according to law.

The above constitutes the solemn declaration or oath taken by all those newly appointed to the office of constable within England and Wales, in accordance with the wording under Sched 4 to the Police Act 1996. This is declared during a ceremony known as the 'attestation', which takes place before a justice of the peace.[1] On analysis, this oath provides an interesting indication as to the constitutional status of a police officer in modern times and, in essence, describes the manner in which police powers should be exercised.

Compared to many policing systems abroad, the system in England and Wales has a number of similarities and distinctions. Perhaps two of the greatest distinctions are based upon the main principle of policing in this country and the basic structure of our police service. With regard to the former, policing in this country is still fundamentally based upon the principle or concept of 'policing by consent'. This means that the police service functions in society with the consent of the majority. This has great advantages compared to many foreign policing systems, which do not enjoy this concept to the extent that it is still evident here. Among other things, this ensures a greater level of public co-operation with the police and has also enabled our police to avoid being fully and permanently equipped with firearms throughout the 20th century and, so far, into the present millennium. Although, in recent years, they have been equipped with a greater range of protective weaponry, such as extendable batons and CS gas spray, these are not intended to be lethal in their effects if used correctly and, so far, we have avoided a permanent para-military police force in this country.

---

1   Newly appointed constables in the Metropolitan Police have taken the attestation before either the Commissioner or an Assistant Commissioner who, technically at least, are also justices of the peace. This practice will discontinue as a result of the Greater London Authority Act 1999, Sched 27, para 83, which provides that all constables in England and Wales will be attested before magistrates. It is this statute which contains the measures under which the new Metropolitan Police Authority has been instituted.

A further distinction between foreign policing and our own domestic system is that this function in England and Wales is currently divided between 43 individual police forces, whereas policing abroad, including Europe, is often under more centralised control. In other words, we do not have a national police service, but a network of individual police forces, responsible for policing specified counties, areas or cities. During times of emergency, these forces may be co-ordinated through a centralised mutual aid procedure, but such occasions are infrequent, one of the most well known in recent times being the miners' dispute during the winter of 1984–85, where police officers from many parts of the country were sent to key mining areas to reinforce the local police presence there.

A BRIEF HISTORICAL OVERVIEW

The general concept of policing in this country is certainly not new; in fact, various forms of law enforcement which were in the nature of policing existed since early Saxon times. Even the term 'constable' originated as far back as the Norman era.

Constables were also evident during the reign of the Tudors and Stuarts but, following a period of apparent decline in the role of such constables, growing concerns during the Georgian period regarding increasing crime and disorder led, ultimately, to the formation of the famous Bow Street Runners. A fragmented system of policing gradually evolved in other parts of London but, in 1785, the London and Westminster Police Bill was introduced, designed to form a co-ordinated policing system for the capital. This was defeated due to fierce opposition and poor management of the Bill in its passage through Parliament, although a more limited version was successfully passed seven years later.[2] However, crime and fears of public disorder continued to rise and, eventually, Sir Robert Peel introduced his famous Bill, which was enacted on 19 June 1829 as the Metropolitan Police Act and, subsequently, the Metropolitan Police was born. The preamble to this landmark statute reads as follows:

> Whereas offences against property have, of late, increased in and near the Metropolis, and the local establishments of nightly police have been found inadequate to the prevention and detection of crime, by reason of the frequent unfitness of the individuals employed, the insufficiency of their number, the limited sphere of their authority and their want of connection and co-operation with each other. And, whereas it is expedient to substitute a new and more efficient system of police in lieu of such establishments of nightly watch and nightly police, within the limits hereinafter mentioned, and to constitute an

---

2   Emsley, C, *The English Police: A Political and Social History*, 2nd edn, 1996, London: Longman.

office of police which, acting under the immediate authority of one of His Majesty's Principal Secretaries of State, shall direct and control the whole of such new system of police within those limits. Be it therefore enacted, etc ...

This signalled the formation of the first modern style professional policing system in this country and, by 1856, all of England and Wales was covered by a network of police forces. It remains a popular belief that the main driving force behind the 1829 Act was the appalling crime rate, particularly in London. Although this was undoubtedly a major factor, there was also another issue which was equal in importance, namely the increase in the level of public disorder that had escalated in the 18th and early 19th centuries:

> The prevention of crime was stressed as the first duty of the new Metropolitan Police constables and the whole system of beat patrols ... was ostensibly designed with this in mind. But the uniform, the discipline and the organisation of the new force suggest that Peel had imported into London many of the policing practices developed in Ireland to deal with civil disorder.[3]

Whilst the military were used to quell rioting in London and other big cities, there were serious tactical and political disadvantages in using armed troops for this purpose. First, long delays were often experienced in transporting troops from their barracks to the scene of public disorder; subsequently, the situation was well out of hand by the time they arrived. Secondly, the only forms of weaponry available to them were potentially lethal, namely bullets or bayonets, the use of which often had drastic consequences in terms of fatal or serious injuries. In contrast, the new police were frequently able to resolve both problems by mainly using wooden truncheons to control riots and, by being deployed throughout London on regular 24 hour patrols, were able to disperse many unruly gatherings before they escalated into full scale disorder.

Although, in their early days, the new police were often regarded with disdain and suspicion by both general populace and even some in authority, they quickly gained the respect still found amongst the majority of the public today. Although some assert that this effect is waning, the policing system in this country is still characterised by the concept of policing by consent, which remains the envy of policing systems in many other parts of the world.

THE STRUCTURE OF POLICING IN ENGLAND AND WALES

As mentioned above, there are currently 43 police forces in England and Wales. This excludes those with special jurisdiction, such as the British Transport Police and the Ministry of Defence Police, who operate in various parts of the country. The 43 police areas include the two forces in London,

---

3   *Op cit*, Emsley, fn 2.

namely the Metropolitan Police and the City of London Police. These two London forces warrant separate coverage as distinct from those outside the capital, and these will be discussed below. At this stage, it should be noted that the chief officers of police for both the London forces are commissioners rather than chief constables, who head police forces outside the capital.

Since 1964, the Home Secretary has had the power to amalgamate police forces and this power now exists under s 32 of the Police Act 1996, where such a move can be made on grounds of efficiency and effectiveness. Prior to enacting the 1996 Act, the Conservative Government announced plans to implement such action, although, to date, this has not occurred. Although the fragmentation of police forces throughout this country lends itself to the notion that policing in England and Wales is not under centralised control, recent developments in the structure of our police service indicates a movement towards this end, which will now be discussed.

In 1962, the Report of the Royal Commission on the Police[4] rejected the concept of a national police force under direct central government control and, in response to its report, the Police Act 1964 was passed, which enshrined the principle legal rules governing the organisation of the police service up until the mid-1990s. An important consequence of this legislation is that policing in this country is governed by three points of power, namely: the Home Secretary, who represents central government and is responsible for the overall supervision of the police service, as well as being answerable to Parliament regarding the service's function; local police authorities, responsible for the overall maintenance of police forces within their jurisdiction and ensuring local accountability; and chief officers of police, responsible primarily for making operational decisions, as well as the routine management of their forces.

The police authorities

The balance of power regarding policing in England and Wales was changed controversially through Pt I of the Police and Magistrates' Courts Act 1994, which was later consolidated into the Police Act 1996, and these provisions, among other things, generally endeavour to make the police service function under a more 'business management' regime.[5] They have also created new style police authorities, in contrast to those which existed earlier. Previously, police authorities outside London consisted of two-thirds local councillors and one-third local magistrates. These bodies varied considerably in size – at the extreme ends, from between six to over 40 members in total, although the

---

4 Cmnd 1728, 1962, London: HMSO
5 Molan, M, *Constitutional Law: The Machinery of Government*, 1997, London: Old Bailey.

proportion of magistrates and councillors was always the same. The Government White Paper, entitled *Police Reform – A Police Service for the 21st Century,* contained, *inter alia,* proposals that police authorities should be set to a prescribed number of 16 members. This was not itself a controversial measure, since some authorities were regarded as too small, whereas, in contrast, others had become too large and unwieldy. The main controversy was that these bodies should consist of eight local councillors, three magistrates and five persons appointed by the Home Secretary, who would also appoint the chairperson, who, in turn, would have the casting vote where necessary. These proposals were severely criticised, both within and outside Parliament, on the grounds that this would have given central government a significant increase in power over local police forces.[6] In the end, the Government modified its original proposals, which included allowing each police authority to elect its own chairperson and increasing the size of each authority to 17 members, of which nine are local councillors, three are local magistrates and five are independent members appointed from a shortlist compiled by the Home Secretary.

There is provision under the Police Act 1996 for the Home Secretary to increase the size of police authorities where appropriate, but the outcome must result in such bodies reaching odd numbers and the composite of councillors, magistrates and independent members approved by the Home Secretary remaining unchanged. Other aspects of these reforms included the transformation of police authorities into corporate bodies which, in turn, must have regard to any objectives determined by the Home Secretary, as well as to formulate annual local policing plans and comply with these accordingly in order to meet performance targets. Also, they must publish an annual report, which includes the extent to which the local policing plan has been complied with, as well as submit reports on relevant police matters to the Home Secretary as required by him.

Many functions of the police authorities remain as they did prior to the Police Act 1996, which include the overall duty to secure the maintenance of an effective and efficient police force by, among other things, acting as its paymaster in terms of local expenditure and controlling the police budget. Police authorities also appoint chief constables and assistant chief constables (the latter in consultation with the chief constable), and may require any of them to retire, although these decisions can be vetoed by the Home Secretary, who can also require a police authority to retire a chief constable on his own initiative. The power of the Home Secretary's veto was last used in 1990 in a dispute with the police authority over the appointment of the chief constable for Derbyshire. Police authorities may also employ civilian staff to assist the

---

6   See Jason-Lloyd, L, 'Who should have power to police the police?' (1993) *The Times,* 24 August; and, also, 'Changes in the police service' (1994) LXVII(2) Police Journal 105, April–June.

police force maintained by it and to enable the authority to discharge its functions, although such employees are under the direction and control of the chief constable.

Further moves towards centralised control?

The Police Act 1997 (not to be confused with the Police Act 1996) contains a number of provisions which have implications for the police service as well as the exercise of certain powers regarding surveillance (see Chapter 4). As far as the structure of the police service is concerned, Pt I of the 1997 Act has placed the National Criminal Intelligence Service (NCIS) on a statutory footing. This organisation is staffed by police and HM Customs and Excise officers, as well as persons from the security services and has, since 1992, been involved with collating and analysing information and other intelligence in respect of matters such as international drug trafficking and money laundering, as well as other specialist crimes, including kidnap, extortion and counterfeit currency. Part II of the Act makes provision for the formation of a National Crime Squad, designed to deal with serious crime. Both these bodies, under the 1997 Act, will have implications in more than one police area.

Under ss 23 and 24 of the Police Act 1996, chief constables have the power to collaborate with other police forces or provide mutual aid where additional officers or other assistance may be provided. The collaboration under s 23 includes sharing resources such as premises, training facilities, technical support and specialised services. An example of the latter includes the use of police helicopters. With regard to s 24, as mentioned above in the introduction to this chapter, the last time mutual aid was used on any mass scale was during the winter of 1984–85, during the series of strikes by the coal mining industry. As a consequence, police officers from many parts of England and Wales were sent to areas where large scale picketing was taking place. Some observers reported that seeing so many different police forces represented in one place gave the impression of a national police force, although this venture only lasted for the duration of one winter. Parallel provisions also exist under s 98 of the Police Act 1996 (previously enacted under s 141 of the Criminal Justice and Public Order Act 1994), whereby chief officers of police may request assistance from any UK police force, which includes providing additional constables. There is also provision for the Home Secretary to act on his own volition, presumably in times of emergency, where he may direct a police force within another part of the UK to provide such assistance. In other words, police officers from Northern Ireland can be called upon to reinforce the police in any part of England, Wales or Scotland, or police in Scotland can be asked to provide mutual aid to any police force in England and Wales or to Northern Ireland, and the police in England and Wales can be called upon to provide assistance to the police in Northern Ireland or to any force in Scotland. One hopes that such an interchange may never be necessary, in view of the prospective turmoil that would necessitate such action.

Mention should also be made regarding the Association of Chief Police Officers (ACPO), which is the representative body of all police chiefs and has existed since 1948. This organisation constitutes a powerful pressure group, capable of influencing central government to a significant extent on a variety of matters affecting policing in this country. It is this body which facilitates co-operation between police forces where necessary.

Policing in London

It should be noted that the police authority in respect of the City of London Police is the Common Council of the City of London, although separate and quite unique arrangements have existed regarding the Metropolitan Police. At the time of writing, transitional arrangements are in place through which a Metropolitan Police Authority has been instituted for the first time. For many years, the issue of accountability of the Metropolitan Police has been severely criticised by a number of commentators. Up until recently, the Home Secretary constituted the police authority for the Metropolis, which has the largest police force in the UK (approximately 26,400 police officers and 11,250 civilian support staff). Although there was provision originally under s 106 of the Police and Criminal Evidence Act 1984 and, more recently, under s 96 of the Police Act 1996 for consultations between the police and local consultative groups, there has never been an actual police authority for the Metropolis of London compared to those that exist in other parts of England and Wales. Therefore, under s 106 of the 1984 Act and then s 96 of the 1996 Act, special provision was made whereby the Home Secretary shall issue guidance to the Metropolitan Police Commissioner in respect of obtaining the views of the community on policing the capital.

Sections 310 to 325 of the Greater London Authority Act 1999 now institutes a police authority for the Metropolis of London. However, in April 1995, a body was formed called the Metropolitan Police *Committee*. This originally consisted of 12 members appointed by the Home Secretary to advise and assist the Metropolitan Police Commissioner in maintaining an efficient and effective police service, and this body was used to prepare for the institution of the Metropolitan Police *Authority* in July 2000. The committee compiled regular annual reports and was under the chairmanship of Sir John Quinton.

The institution of the Metropolitan Police Authority is inextricably linked with the formation of the Greater London Authority, since the new police authority consists of 23 members, 12 of which are selected by the Mayor of London and are members of the Greater London Assembly, including the Deputy Mayor. The Metropolitan Police Authority may select its own chairperson from among its own members and this does not discount the Deputy Mayor of London. Other members of the new police authority include seven independent persons and four magistrates. The independent faction includes one person appointed directly by the Home Secretary, who is Sir John Quinton, former chairman of the Metropolitan Police Committee mentioned above. The four magistrates on the new police authority have been appointed by the Greater London Magistrates' Courts Association.

In effect, the powers and duties of the new police authority are almost identical to those which function outside the Metropolitan Police area. These include publishing annual reports, consultations with local communities and setting objectives.

The introduction of the Metropolitan Police Authority has automatically resulted in abolishing the post of the Receiver, whose functions will, to a large extent, be performed by the new police authority, especially matters regarding finance, responsibility for which will move to the Treasurer. The new body will also play a role in recommending to the Home Secretary the appointment of future commissioners, their deputies, assistant commissioners and commanders. However, whilst a similar selection procedure may be used to appoint the Commissioner, as in the police authorities outside London regarding their chief constables, this will be modified to take into account the need to protect the national interest and the international obligations of the Metropolitan Police Service, and not just its local remit. This is a particularly sensitive issue, which has constituted one of the primary objections in the past to having a police authority for the Metropolis (see the coverage of the role of the Home Secretary below). The Metropolitan Police Authority will be expected to account for its actions when summoned before the Greater London Assembly in much the same way as do representatives of police authorities outside London when under scrutiny by their respective local authorities.

THE CONSTITUTIONAL AND GENERAL LEGAL STATUS OF THE POLICE

Historically, many constitutional lawyers have expressed varying opinions regarding the legal status of police officers. Notwithstanding the recent reforms of the police service mentioned above, there is common agreement that police officers are not servants of central government, but are officers of the Crown or of the State. Interestingly, whilst the police service is part of the executive aspect of our constitutional framework, it also has a significant measure of independence from it. As mentioned in other parts of this chapter, chief officers of police are not subject to direct orders from any person or body in relation to operational matters although, ultimately, they are answerable to their police authorities and the Home Secretary for their actions.

The general legal status of the police, which is of prime interest to certain sections of the populace, is their liability for wrongful acts in the course of their duty. In view of the wide duties and responsibilities incumbent upon the average police officer, inevitably, things will go wrong from time to time. There is, of course, the complaints procedure in dealing with grievances against police actions (see Chapter 8) and, also, the police are not immune from criminal prosecutions in extreme circumstances, but to what extent are individual police officers liable for civil wrongs (torts) such as negligence, trespass and false imprisonment? Under the common law, a police officer was personally liable for his or her wrongful or unlawful acts although, prior to the Police Act 1996, it was left to police authorities as to whether they were prepared to pay an officer's damages and legal costs. Under s 88 of the 1996 Act, chief constables are now vicariously liable for torts committed by their police officers in the course of their duties. Costs and damages incurred as a result or claims settled out of court are paid from the local police budget, provided the police authority gives its approval in the case of the latter. Whether the chief constable has been sued or not, the police authority may pay damages or costs awarded against a police officer within that force.

It is important to mention that police officers are not essentially employees, but holders of a public office determined principally by statute. They can be dismissed only under regulations which deal with breaches of discipline, such as misuse of authority, neglect of duty, racist behaviour, insubordination and other transgressions which bring the police service into disrepute (see, also, Chapter 8). But police officers are certainly not subject to unlimited privileges and immunities, as illustrated in the following commentary:

> Indeed, legislation restricts the freedom of a police officer in a way in which no employer could by a contract of employment. Thus, police officers are not allowed to be members of a trade union or of any association which seeks to control or influence the pay or conditions of service of any police force; instead, there are Police Federations for England and Wales and for Scotland, which represent police officers in all matters of welfare and efficiency, other than questions of promotion affecting individuals, and with limited powers in relation to discipline. Police regulations impose a great many restrictions upon the private life of serving police officers, including one of constitutional importance, namely that a police officer 'shall, at all times, abstain from any activity which is likely to interfere with the impartial discharge of his duties or which is likely to give rise to the impression amongst members of the public that it may so interfere; and, in particular, [he] shall not take any active part in politics'.[7]

---

7   Bradley, A and Ewing, K, *Constitutional and Administrative Law*, 12th edn, 1997, London: Longman.

Other obligations are incumbent upon police officers apart from the above duties. These include restrictions on where they may live and being obliged to report for duty with little or no prior notice under urgent circumstances. An off duty police officer may even be expected to place him or herself on duty immediately, in the event of being confronted with a particularly serious situation which may demand instant police intervention. In essence, a police officer is always on duty, hence the requirement that they carry their warrant cards at all times. This brings us to the well worn definition of a police officer who is described as a citizen in uniform *and/or the holder of a warrant card*, who has been given additional powers in the execution of his or her duty (the words in italics are mine and apply to non-uniformed officers). Is this now an accurate definition, in view of the substantial increases in police powers since it was first formulated? Can the average police officer be regarded as an ordinary citizen, even when off duty, in view of the observations made above?

Chief constables

With the exception of the two London forces, which were discussed above, chief officers of police in the remaining 41 police areas in England and Wales are known as chief constables. The unique constitutional status of chief constables has been described as follows:

> A chief constable is nobody's servant, but an independent officer, upon whom powers and duties are directly conferred by law for the benefit of the populace. His constitutional status remains anomalous and puzzling, even after the re-organisation of the police system implemented by the Police Act 1964. It is still not clear whether anyone is entitled to give him instructions as to the performance of any of his duties, or to what extent the Home Secretary is answerable for decisions taken by chief constables outside the Metropolis.[8]

The Police Act 1996 re-asserts that chief constables are responsible for the direction and control of their respective police forces. However, when making operational and other decisions, he or she must have regard to the local policing plan mentioned above. In *R v Commissioner of Police for the Metropolis ex p Blackburn* (1968), at p 135, Lord Denning MR gave the following guidance regarding the legal status of chief officers of police:

> The office of Commissioner of Police within the Metropolis dates back to 1829, when Sir Robert Peel introduced his disciplined force. The commissioner was a justice of the peace specially appointed to administer the police force in the Metropolis. His constitutional status has never been defined either by statute or by the courts. It was considered by the Royal Commission on the Police in their report (Cmnd 1728). I have no hesitation, however, in holding that, like every constable in the land, he should be, and is, independent of the executive.

---

8   De Smith, S and Brazier, R, *Constitutional and Administrative Law*, 7th edn, 1994, London: Penguin.

He is not subject to the orders of the Secretary of State, save that, under the Police Act 1964, the Secretary of State can call on him to give a report, or to retire in the interests of efficiency. I hold it to be the duty of the Commissioner of Police, as it is of every chief constable, to enforce the law of the land. He must take steps so to post his men that crimes may be detected and that honest citizens may go about their affairs in peace. He must decide whether or not suspected persons are to be prosecuted and, if need be, bring the prosecution or see that it is brought but, in all these things, he is not the servant of anyone, save of the law itself. No Minister of the Crown can tell him that he must or must not keep observation on this place or that; or that he must or must not prosecute this man or that one. Nor can any police authority tell him so. The responsibility for law enforcement lies on him. He is answerable to the law and to the law alone. That appears sufficiently from *Fisher v Oldham Corporation* (1930) and the Privy Council case of *Attorney General for New South Wales v Perpetual Trustee Co Ltd* (1955).

Chief constables have the responsibility for appointing, promoting and, where necessary, disciplining (including dismissing) all officers below the rank of assistant chief constable. The appointment of special constables and police cadets also falls within the responsibility of chief constables under the 1996 Act, which also requires that they submit annual reports to the Home Secretary and their police authority, as well as any additional reports as requested by either, including the submission of criminal statistics to the Home Secretary. Although there are now fairly exhaustive mechanisms in place regarding the accountability of chief constables, the fact remains that no one can give such a person direct orders, especially in terms of operational matters. Even the judiciary have shown great reluctance in interfering with the decisions of police chiefs, particularly with regard to the deployment of manpower and resources,[9] although the judges have warned that the exercise of police discretion is reviewable in the courts.[10] This was recently demonstrated in *R v Commissioner of Police for the Metropolis ex p Free Tibet Campaign and Others* (2000), where it was held that the Metropolitan Police had acted unlawfully by, *inter alia*, removing banners and using vans to block peaceful protestors from the view of the visiting Chinese President during an official visit to London.

The Home Secretary and the police

As mentioned above, p 7, a new Metropolitan Police Authority was instituted in July 2000 under the Greater London Authority Act 1999. Until this time, the

---

9   See *Harris v Sheffield United Football Club Ltd* (1987), where Neill LJ stated: 'I see the force of the argument that the court must be very slow before it interferes in any way with a decision of a chief constable about the disposition of his forces.' See, also, *R v Chief Constable of Sussex ex p International Trader's Ferry Ltd* (1997).

10 See *R v Commissioner of Police for the Metropolis ex p Blackburn (No 1)* (1968) and *R v Commissioner of Police for the Metropolis ex p Blackburn (No 3)* (1973).

Home Secretary retained his role as the police authority for the Metropolis of London, assisted by the transitional Metropolitan Police Committee. Even though the new authority has commenced its duties, the Home Secretary is still in a position to exert some influence regarding the policing of the capital. This includes having the ultimate say regarding the appointment of new commissioners. It was noted on p 7, above, that the Metropolitan Police Authority is, in essence, very similar to the police authorities elsewhere in England and Wales. There is one important exception to this statement and this relates to the fact that the Metropolitan Police Service plays an important role in matters which go beyond just policing the capital. As mentioned earlier, the Metropolitan Police perform national as well as international functions, which are of a very sensitive nature, both politically and otherwise. This has constituted a powerful argument in the past against it having its own police authority. In order to ensure the effective performance of its national and international policing functions, para 104 of Sched 27 to the Greater London Authority Act 1999 provides that, if the Home Secretary is not satisfied with the standard of performance of the Metropolitan Police in its national and international functions, then he may direct the Metropolitan Police Authority to take such measures as may be specified in that direction. The definition of such functions under these provisions includes the personal protection of VIPs, as well as their property, national security, counter-terrorism or 'the provision of services for any other national or international purpose'.

Notwithstanding the overall effects of these changes, the Home Secretary will still be the most singularly prominent figure in respect of the policing of this country. Under the Police Act 1996, which has preserved many of the powers held by him under the Police Act 1964, the Home Secretary, under s 37, may determine policing objectives in all areas, having made prior consultations with the relevant police authorities and their police chiefs. This may also include him requiring police authorities, under s 38, to set performance targets in order to achieve this end. Under s 42 of the 1996 Act, the Home Secretary may require a police authority to dismiss a chief constable (or an assistant chief constable) following an inquiry if necessary and, if representations are made by that officer, a hearing must be convened (see *Ridge v Baldwin* (1964), where the principle of the right to a fair hearing was extended to a former chief constable, who had been dismissed from his post by a borough police authority, and that committee had not initially given him the opportunity to present his case in defence). The right to make representations where a police authority dismisses a chief constable is provided for under s 11 of the 1996 Act. Other provisions under the 1996 Act include the Home Secretary's power to order inquiries into specific incidents (the Scarman Report on the Brixton riots, for example), the appointment of inspectors of constabulary in order to assess the efficiency of individual forces, the making of regulations regarding the administration of the police service as a whole, including matters affecting national pay and conditions, as well as issuing Home Office circulars for the guidance of the police service.

In *R v Secretary of State for the Home Department ex p Northumbria Police Authority* (1988), police authorities in several areas, including Northumbria, sought to challenge the Home Secretary's actions regarding the issue of certain riot control equipment. Following the inner city riots in 1981, it had been apparent that the police could no longer effectively control serious disturbances using their existing standard equipment, which was largely confined to truncheons and long shields, especially when dealing with rioters throwing missiles, including fire bombs. This was acknowledged in the Scarman Report, and it was recommended that the police should be issued with stand-off weaponry, such as CS gas and plastic bullets. The police authorities mentioned above objected to such devices being issued to their police officers and refused to authorise their purchase. The Home Secretary then issued a circular to all chief constables, advising them of the availability of such equipment on permanent loan, in the event of their police authorities refusing to authorise the purchase of CS gas and plastic bullets. The Court of Appeal held that the Home Secretary had acted lawfully on two grounds. First, under ss 4 and 5 of the Police Act 1964, powers to effect the supply of equipment to the police were vested in chief constables and police authorities. However, under s 41, the Home Secretary also had powers to supply central or common services to the police service as a whole. It was held that the Home Secretary had lawfully exercised this power, as riot control equipment fell within this definition. Secondly, it was held that, in acting in this manner, the Home Secretary had correctly exercised the prerogative power to keep the Queen's peace, which was unaffected by the 1964 Act.

The Inspectorate of Constabulary

With regard to all police forces in England and Wales, many decisions of any Home Secretary and, indeed, chief police officers, are likely to be influenced by the findings of the Inspectorate of Constabulary, a body first instituted in 1856, which inspects the efficiency and effectiveness of all police forces. The inspectorate currently consists of five inspectors of constabulary[11] who are former chief police officers, headed by a chief inspector of constabulary, who, among other things, are together responsible for laying an annual report on the Inspectorate's work before Parliament. Her Majesty's inspectors of constabulary are appointed by the Queen, on the recommendation of the Home Secretary, and are empowered to inspect all police forces in England

---

11 One inspector of constabulary is expected to retire fairly soon and it has not yet been decided as to whether a direct replacement will be sought.

and Wales, including the Metropolitan Police which, up until fairly recently, were exempt from their scrutiny.

General operational policing in England and Wales

All recruits to the police service are initially attested as constables (including part time voluntary police officers in the special constabulary, who are discussed below). This is the rank in which all police men and women must begin, regardless of educational attainment or other qualities which may result in promotion during their service. This constitutes one of the many features of the police service in England and Wales, distinct from the armed forces, where there is an officer class to which suitable new entrants may immediately enter. As a consequence, all senior officers within the police service, including those who head such forces, have progressed through all the ranks, starting with the rank of constable. The first Metropolitan Police Commissioner to have risen through all the ranks was Sir Joseph Simpson, who took office as Commissioner in 1958. This is now the normal route for all police chiefs throughout England and Wales. However, there is an accelerated promotion scheme for suitable new recruits or those who demonstrate exceptional abilities soon after joining. This, among other things, involves attendance at the Police Staff College, where recruits are taught advanced management practices, as well as learning senior command skills.

All new recruits, even the most promising, have to satisfactorily complete their initial two year probationary period as constables, which provides all police officers with an essential introduction to police duties. (see Figure 1, which depicts the overall rank structure within the police service in England and Wales). Certain aspects of the police rank structure were reformed around the early 1990s as a result of the Sheehy Report,[12] which endeavoured, *inter alia*, to streamline the management of the police service by removing some of the more senior ranks. In the end, the ranks of chief superintendent and deputy chief constable were removed, although some existing holders of those ranks were allowed to keep them. Eventually, it was intended that these posts would cease to exist, as well as deputy assistant commissioners in London. However, these substantive ranks are due to be restored in the not too distant future and, already, some officers are wearing the insignias of the hereto abolished senior ranks, hence their inclusion in Figure 1.

The general requirements for entry into the police service are contingent upon good health, character, education and appearance, and also upon British nationality. There are varying requirements between forces regarding upper and lower age limits; at one time, minimum height requirements were quite

12 Sheehy Commission, *Inquiry into Police Responsibilities and Rewards*, Cm 2280, 1993, London: HMSO.

Figure 1: the police rank structure

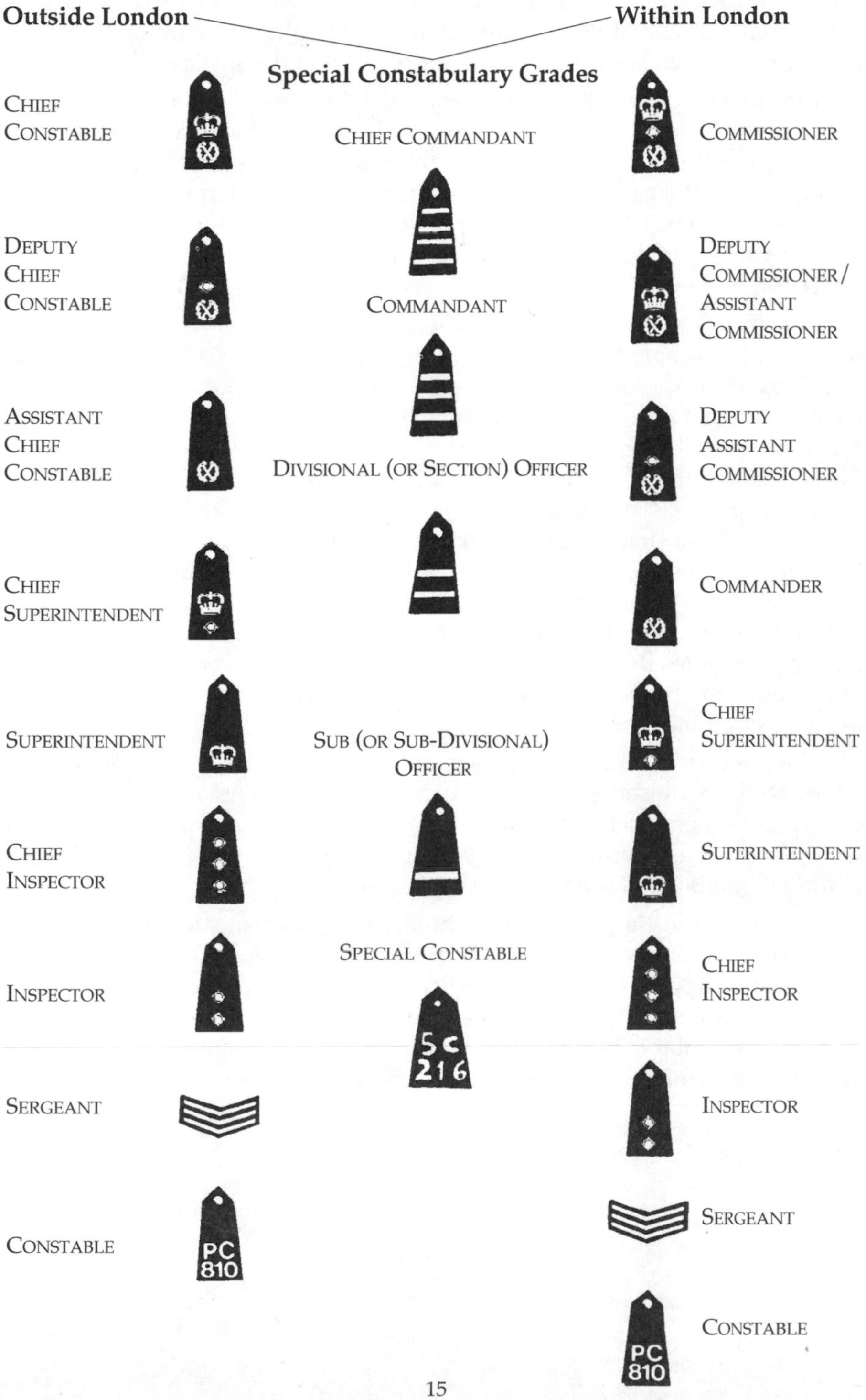

Outside London ⟍　　　　　　　　　⟋ **Within London**

Special Constabulary Grades

Outside London		Special Constabulary Grades		Within London
CHIEF CONSTABLE		CHIEF COMMANDANT		COMMISSIONER
DEPUTY CHIEF CONSTABLE		COMMANDANT		DEPUTY COMMISSIONER / ASSISTANT COMMISSIONER
ASSISTANT CHIEF CONSTABLE		DIVISIONAL (OR SECTION) OFFICER		DEPUTY ASSISTANT COMMISSIONER
CHIEF SUPERINTENDENT				COMMANDER
SUPERINTENDENT		SUB (OR SUB-DIVISIONAL) OFFICER		CHIEF SUPERINTENDENT
CHIEF INSPECTOR				SUPERINTENDENT
INSPECTOR		SPECIAL CONSTABLE		CHIEF INSPECTOR
SERGEANT				INSPECTOR
CONSTABLE				SERGEANT
				CONSTABLE

strictly adhered to. This rule has been relaxed for several years. Efforts are being made in an endeavour to make the police service more representative of the overall population in this country, by focusing recruitment on the ethnic community, which is still under-represented within this service.

The training of recruits initially requires 18–19 weeks' full time attendance at one of the police training centres, located in regions throughout the country. Training remains a prevalent feature throughout the two year probationary period, which takes the form of practical street experience under varying degrees of supervision, but interspersed with classroom instruction. The precise training programmes of probationary constables vary between the police forces.

In terms of specialist opportunities, the police service possibly has no parallel. A constable having satisfactorily completed his or her probationary period is given the opportunity to either continue working in uniform at a local police station (divisional or sub-divisional level) or to enter any of a range of specialist areas immediately or at some other stage in their career. These include the Criminal Investigation Department, traffic division, the mounted police, the drugs squad, communications, the vice squad, dog handlers, Special Branch, VIP protection, the National Crime Squad, internal investigations, public order control, training, youth and community work and many more. But many prefer to remain as uniformed officers in the local police divisions, believing that policing at this level can provide all the variety and opportunities that specialist work can bring. There is considerable merit in this assertion, since police work is equally dependant upon both specialist, as well as 'routine', police duties.

The command structure of each police force varies from area to area, although there are certain characteristics that all forces have in common. The headquarters and local command structure of a typical provincial police force is depicted in basic form in Figure 2, whereas the more complex organisation of the Metropolitan Police Service is represented in Figure 3.

Whatever rank a police officer holds, the numerous statutes covering police powers refer to all police officers as holders of the office of 'constable', unless specific ranks are stipulated for certain procedural purposes. The fundamental tenet that all police officers hold the office of constable also applies to voluntary, part time police officers, who are members of the special constabulary, which will be discussed in the next section.

Figure 2: the headquarters command structure of a police force

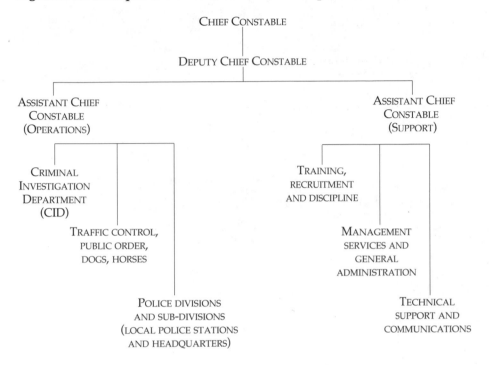

THE LOCAL COMMAND STRUCTURE OF A POLICE FORCE

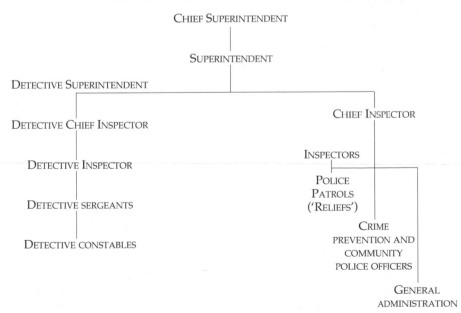

Figure 3: the Metropolitan Police Service

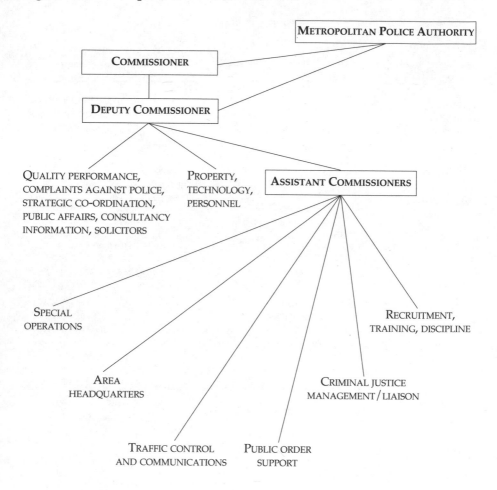

The special constabulary

Fairly extensive coverage of this aspect of the police service will be made here, since it is a relatively understudied subject[13] and, it is submitted, warrants discussion here. The special constabulary is a very old institution which, in its original form, pre-dates the formation of the Metropolitan Police in 1829 by over 150 years. Although the early justices of the peace and Lords of the Manor were expected to appoint officers to enforce the law, they frequently neglected this duty and, in 1673, a statute was passed, which enabled two magistrates to appoint special constables within their respective districts. However, it was the Special Constables Act 1831 which placed this force on the general footing upon which the modern special constabulary is now based. Since then, the 'specials', as they are commonly termed, have achieved notable places within the history of the modern police service. For example, in 1848, the largest single enrolment of special constables occurred in response to fears of serious disorder arising from the Chartist movement. This resulted in no fewer than 170,000 specials being deployed in central London. The anticipated trouble was averted, since the number of specials outnumbered the protestors by over three to one. It was during both World Wars that the specials particularly excelled and often formed the bulwark of operational policing throughout many parts of the country. However, they were also involved in other high profile roles during certain events between the war years. From 1919 to 1926, they assisted in maintaining order during a series of major industrial disputes, including the General Strike, and, during the early 1930s, they were used extensively during a series of demonstrations in London resulting from mass unemployment.[14]

In more modern times, the special constabulary is an auxiliary force within the police service, which consists of men and women who serve as part time, unpaid police officers who work in a voluntary capacity. At present, there are about 18,000 specials throughout England and Wales and, not surprisingly, the greatest representation is to be found within the Metropolis of London, which has about 1,300, although this should be viewed against the number of regular police officers in that force, which total over 26,000. Although Derbyshire, for instance, has only about 350 specials, the ratio is much higher, compared to about 1,600 regular police officers in that force (about one in five police officers in that county are specials and similar ratios are reflected in some other parts of the country, whilst some are much smaller). Specials receive no payment for their services, although they receive limited out of pocket expenses, such as travel and meal allowances, together with a boot or

---

13 There are some exceptions. These include Gill, M and Mawby, R, *A Special Constable: A Study of the Police Reserve*, 1990, Aldershot: Avebury; and, also, Barron, T, *The Special Constable's Manual*, 1997, London: Police Review.

14 *The Metropolitan Special Constabulary: An Illustrated History from 1831 to Today*, 1981, London: New Scotland Yard.

shoe allowance. They also receive reimbursement for any loss of earnings, for example, where they attend court. Their police work is confined to whatever spare time they can devote to this end. This often involves a significant sacrifice in certain cases, since many have demanding commitments elsewhere but, in any event, they are generally expected to perform at least eight hours voluntary duty per month.

It is important to note that specials have full police powers, the same as regular police officers, but with one variation. Whereas members of the regular police service may exercise their powers anywhere in this country, specials are restricted to the use of police powers within their respective police areas and within those police areas which immediately border on to their own. The exception to this general rule are specials in the City of London, who may exercise their police powers in the Metropolitan Police area as well as the counties which border onto the Greater London boundaries. Also, if specials are seconded to a different police area under mutual aid, they will have full police powers within that area. With some variations, specials are basically equipped with the same uniform as regular full time police officers, as well as certain protective clothing and equipment. The latter are necessary, because specials, as well as regular police officers, often face the same risks when on duty.

A grade (but not 'rank') structure exists within the special constabulary for those wishing to acquire additional responsibility (see Figure 1). This places graded officers within the special constabulary in authority above specials without or with lower grades, but this cannot be exercised towards regular police officers, who supersede specials of any status. Some specials join the regular force having initially served in a voluntary capacity and feel that they wish to make a full time career within the police service. In this respect, a person joining the special constabulary acquires an excellent introduction to operational policing. As mentioned on p 11, above, special constables, as well as regular police officers, are appointed by chief officers of police.

CHAPTER 2

POLICE POWERS OF STOP AND SEARCH

INTRODUCTION

The powers of the police to stop and search, particularly in public, has been the subject of particular scrutiny in recent years. The excessive use of such powers was held to have been a major contributory factor to the underlying resentment, notably between younger people and the police, which led to the inner city riots in 1981. It is important to note that this chapter will examine the law and procedures governing stops and searches by the police who have not, at that stage, made an arrest. Police powers to search either persons or premises, once an arrest has been effected, will be discussed in Chapters 3 and 4.

The Royal Commission on Criminal Procedure,[1] as part of its remit, examined the then existing laws governing police powers of stop and search. These largely consisted of a patchwork of local Acts of Parliament, which lacked any standard procedures or uniform application nationally:

> The Philips Royal Commission identified two main defects in the existing law. First, police powers to stop and search varied from one part of the country to another. In London, for instance, the police could use the powers under s 66 of the Metropolitan Police Act 1839 to stop and search for stolen goods and similar local powers existed in Birmingham, Manchester, Liverpool and Rochdale, but equivalent powers did not exist in most other parts of the country. Secondly, existing powers were either inadequate or, at best, uncertain and required clarification or redefinition.[2]

As a result, the Royal Commission recommended that uniform powers of stop and search should be given to the police throughout England and Wales, although the Government rejected the idea of a single or general power covering every eventuality. In consequence, a major reform of police powers of stop and search, as well as other powers, was enacted under the Police and Criminal Evidence Act 1984.

---

1   Philips Royal Commission.
2   Zander, M, *The Police and Criminal Evidence Act 1984*, 3rd edn, 1995, London: Sweet & Maxwell.

THE POLICE AND CRIMINAL EVIDENCE ACT 1984

This statute (commonly known as PACE) constituted the greatest single reform of police powers, certainly during the 20th century, to the extent that the bulk of police powers are either contained or consolidated within this statute. The main elements of PACE are: powers to stop and search (Pt I); powers of entry, search and seizure (Pt II); arrest (Pt III); detention (Pt IV); questioning and treatment of persons by police (Pt V); Codes of Practice (Pt VI); documentary evidence (Pt VII); evidence in criminal proceedings (Pt VIII); and police complaints and discipline (Pt IX), together with general police matters and miscellaneous provisions. Since its original enactment, a number of provisions under PACE have been subject to amendment by other statutes, as well as clarification resulting from judicial decisions. These will be explained at the appropriate stages in this book, which will cover the relevant aspects of this Act.

PACE took almost two years to be passed. Certain clauses in the Police and Criminal Evidence Bill attracted fierce opposition, both within and outside Parliament, and its passage was further delayed by the general election in May 1983. Although enacted in October 1984, nearly all of PACE did not come into effect until 1986, such was the extent of preparation needed for the operation of its new provisions. As far as the police service itself was concerned, all police officers had to be retrained under the new provisions and procedures of PACE, in time for its implementation.

As mentioned above, statutes affecting police powers refer to police officers in general as constables. This is because all police officers hold the office of constable, whether they be a police constable, chief constable or special constable, as well as the relevant ranks between them. The exception to this rule is where certain ranks are stipulated for specific procedures. For example, under s 4 of PACE, only a police superintendent or above may authorise road blocks (see later in this chapter for further coverage of this topic).

It must be stressed that whilst the bulk of police powers are enshrined under PACE, not all of them are. A number of statutes have been enacted before and after PACE which affect police powers that have not been included under its provisions. However, many of them are linked to certain procedures under PACE and, in effect, work through it, the common link being the Codes of Practice (see below). These affect, for example, the power to stop and search for controlled drugs under s 23 of the Misuse of Drugs Act 1971 and the power to stop and search for firearms under s 47 of the Firearms Act 1968. Although these specific powers to stop and search are contained within those statutes and not PACE, these powers are still subject to the various safeguards under the Codes of Practice. This will be discussed in more detail later in this chapter (see, also, Figure 4, which illustrates some of the principal police powers, both under PACE and other statutes, as well as the common law).

Figure 4: some sources of police powers

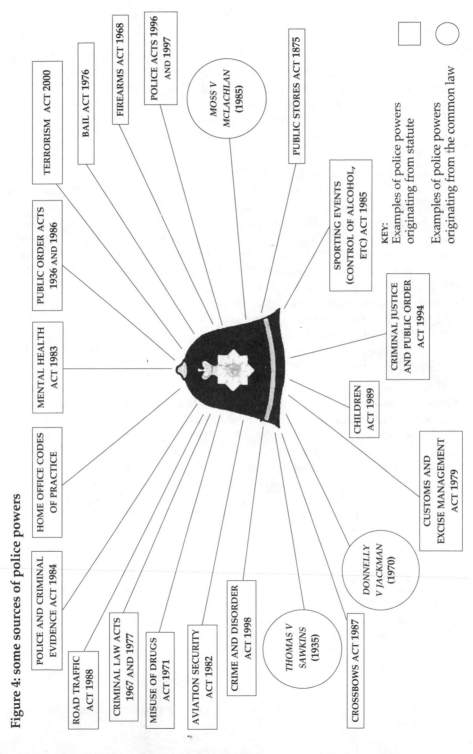

KEY:

Examples of police powers originating from statute

Examples of police powers originating from the common law

TERRORISM ACT 2000

BAIL ACT 1976

FIREARMS ACT 1968

POLICE ACTS 1996 AND 1997

MOSS V MCLACHLAN (1985)

PUBLIC STORES ACT 1875

PUBLIC ORDER ACTS 1936 AND 1986

SPORTING EVENTS (CONTROL OF ALCOHOL, ETC) ACT 1985

MENTAL HEALTH ACT 1983

CRIMINAL JUSTICE AND PUBLIC ORDER ACT 1994

HOME OFFICE CODES OF PRACTICE

CHILDREN ACT 1989

POLICE AND CRIMINAL EVIDENCE ACT 1984

CUSTOMS AND EXCISE MANAGEMENT ACT 1979

ROAD TRAFFIC ACT 1988

CRIMINAL LAW ACTS 1967 AND 1977

MISUSE OF DRUGS ACT 1971

AVIATION SECURITY ACT 1982

CRIME AND DISORDER ACT 1998

DONNELLY V JACKMAN (1970)

THOMAS V SAWKINS (1935)

CROSSBOWS ACT 1987

THE CODES OF PRACTICE

It has already been noted that PACE is accompanied by the Codes of Practice, mentioned above under Pt VI (more specifically, under ss 66 and 67, as well as s 60 under Pt V). The Codes of Practice exist as a separate publication and are designed to assist in the interpretation and clarification of the relevant provisions of PACE, in addition to providing essential guidance to those who use its powers. For this reason, they will be referred to extensively throughout most of this book.

The Codes of Practice have also been subject to many changes. The first edition took effect on 1 January 1986 and the second on 1 April 1991 but, since then, further changes have necessitated the publication of more editions, particularly the Codes affecting powers of stop and search. The latest edition was published in 1999[3] and consists of the following five Codes under a single consolidated booklet: (A) Code of Practice for the exercise by police officers of statutory powers of stop and search (this took effect from 1 March 1999); (B) Code of Practice for the searching of premises by police officers and the seizure of property found by police officers on persons or premises; (C) Code of Practice for the detention, treatment and questioning of persons by police officers; (D) Code of Practice for the identification of persons by police officers; and (E) Code of Practice on tape recording of interviews with suspects (the last four Codes took effect on 10 April 1995).

The existing Codes of Practice are currently being reviewed by the Home Office, especially Code C, and it is intended that a new edition may be published in 2001. Certain police powers and duties are enshrined only in the Codes of Practice and do not appear in PACE. The prime example is Code E, which makes provision for the tape recording of interviews, which is merely mentioned under s 60 of PACE.

POWERS OF STOP AND SEARCH UNDER PACE

Under s 1 of PACE, if a constable has reasonable grounds to suspect that stolen or prohibited articles are being carried, that police officer may stop, detain and search persons or vehicles (including anything or anyone in the vehicle or anything on it), and seize such items if found (see Figure 5). This power may be exercised in any public place. It should be noted that, if persons within a vehicle are searched, there must be reasonable grounds to suspect that they are personally carrying such items in order to justify searching them.

---

3   Home Office, *Police and Criminal Evidence Act 1984 (s 60(1)(a) and s 66): Codes of Practice*, rev edn, 1999, London: Stationery Office.

Figure 5: police powers to stop, detain and search under PACE

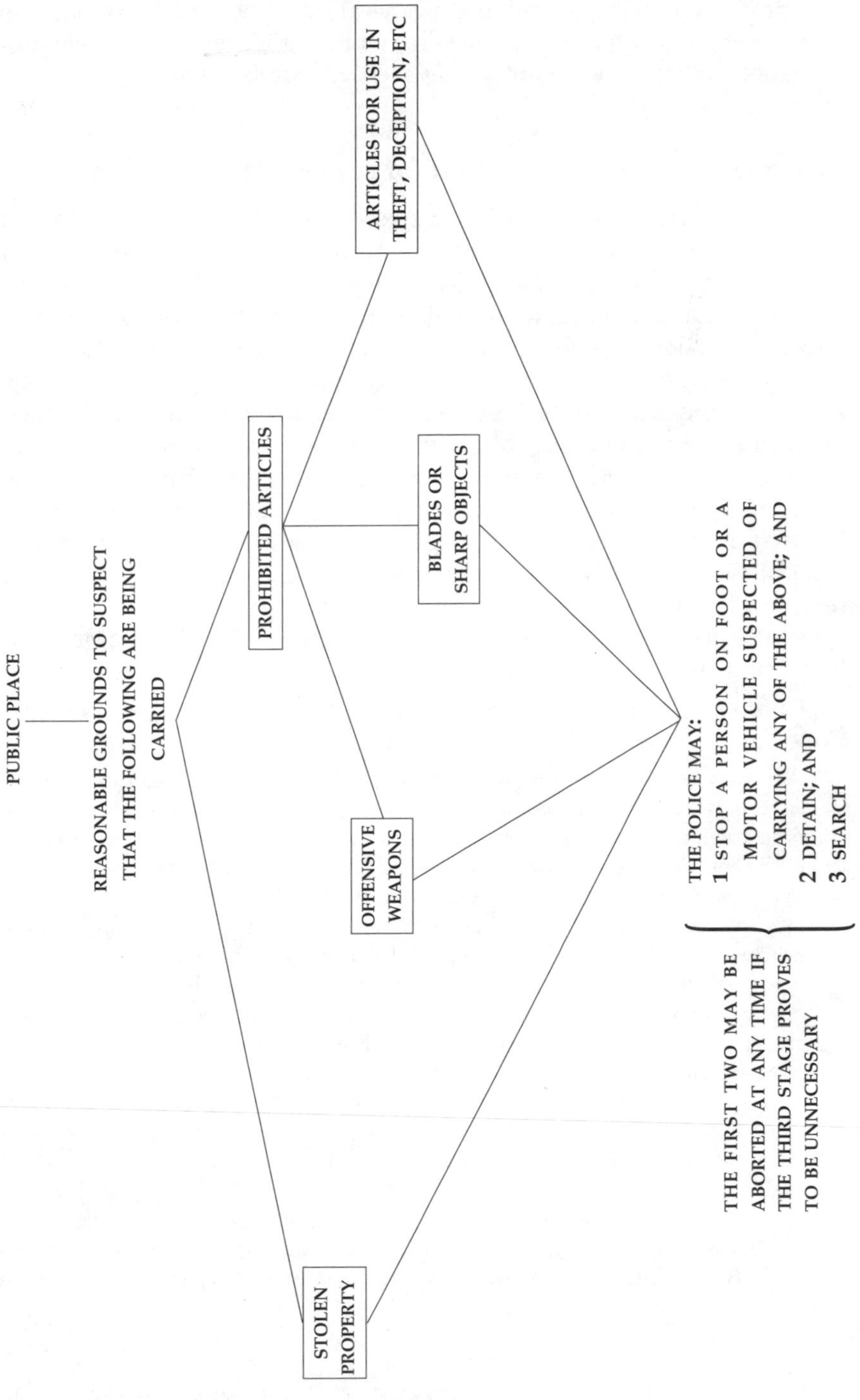

PUBLIC PLACE

REASONABLE GROUNDS TO SUSPECT
THAT THE FOLLOWING ARE BEING
CARRIED

PROHIBITED ARTICLES

ARTICLES FOR USE IN
THEFT, DECEPTION, ETC

BLADES OR
SHARP OBJECTS

OFFENSIVE
WEAPONS

STOLEN
PROPERTY

THE POLICE MAY:
1 STOP A PERSON ON FOOT OR A
MOTOR VEHICLE SUSPECTED OF
CARRYING ANY OF THE ABOVE; AND
2 DETAIN; AND
3 SEARCH

THE FIRST TWO MAY BE
ABORTED AT ANY TIME IF
THE THIRD STAGE PROVES
TO BE UNNECESSARY

The above paragraph provides a general statement of s 1. We now have to examine the following points, namely: what constitutes 'reasonable grounds to suspect', what is the definition of stolen or prohibited articles and what is a public place?

Reasonable grounds to suspect (or reasonable suspicion)

The term 'reasonable grounds for suspecting' or 'reasonable grounds to suspect' is mentioned in PACE under a number of provisions and not just s 1, but this statute does not define its meaning. Therefore, we have to examine a variety of sources in order to ascertain both its definition and how it should be applied. To begin with, the question of reasonable suspicion is tested objectively, meaning: '... facts and circumstances which would lead an impartial third party to form the belief or suspicion in question.'[4] One of the main complaints from particularly young people in the areas affected by the inner city riots of 1981, especially those from the ethnic community, was that the police had arbitrarily or randomly exercised their stop and search powers just by virtue of the fact that those persons were on the street. In some cases, the police were alleged to have made statements that they merely had a feeling that those suspects were generally 'up to no good'. The latter constitutes a purely *subjective* approach to suspicion, which is forbidden under PACE and the Codes of Practice.

Guidance as to what constitutes the *objective* test of suspicion is given in Code A, in paras 1.6 and 1.7, which state:

> Whether reasonable ground for suspicion exists will depend on the circumstances in each case, but there must be some objective basis for it. An officer will need to consider the nature of the article suspected of being carried in the context of other factors, such as the time and place, and the behaviour of the person concerned or those with him. Reasonable suspicion may exist, for example, where information has been received, such as: a description of an article being carried or of a suspected offender; a person seen acting covertly or warily or attempting to hide something; or a person carrying a certain type of article at an unusual time or in a place where a number of burglaries or thefts are known to have taken place recently. But the decision to stop and search must be based on all the facts which bear on the likelihood that an article of a certain kind will be found ... reasonable suspicion can never be supported on the basis of personal factors alone, without supporting intelligence or information. For example, a person's colour, age, hairstyle or manner of dress, or the fact that he is known to have a previous conviction for possession of an unlawful article, cannot be used alone or in combination with each other as the sole basis upon which to search that person. Nor may it be founded on the basis of stereotyped images or groups as more likely to be committing offences.

---

4   Lidstone, K and Palmer, C, *Bevan and Lidstone's The Investigation of Crime: A Guide to Police Powers*, 2nd edn, 1996, London: Butterworths.

However, the above guidance was modified by paras 1.6A and 1.7AA, which were inserted on 15 May 1997. These broadened the basis of what constituted objectively based suspicion as follows:

> ... reasonable suspicion may be based upon reliable information or intelligence which indicates that members of a particular group or gang, or their associates, habitually carry knives unlawfully or weapons or controlled drugs ... where there is reliable information or intelligence that members of a group or gang who habitually carry knives unlawfully or weapons or controlled drugs and wear a distinctive item of clothing or other means of identification to indicate membership of it, the members may be identified by means of that distinctive item of clothing or other means of identification.

The concluding words 'other means of identification' are defined in note 1H of Code A as: 'Other means of identification might include jewellery, insignias, tattoos or other features which are known to identify members of the particular gang or group.'

Why the change to the criteria which now constitutes objectively based suspicion? This can be summarised in the following statement:

> According to the Home Office Consultation Paper that was sent to all chief officers of police on 19 March 1997, the above changes reflected the previous government's concern regarding knife-carrying gangs. The consultation document went on to say that the earlier Codes of Practice had left the police uncertain as to whether they may search persons known to them as part of a gang which regularly carried knives or where persons were not known to them, but were associated with such groups, by virtue of their wearing some distinctive item of dress identifiable with them. In these circumstances, the main impediment to the exercise of reasonable cause for suspicion under s 1 of the Police and Criminal Evidence Act was the earlier requirement that it can never be supported on the basis of personal factors alone, such as hairstyle or manner of dress. The amendments proposed at that time were intended to remove this uncertainty and clarify that reasonable cause to suspect that persons may be carrying the relevant prohibited articles may be extended to include the circumstances mentioned above.[5]

The upshot of these provisions is that, *normally*, the police cannot justify stopping and searching a person just because of his or her appearance. However, the situation may be different where the police receive reliable information or intelligence that a group or gang habitually and unlawfully carry knives, weapons or controlled drugs, and membership of it is denoted by the wearing of distinctive clothing or other means of identification. This may still constitute an objective ground for suspecting that a person wearing such identification may be carrying such items unlawfully.

---

5   Jason-Lloyd, L, 'Changes to Code A of the Police and Criminal Evidence Act 1984' (1997) 161 JP 715.

The issue of reasonable suspicion has been subject to judicial interpretation in a number of cases, which include the following. In *Black v DPP* (1995), the police entered premises belonging to the defendant's brother in accordance with a search warrant under the Misuse of Drugs Act 1971. While the search was in progress, the defendant arrived, carrying a bag and was suspected by the police of attending the premises in order to buy or sell drugs. The police wished to search the defendant and asked him to enter the premises for this purpose, but he became aggressive, threw the bag down and then attempted to leave the premises. He was charged and later convicted of obstruction under s 23(4)(a) of the 1971 Act. The Divisional Court held that a person merely arriving at the address of a known drug dealer did not amount to conduct which constituted reasonable grounds for suspecting that person of possessing a controlled drug and that the defendant's behaviour after he was detained could not retrospectively provide such grounds. The defendant's conviction was quashed.

In *Samuels v Commissioner of Police for the Metropolis* (1999), S sued the police for damages under what may generally be termed unlawful detention. Earlier, he had been acquitted of the charge of assault on police. S was stopped by a police officer whilst walking home and was asked where he was going. S did not venture any significant information and stated that he had the right to go where he wanted. He then continued his journey but, when he was nearly home, the police officer stated that he wished to search S, because he suspected him of being in possession of a prohibited article. The officer later gave evidence that he thought S may have been carrying a screwdriver and his manner of walking was suspicious. It was ruled by the trial judge that the stop and search of S was based on reasonable grounds. The Court of Appeal, however, had to consider whether that suspicion was reasonable. In allowing the appeal, the court held that, if the police officer did not have the prerequisite reasonable suspicion before he approached S, then the conduct of S immediately afterwards could not transform an unreasonable suspicion into one which was reasonable.

It is important to note that a police officer does not have the power to stop a person against their will in order to establish any grounds for suspicion; neither may a person's refusal to answer questions constitute reasonable suspicion. In *Rice v Connolly* (1966), it was held that citizens are under no *general* legal duty to answer questions put to them by the police. However, such refusal may reinforce a police officer's existing suspicion, but this may not singularly justify stopping and detaining a person. The essence of reasonable suspicion, within the context of PACE, is that there must be a tangible and positive condition present to justify the use of police powers of stop and search under s 1.

Under more recent legislation, namely ss 60 and 81 of the Criminal Justice and Public Order Act 1994, a number of stop and search powers have been conferred upon the police which do not require reasonable suspicion as a prerequisite for these powers to be exercised. These important new developments will be discussed in the final part of this chapter.

Another important term used frequently in PACE is 'reasonable grounds for believing' or 'reasonable grounds to believe'. What is the difference between reasonable grounds to *believe* and reasonable grounds to *suspect*? First, a much higher criteria is set when the exercise of certain police powers require reasonable belief, rather than suspicion. This is because many of the powers requiring reasonable belief generally impose a greater restriction on the liberty of those against whom they are being used. Belief is therefore much closer to certainty than suspicion:

> If, therefore, there are 10 steps from mere suspicion to a state of certainty, or an acceptance that something is true, then reasonable suspicion may be as low as step two or three, whilst reasonable belief may be as high as step nine.[6]

Secondly, it has been propounded that many of the powers under PACE that require reasonable belief are often exercised following decisions made as a result of consultation and reflection, whereas many powers requiring reasonable suspicion are often made in street situations, requiring quick, if not instant, decisions.[7]

Stolen and prohibited articles

The definition of *stolen articles* not only includes property actually stolen by the suspect, but also property being dishonestly handled by him or her. In effect, any property dishonestly obtained falls within the scope of s 1, whether or not obtained in this country.[8]

Prohibited articles fall under two main categories, namely offensive weapons and articles for use in theft or cheat. The definition of offensive weapons is best explained by referring to the three main classes of articles which fall under this heading. First, there are items which are made specifically for the purpose of inflicting physical harm, such as bayonets and knuckledusters. Secondly, there are weapons which have been adapted in order to cause injury, where an ordinary object has been transformed into something capable of achieving this purpose. Examples include a broom handle with a nail or spike driven through it or a metal comb being sharpened at one end to produce a razor-sharp edge. Finally, there is the third category of offensive weapons, which are neither *made* nor *adapted*, but are simply *intended* to be used to cause injury. Such items are ordinary objects, which are

---

6   *Op cit*, Lidstone and Palmer, fn 4.
7   *Op cit*, Lidstone and Palmer, fn 4.
8   *Op cit*, Lidstone and Palmer, fn 4.

intended to cause physical harm, even though they have not had their substance or form altered. Examples include bunches of keys, belts and walking sticks.[9] In summary, offensive weapons may either be *made*, *adapted* or may fall into neither category but may be *intended* to be used as a weapon.

Having an offensive weapon in a public place, without lawful authority or reasonable excuse, is an offence under s 1 of the Prevention of Crime Act 1953. The meaning of 'public place' is defined below, but the interpretation of the terms 'lawful authority' and 'reasonable excuse' will now be discussed. Lawful authority simply includes certain classes of persons who are allowed to carry what would otherwise be regarded as offensive weapons, but for their professional duty. This includes the carrying of axes by firefighters and batons by police officers. The defence of reasonable excuse covers a variety of situations where the circumstances under which a person carries an offensive weapon negates any intention to cause harm. Since the introduction of s 1 of the Prevention of Crime Act 1953, there has been a considerable build up of case law in an endeavour to clarify what constitutes 'reasonable excuse'. These cases indicate that the courts interpret this term very narrowly in order to, *inter alia*, deter citizens taking the law into their own hands. For example, in *Houghton v Chief Constable of Greater Manchester* (1987), it was held that carrying a police truncheon only to authenticate a police uniform being worn on the way to or from a fancy dress party fell within the definition of reasonable excuse. But, in *R v Peacock* (1973), the court warned that, where a weapon was being carried for self-defence purposes, generally, only those fearing immediate attack would be able to rely on the defence of reasonable excuse. This obviates those who carry offensive weapons in response to a general or widespread fear of being attacked, such as people carrying knives while walking the streets, because of a high number of muggings in their neighbourhood, or taxi drivers carrying coshes in their cabs, because of colleagues being robbed. However, in *Evans v Hughes* (1972), it was held that the carrying of a weapon a week after an attack could constitute a reasonable excuse.[10]

The above provisions have been augmented by s 139 of the Criminal Justice Act 1988, which created the offence of having articles with blades or sharp points in public places without lawful authority or reasonable excuse. In effect, this extended the law regarding possession of offensive weapons, although it does not apply to folding pocket knives with a blade less than three inches in length when exposed. Blades and sharp points prohibited under s 139 are also included under the heading of prohibited articles for the purposes of s 1 of PACE.

The second meaning of the term 'prohibited articles' applies to articles made, adapted to be used or intended to be used in burglary, theft, taking a

---

9   Jason-Lloyd, L, 'The Offensive Weapons Act 1996 – an overview' (1996) 160 JP 931.
10   *Ibid.*

motor vehicle without consent or obtaining property by deception. These have included a variety of housebreaking implements, such as jemmies, screwdrivers and skeleton keys, although it has also included less obvious items such as gloves, adhesive tape (to muffle the sound of breaking glass) and credit cards (to open locks as well as to commit offences of deception).

Definition of 'public place'

Under s 1(1) of PACE, police powers of stop and search may be exercised as follows:

(a) in any place to which, at the time when he proposes to exercise the power, the public or any section of the public has access, on payment or otherwise, as of right or by virtue of express or implied permission; or

(b) in any other place to which people have ready access at the time when he proposes to exercise the power, but which is not a dwelling.

The above generally includes the streets, parks and garage forecourts, as well as museums, cinemas, supermarkets, football grounds and public houses. It has also been subscribed that any open ground or fenced land with an open gate, or even a building, which is not a dwelling, with an unlocked, unattended door, can fall under the description of a public place. In effect, these are places where ready access can be gained rather than right of access although, ultimately, it is for the courts to decide in such cases.[11] However, this does not include schools and universities.[12] It was largely because of the exclusion of schools from the ambit of public places that the Offensive Weapons Act 1996 was enacted, in order to give the police powers to search such places and persons in them for offensive weapons and knives (see the coverage of the 1996 Act on p 108).

It has been generally mentioned above that police stop and search powers under s 1 of PACE may not be exercised in a dwelling. This includes persons or vehicles in any garden, yard, land or building which constitutes a dwelling, unless the police have reasonable cause to *believe*[13] that the person or individual in charge of the vehicle does not reside there, and that the resident has not given his or her express or implied permission for the person or the vehicle to be there; in other words, being or driving there without the resident's consent. This is designed to prevent suspects randomly fleeing into a person's residence or driving into a garden or yard belonging to a residence, in order to avoid being searched.

---

11 Levenson, H, Fairweather, F and Cape, E, *Police Powers: A Practitioner's Guide*, 1996, London: Legal Action Group.

12 *Op cit*, Zander, fn 2.

13 See the discussion above, regarding the difference between reasonable *suspicion* and reasonable *belief*.

Definition of a 'vehicle'

Some obvious, and even amusing, definitions have arisen as to what constitutes a vehicle for the purposes of police stop and search powers. The most well known are motor vehicles such as cars, vans, lorries, coaches, buses and motorcycles. As a result of case law, 'vehicles' have also included aircraft, hovercraft, ships, boats, rafts, trams, bicycles, horse-drawn carts, handcarts and trailers. The definition has even included perambulators and an empty poultry shed drawn by a tractor![14] In essence, it is assumed that a vehicle would be known when one saw it.

SEARCH PROCEDURE

The conduct of a search under PACE is governed by ss 2 and 3, as well as paras 2, 3 and 4 of Code A. As far as persons are concerned, the first step is to *stop* that person or the vehicle in which they are being carried. The second stage is to *detain* them. It does not always follow that a *search* is then made because, according to para 2.2 of Code A:

> Before carrying out a search, the officer may question the person about his behaviour or his presence in circumstances which gave rise to the suspicion, since he may have a satisfactory explanation which will make a search unnecessary. If, as a result of any questioning preparatory to a search, or other circumstances which come to the attention of the officer, there cease to be reasonable grounds for suspecting that an article is being carried of a kind for which there is a power of stop and search, no search may take place.

In other words, if the suspect has been stopped and detained, the procedure may be aborted at any stage if it subsequently comes to light that a search is unnecessary. Under para 2.3 of the Code, this will often occur as a result of satisfactory answers being given as to the suspect's conduct, which gave rise to the police officer's initial suspicion. However, it goes on to warn that reasonable grounds for suspicion cannot be retrospectively provided by such questioning or refusal to answer any questions at all. The power to abort the procedure where a search becomes unnecessary is to be found under s 2(1) of PACE (see, also, Figure 5).

SEARCHING OF PERSONS

Following the stopping and subsequent detention of a person on foot or in a vehicle, if the police officer still contemplates a search, then, under s 2(2) of

14   Lidstone and Palmer, *op cit*, fn 4.

PACE, it is the duty of that officer to bring the following to the attention of the suspect:

(1) if the police officer is not in uniform, he or she must produce documentary evidence (usually a warrant card), confirming their status as a police officer;

(2) if that police officer is in uniform (which must be the case if a moving vehicle is stopped), that officer must state the following to the suspect (s 2(3)):

(a) the police officer's name and station to which attached (in cases linked to terrorism, for personal safety reasons, the police officer does not have to give his or her name, but their number instead);

(b) the object of the proposed search;

(c) the grounds for making the search;

(d) that the person is entitled to a record of the search if applied for within a year following the incident. Under s 2(4), this requirement may be waived in the circumstances mentioned below under the completion of the search procedure.

Any search which then follows must be conducted strictly in accordance with the provisions under s 2(9)(a) of PACE and s 3 of Code A, augmented by Annex A to Code C. Under s 2(9)(a), a suspect must not be required to remove any clothing in public other than an outer coat, jacket or gloves. Section 3 of the Code gives essential guidance as follows:

3.1 Every reasonable effort must be made to reduce to the minimum the embarrassment that a person being searched may experience.

3.2 The co-operation of the person to be searched shall be sought in every case, even if he initially objects to the search. A forcible search may be made only if it has been established that the person is unwilling to co-operate ... [see p 37, below, on the use of force].

3.3 The length of time for which a person or vehicle may be detained will depend on the circumstances, but must, in all circumstances, be reasonable and not extend beyond the time taken for the search ...

3.5 Searches in public must be restricted to superficial examination of outer clothing. There is no power to require a person to remove any clothing in public other than an outer coat, jacket or gloves ...[15] Where, on reasonable grounds, it is considered necessary to conduct a more thorough search (for example, by requiring a person to take off a T-shirt), this shall be done out of public view, for example, in a police van or police station if there is one nearby. Any search involving the removal of more than an outer coat, jacket, gloves ... may only be made by an officer of the same sex as the

---

15 However, note for guidance 3A under Code A states: '... although there is no power to require a person to do so, there is nothing to prevent an officer from asking a person to voluntarily remove more than an outer coat, jacket or gloves ...'

person searched and may not be made in the presence of anyone of the opposite sex, unless the person being searched specifically requests it ... No search involving exposure of intimate parts of the body may take place in a police van ...

Strip searches

Under para 10 of Annex A to Code C, the justifications for making strip searches are as follows:

10 A strip search may take place only if it is considered necessary to remove an article which a person would not be allowed to keep, and the officer reasonably considers that the person might have concealed such an article. Strip searches shall not be routinely carried out where there is no reason to consider that articles have been concealed.

Where a strip search is necessary and involves the exposure of intimate parts of the body, the following rules under para 11 of Annex A to Code C will apply:

11 ...

(a) a police officer carrying out a strip search must be of the same sex as the person searched;

(b) the search shall take place in an area where the person being searched cannot be seen by anyone who does not need to be present, nor by a member of the opposite sex (except an appropriate adult who has been specifically requested by the person being searched);

[See Chapter 6 for the definition of 'appropriate adult'.]

(c) except in cases of urgency, where there is a risk of serious harm to the person detained or to others, whenever a strip search involves exposure of intimate parts of the body, there must be at least two people present other than the person searched and, if the search is of a juvenile or a mentally disordered or mentally handicapped person, one of the people must be the appropriate adult. Except in urgent cases as above, a search of a juvenile may take place in the absence of the appropriate adult only if the juvenile signifies in the presence of the appropriate adult that he prefers the search to be done in his absence and the appropriate adult agrees. A record shall be made of the juvenile's decision and signed by the appropriate adult. The presence of more than two people, other than an appropriate adult, shall be permitted only in the most exceptional circumstances;

(d) the search shall be conducted with proper regard to the sensitivity and vulnerability of the person in these circumstances and every reasonable effort shall be made to secure the person's co-operation and minimise embarrassment. People who are searched should not normally be required to have all their clothes removed at the same time, for example, a man shall be allowed to put on his shirt before removing his trousers, and a woman shall be allowed to put on her blouse and upper garments before further clothing is removed;

(e) where necessary, to assist the search, the person may be required to hold his or her arms in the air or to stand with his or her legs apart and to bend forward, so that visual examination may be made of the genital and anal areas, provided that no physical contact is made with any body orifice;

(f) if, during a search, articles are found, the person shall be asked to hand them over. If articles are found within any body orifice other than the mouth, and the person refuses to hand them over, their removal would constitute an intimate search, which must be carried out in accordance with the provisions of Pt A of this Annex:

(g) a strip search shall be conducted as quickly as possible and the person searched allowed to dress as soon as the procedure is complete.

Where a strip search is carried out, a record shall be made which must include the reason for it, those present during the search and any result accruing from it.

Intimate searches

It should be emphasised that a strip search is distinct from an *intimate* search, the latter being more intrusive, since it involves the searching and examination of the body orifices except the mouth. Intimate searches can only take place at a police station or in medical premises following an arrest and where certain items may be concealed in a person's body; therefore, this subject is covered in Chapter 6. The above rules regarding strip searches also apply to persons who have been detained by the police following an arrest and are also applicable to Chapter 6.

VEHICLES

Moving vehicles

Under s 2(9)(b), only a police officer in uniform may stop a moving vehicle. With regard to motor vehicles, this, *inter alia*, has a practical application, since a plain clothes officer would be indistinguishable from any other citizen and drivers of such conveyances would be unlikely to stop. Section 2(9)(b), however, does not prevent a vehicle being searched by a non-uniformed police officer once it has already stopped or is parked unattended. There is a general power for uniformed police officers to stop motor vehicles under s 163 of the Road Traffic Act 1988 and, once a vehicle has been stopped, the powers of s 1 of PACE can then be applied. It should be noted that if reasonable suspicion is focused on something which the vehicle may be carrying, the power to search should be confined to the vehicle and anything in or on it. This should not extend to anyone in the vehicle, unless they are reasonably suspected of carrying stolen or prohibited articles themselves. This being the case, the same search procedures mentioned above will apply as they do to persons who are not in vehicles. Whether or not just the vehicle is searched, the person in charge of the vehicle (usually the driver) should also be given the same information as persons who are about to be searched namely, the officer's name and station, the grounds and object of the search and the availability of a record of the search if applied for within a year (subject to the exceptions mentioned below). Apart from the overall requirement under Code A that any search should be conducted with reasonable expedition (para 3.3), in *Lodwick v Saunders* (1985), it was held that a police officer is entitled to detain a vehicle for a reasonable time in order to carry out the necessary procedures, so as to make an arrest if the vehicle is suspected of being stolen.

Unattended vehicles

Unattended vehicles may be searched but, since the person in charge of it will not be present, it is, of course, not possible for the police to convey to that person the name of the officer conducting the search, his or her station to which attached and the grounds and object of the search. In such circumstances, s 2(6) of PACE states that, if possible, a notice should be left inside or on the vehicle, in which the officer should identify his or herself and the station to which attached and information that the vehicle has been searched. There should also be mention that an application for compensation in respect of any damage caused by the search may be made and to where it should be directed, and that the person in charge of the vehicle is entitled to a record of the search within a year of the incident (s 3(8) and (9) of PACE and para 4.9 of Code A). Under para 4.10 of Code A, the vehicle must, if practicable, be left secure.

Road blocks

For a number of years, the police have had powers under both the common law and statute to stop vehicles, including the use of road blocks. The most frequently used is s 163 of the Road Traffic Act 1988, which gives a constable in uniform the power to stop any vehicle for a variety of reasons, although this is often confined to road traffic matters, such as the need to check on driving documents or the vehicle's general roadworthiness. More specifically, s 4 of PACE enables the police to conduct such a procedure in order to carry out road checks using the power under s 163 if the following conditions exist: where a serious arrestable offence is reasonably believed to have been or is likely to be committed and there are reasonable grounds to suspect that the culprit is or will be in the area (the definition of a serious arrestable offence can be found in Chapter 3, p 67); where there are reasonable grounds for believing that witnesses to a serious arrestable offence are likely to be traced; and where it is reasonably suspected that a person unlawfully at large is or about to be in the area.

The authorisation of road checks must be made in writing by a police officer of at least the rank of superintendent and such authority lasts for up to seven days, but can be renewed, where appropriate, although not for periods exceeding seven days. Every written authorisation shall specify the name of the officer giving it, the purpose of the road check and the locality in which the vehicles are to be stopped. In an emergency, a police officer below that rank may make such an authorisation, but is under a duty to make a written record of the time at which it is given and to inform an officer of at least the rank of superintendent that it has been given as soon as is practicable. That officer may then either continue or discontinue the road check. Persons in charge of vehicles stopped in the course of road checks are entitled to a written statement of the purpose of the check if made within 12 months of the incident.

The police also have powers under the common law to stop vehicles. In *Moss v McLachlan* (1985), it was held that the police had acted lawfully in setting up road blocks and turning vehicles away, in order to prevent a breach of the peace (see Chapter 3, p 72). As mentioned earlier, this case was decided in the wake of the miners' strike during the winter of 1984–85, where the police stopped pickets travelling to a colliery whose purpose was to reinforce the strength of pickets already there. Such places were often the scenes of violent confrontations between the police and striking miners and, therefore, a breach of the peace was apprehended.

FURTHER SEARCH PROCEDURES

The use of force

Section 117 of PACE states:

> Where any provision of this Act:
>
> (a) confers a power on a constable; and
>
> (b) does not provide that the power may only be exercised with the consent of some person, other than a police officer, the officer may use reasonable force, if necessary, in the exercise of the power.

This means that, if necessary, a person may be forcibly searched, although the degree of force used must always be reasonable in all the circumstances.

Section 117 applies to all coercive powers under PACE, including the power to make arrests (see Chapter 3). The issue of what constitutes reasonable force is decided on its own merits, although some guidance has been derived from a build up of case law discussed in Chapters 8 and 9.

The completion of the search procedure

Any stolen or prohibited article found in the course of a search under s 1 may be seized (s 1(6)) and an arrest usually follows (see Chapter 3). In any event, under s 3(1), the police officer must make a written record of the search, unless it is impracticable to do so. The latter will include instances where the officer has searched a large number of persons in a short space of time, such as at a major sporting event, or in situations involving public disorder (para 4.1 of Code A). Where this is possible, the record does not have to be written contemporaneously with the incident, but as soon as is practicable afterwards. This delay may also be necessary due to other urgent duties or bad weather, for instance (s 3(2) of PACE and para 4.2 of Code A).

Under s 3(3), the police officer must include the suspect's name in the record if known, but there is no compulsion for his or her name to be given and, therefore, the suspect must not be detained for this purpose. Failure to obtain the name of the suspect must be substituted by a description of him or her (s 3(4)) and, under s 3(5), a description of any vehicle searched must also be included. Paragraphs 4.4 to 4.7A of Code A state that a suspect's date of birth should also be sought in addition to his or her name and that the following information must be recorded, even if none of these details are forthcoming: a description of the suspect if the name is withheld; a note of the person's ethnic origin; a description of any vehicle searched, together with its registration number; the grounds and object of the search; the date, time and place of the search; the results of the search; any injury or damage to property resulting from it; and, finally, the police officer's identity and duty station, except in cases linked to terrorism, where, usually, the officer's warrant number is recorded.

Under s 3(7) to (9) of PACE, any person searched or the owner or person in charge of any vehicle searched may obtain a copy of any record made within 12 months of the incident. All the above information obtained from individual searches under s 1 of PACE must be recorded on a standard form supplied for this purpose, known as the National Search Record (para 4.3 of Code A).

Informal police procedures

The police are not strictly bound to resort to their substantive powers of stop and search in every instance. The following notes for guidance under Code A make it very clear that less formal police procedures are permissible, but subject to certain safeguards:

1B This code does not affect the ability of an officer to speak to or question a person in the ordinary course of his duties (and in the absence of reasonable suspicion) without detaining him or exercising any element of compulsion. It is not the purpose of the code to prohibit such encounters between the police and the community with the co-operation of the person concerned and neither does it affect the principle that all citizens have a duty to help police officers to prevent crime and discover offenders.

1D Nothing in this code affects:

(a) the routine searching of persons entering sports grounds or other premises with their consent, or as a condition of entry; or

(b) the ability of an officer to search a person in the street with his consent where no search power exists. In these circumstances, an officer should always make it clear that he is seeking the consent of the person concerned to the search being carried out by telling the person that he need not consent and that, without his consent, he will not be searched.

1E If an officer acts in an improper manner, this will invalidate a voluntary search. Juveniles, people suffering from a mental handicap or mental disorder and others who appear not to be capable of giving an informed consent should not be subject to a voluntary search.

There have been some misgivings regarding the use of voluntary or consensual searches by the police. It has been pointed out, *inter alia*, that a person who provides such consent is not covered by the procedural safeguards that apply in the case of searches under s 1 of PACE. There has also been some suggestion that, even where a substantive power to search does exist, the police may still try and obtain the consent of the suspect in order to avoid 'the procedural burdens of a statutory search', notwithstanding the note for guidance under note 1D(b) stated above.[16]

It is quite common for the police to speak to or even question people on an informal basis in the course of everyday patrol duties, and this can be used as an informal and even subtle means to confirm or repudiate any form of suspicion, rather than resort to the more authoritarian use of substantive powers. As mentioned above, under the section dealing with reasonable suspicion, there is no *general* legal duty for citizens to answer questions put to them by the police.[17] This was held in *Rice v Connolly* (1966), where two police

---

16 *Op cit*, Lidstone and Palmer, fn 4.

17 There are some specific provisions that impose a legal duty to answers questions. For instance, the requirement under the Road Traffic Act 1988, s 169, where there is a legal duty for a person to provide their name and address, and also under the Criminal Justice Act 1987, where there is the requirement for answers to be given during certain investigations into serious fraud, as well as similar provisions under the Companies Act 1985.

officers approached a man in the street and asked him questions regarding his movements that night. He gave an incomplete answer and walked away. His conviction for wilfully obstructing police was quashed, on the grounds that, whilst there was a moral obligation to assist the police, he was under no legal obligation to answer their questions. This is in contrast to *Ricketts v Cox* (1982), where, in a similar scenario, the suspect was asked questions by the police, but he responded with hostility and abuse instead of passive silence, and his conviction for wilfully obstructing police was subsequently upheld. A number of cases have been decided which confirm that, unless the police have a specific power to detain a person (such as under s 1 of PACE or where they have made an arrest), they will be acting outside the scope of their powers if they restrict a person's liberty. In *Kenlin v Gardiner* (1967), a youth in company with another attempted to run away when being questioned by the police He was restrained and a police officer was assaulted in the ensuing scuffle. Both youths were convicted of assault on police, but their convictions were quashed, on the grounds that the police had unlawfully detained the youth; therefore, the police officer was not acting in the course of his duty. In *Collins v Wilcock* (1984), a woman police officer spoke to another female in the street who was suspected of soliciting for prostitution. The suspect walked away when questioned and the police officer took her by the arm in order to compel her to remain. The female scratched the police officer's arm and was charged with assault on a police officer. Her conviction was quashed, on the grounds that the police officer did not have the power to forcibly detain the suspect in order to answer questions and that, in scratching the officer's arm, she was using reasonable force to free herself from what amounted to false imprisonment. Also, in *Bentley v Brudzinski* (1982), it was held to have been unlawful where a police officer stated 'just a minute' whilst placing his hand on the person's shoulder at the same time. Both this case and *Collins v Wilcock* exemplify the fact that, where a police officer touches a person in such a manner as to indicate that officer's intention to delay or detain that person, such action will be unlawful.[18] However, the courts have been prepared to exclude trivial interference with a person's liberty from the ambit of these cases, as in *Donnelly v Jackman* (1970), where it was held that the police may take reasonable steps to attract a person's attention, for instance, by tapping them on the shoulder. Also, in *Mepstead v DPP* (1996), it was held that a police officer was not acting unlawfully by briefly holding a person's arm in order to draw his attention to another police officer, who was talking to him to try to calm him down. This constituted the police officer acting within the execution of his duty, even though he was not making an arrest at the time.

---

18 Stone, R, *Entry, Search and Seizure: A Guide to Civil and Criminal Powers of Entry*, 3rd edn, 1997, London: Sweet & Maxwell.

Other stop and search powers

Section 1 of PACE is by no means the only stop and search power available to the police, although it is the most widely used. A number of statutory provisions conferring such powers on the police for other purposes existed before PACE and some have been enacted since 1984. The former include s 6 of the Public Stores Act 1875, which empowers a constable to stop, detain and search any vessel, boat or vehicle where, *inter alia*, there is reason to suspect that any of Her Majesty's stores may be found which have been stolen or unlawfully obtained; also, s 23 of the Misuse of Drugs Act 1971 empowers the police to search a person and any vessel or vehicle where he or she suspects that a person is in possession of a controlled drug; s 47 of the Firearms Act 1968 has also been preserved by PACE. This power enables the police to stop and search persons or vehicles where they have reasonable cause to suspect that a firearm is being carried in a public place or elsewhere, with the intention to commit certain unlawful acts.

Statutory stop and search powers conferred on the police since PACE include s 7 of the Sporting Events (Control of Alcohol, etc) Act 1985, which empowers the police to search certain vehicles for alcohol *en route* to or from football matches; also, s 4 of the Crossbows Act 1987 enables the police to search persons or vehicles reasonably suspected of unlawfully carrying crossbows or parts of such devices, although there is an age restriction in such cases, where the suspect must be under 17 years of age.

MORE RECENT POWERS TO STOP AND SEARCH VEHICLES AND PEDESTRIANS

During the 1990s, a number of other stop and search powers have been conferred upon the police in response to increasing concerns regarding public safety. These are to be found under the Criminal Justice and Public Order Act 1994, the Prevention of Terrorism (Temporary Provisions) Act 1989 and, also, the Offensive Weapons Act 1996, although the latter will be covered in Chapter 4, since the stop and search powers in this instance are contingent upon entry into school premises.

Section 60 of the Criminal Justice and Public Order Act 1994

These provisions, as originally enacted, have since been amended by s 8 of the Knives Act 1997 and s 25 of the Crime and Disorder Act 1998. The overall purpose of s 60 of the 1994 Act is to prevent incidents of serious violence by providing the police with additional stop and search powers, over and above those which exist under s 1 of PACE (see Figure 6).

Figure 6: s 60 of the Criminal Justice and Public Order Act 1994, amended by s 8 of the Knives Act 1997 and ss 25–27 of the Crime and Disorder Act 1998[19]

Inspector or above reasonably believes that:

| Incidents of serious violence may occur in any locality in his area. | AND | It is expedient to give an authorisation under s 60 to prevent their occurrence. | OR | *That persons are carrying dangerous instruments or offensive weapons in any locality in his police area without good reason.* |

That officer may give written authorisation (*specifying the grounds*) for uniformed police officers to stop/search vehicles or persons within that specified locality for up to 24 hours. (*If authorisation given by an inspector, a superintendent or above must be informed as soon as it is practicable to do so.*)

↓

An authorisation under s 60 empowers any uniformed police officer:

To stop any pedestrian and search him or anything carried by him for offensive weapons or dangerous instruments ...

↓

AND/OR
↓

To stop any vehicle and search it, its driver and any passenger for offensive weapons or dangerous instruments.

A uniformed police officer may, in the exercise of these powers, stop any person or vehicle and make any search he thinks fit, whether or not he has any grounds for suspecting that the person or vehicle is carrying weapons or articles of that kind.

A uniformed police officer may seize any dangerous instrument or article reasonably suspected to be an offensive weapon.

The drive of a vehicle stopped under s 60 shall be entitled to a written statement that the vehicle was stopped if applied for within 12 months.

A person searched under s 60 shall be entitled to a written statement that he was searched if applied for within 12 months.

To require any person to remove any item which the police officer reasonably believes is being worn wholly or partly for the purpose of concealing his identity.

↓

A uniformed police officer may seize any item reasonably believed to be intended to be worn wholly or mainly for the above purpose (although no special search power is available for the purpose of finding masks, etc).

Failure to remove an item as above when required by a uniformed police officer is an arrestable offence under s 24(2) of PACE.

An authorisation under s 60 may be extended for a further 24 *hours, but only by a superintendent or above.*

19   Knives Act 1997 and Crime and Disorder Act 1998 provisions are shown in italics.

Since the enactment of PACE, the police had complained that the s 1 requirement of reasonable suspicion that persons were carrying dangerous articles, such as offensive weapons and knives, constituted a serious impediment in preventing violent crime. This was a particular problem where large numbers of potential suspects were in a particular locality and reasonable suspicion could be attributed to some, but not all, of them. In response to this difficulty, s 60 of the Criminal Justice and Public Order Act 1994 (as amended) enables police inspectors (or chief inspectors) to make a written authorisation enabling *uniformed* police officers to exercise stop and search powers in places within their police area where incidents of serious violence are anticipated or where potential troublemakers are passing through. However, inspectors must inform a police officer of at least the rank of superintendent that such an authorisation has been made by them as soon as is practicable. These authorisations must be based on reasonable belief that such action is necessary or that persons are carrying dangerous instruments or offensive weapons in any part of that police area without good reason. The authorisation should specify the grounds on which it is given, the locality where these powers may be exercised and the time scale during which these powers may be used. According to the notes for guidance in Code A, authorising officers should, *inter alia,* observe the following:

1F ... the officer should set the minimum period he considers necessary to deal with the risk of violence, the carrying of knives or offensive weapons, or terrorism ...

1G It is for the authorising officer to determine the geographical area in which the use of the powers are to be authorised. In doing so, he may wish to take into account factors such as the nature and venue of the anticipated incident, the numbers of people who may be in the immediate area of any possible incident, their access to surrounding areas and the anticipated level of violence. The officer should not set a geographical area which is wider than that he believes necessary for the purpose of preventing anticipated violence, the carrying of knives or offensive weapons, or terrorism.

It will be observed that the above guidance also refers to terrorism. The application of this aspect of Code A to the prevention of acts of terrorism will be covered below under ss 13A and 13B of the Prevention of Terrorism (Temporary Provisions) Act 1989.

The maximum period that an authorisation under s 60 may be in force is 24 hours, although this may be extended by up to a further 24 hours, but only by a police officer of at least the rank of superintendent. This may be done only once, since a new authorisation has to be made if further use of these powers is necessary.

When an authorisation is in force, it confers wide powers of stop and search upon uniformed police officers in those locations specified in it. Under s 60(4) and s 60(4A) of the 1994 Act, those powers enable uniformed police officers at the scene to do the following:

    (a) stop any pedestrian and search him or anything carried by him for offensive weapons or dangerous instruments; or

    (b) stop any vehicle and search the vehicle, its driver and any passenger for offensive weapons or dangerous instruments.

(4A) ...

    (a) to require any person to remove any item which the constable reasonably believes that person is wearing wholly or mainly for the purpose of concealing his identity;

    (b) to seize any item which the constable reasonably believes any person intends to wear wholly or mainly for that purpose.

Section 60(4A) was inserted by s 25(1) of the Crime and Disorder Act 1998, in order to overcome the problem of people who wear masks to avoid being identified when carrying out violent offences. It is important to note that there is no power for the police to search for such items, although they can be seized in the course of other search powers being exercised at the time. Likewise, offensive weapons and dangerous instruments may also be seized although, of course, there is the express power for the police to search for such items.

However, it is s 60(5) that provides the most controversial aspect of these powers, by stating:

    (5) A constable may, in the exercise of the powers conferred by sub-s (4) above, stop any person or vehicle *and make any search he thinks fit, whether or not he has any grounds for suspecting that the person or vehicle is carrying weapons or articles of that kind* [emphasis added].

At first sight, the above provisions would seem to confer almost unfettered stop and search powers upon the police within the times and locations specified in an authorisation. This begs the following questions: does this mean that the police can effect random searches?; are there limits as to the extent of a search in view of the words '... and make any search he thinks fit'?; can these powers be exercised anywhere, since no mention is made of their restriction to public places?; does the power to require the removal of face coverings extend to those wearing them for religious purposes?; and, since there are no express powers to detain for the purposes of a search or to use force if necessary, as in ss 1 and 117 of PACE respectively, can persons simply walk or drive away when stopped?[20] The answers to the first four questions can be found in Code A, which states that such searches must conform to the same general procedures as those applicable to ss 1, 2 and 3 of PACE. These include the requirement for police officers to state their name (except in terrorist investigations), their station, the grounds or authorisation of the

---

20 For a useful discussion on most of these issues, see Card, R and Ward, R, *The Criminal Justice and Public Order Act 1994*, 1994, Bristol: Jordans.

search and the object of it (para 2.4); that, regardless of the power being exercised, the selection and treatment of those questioned or searched is not to be based upon prejudice, but on objective factors (note for guidance 1AA); searches *in public* must be restricted to a superficial examination of outer clothing and that there is no power to require the removal of any clothing *in public*, other than an outer coat, jacket or gloves (para 3.5); if there may be religious sensitivities where a person is asked to remove a face covering (such as a Muslim woman wearing a face covering for religious purposes), the item should be removed away from public view and, where practicable, in the presence of an officer of the same sex and out of sight of anyone of the opposite sex (note for guidance 1AA).

It is stressed that nearly all of the above guidance applies to all searches, including those under ss 1, 2 and 3 of PACE, as well as those applicable to s 60 of the 1994 Act and, (subject to certain modifications), searches to prevent acts of terrorism, which will be discussed below. In *Osman v DPP* (1999), a fair was being held in a public park and two police officers, acting under a s 60 authorisation, asked the defendant if he was going to attend the fair and, if so, they were going to search him for weapons. None of the officers stated their names or stations and then proceeded to take the defendant by the arms. He responded by swearing and then demanded to be taken to the police station in order to be searched. Fearing that he may have a weapon, the police officers continued to search him and were assaulted. The defendant's conviction for assault on police was quashed on the grounds that the search was unlawful by virtue of the officers' failure to comply with the correct search procedure. They were therefore not acting in the course of their duty.

With regard to detaining for the purposes of a search, it has been subscribed that to stop for the purposes of a search should also mean to detain as well. Also, failure to remain for the purposes of a search could amount to the offence of obstructing police in the execution of their duty and further resistance, resulting in the use of unlawful force against them, could lead to a charge of assault on police.[21] There is also a specific offence under s 60(8) of failing to stop when required to do so for a constable in the exercise of these powers. This could also be construed as failing to remain. Also, it is an offence under s 60(8) for failure to remove an item (face covering) when required to do so by a police officer. The maximum penalty on summary conviction for these offences is one month's imprisonment and/or a level 3 fine on the standard scale (currently £1,000).

Oddly, whilst failure to remove a mask constitutes an arrestable offence (see Chapter 3 as to the meaning of this term), there is no specific arrest power attached to failing to stop for the police. It is submitted that, in such circumstances, the police may resort to their powers under s 25 of PACE

---

21 *Op cit*, Card and Ward, fn 20.

where appropriate ('general arrest conditions', which are discussed in Chapter 3, p 68), or arrest the suspect for the offence of obstructing police or for any other matters that may emerge in the course of the incident for which there may be an arrest power.

Finally, as a result of an amendment to the original s 60 by s 8 of the Knives Act 1997, all persons searched (whether pedestrians or those in vehicles) and drivers of vehicles stopped are entitled to a written statement covering the incident if applied for within 12 months of its occurrence. Previously, only drivers of vehicles and pedestrians fell within the ambit of these provisions. Paragraph 2.6 of Code A states that all persons stopped and searched must be informed of their entitlement to such a record, unless it is impracticable to make such a record in the first instance.

Sections 13A and 13B of the Prevention of Terrorism (Temporary Provisions) Act 1989

The genesis of the current provisions under ss 13A and 13B of the 1989 Act is rather complicated. Section 81 of the Criminal Justice and Public Order Act 1994 created new police powers to stop and search vehicles and persons in order to prevent acts of terrorism. These were inserted into the Prevention of Terrorism (Temporary Provisions) Act 1989 under a new s 13A. The new powers applied to vehicles and their occupants as well as pedestrians. Section 1 of the Prevention of Terrorism (Additional Powers) Act 1996 expanded the provisions under s 81 by, *inter alia*, amending s 13A and creating a new s 13B under the 1989 Act. As a result, s 13A now applies to stop and search powers relating to vehicles and their occupants, and s 13B applies to pedestrians only (see Figure 7). These provisions share a number of features in common with s 60 of the 1994 Act, although there are also some marked differences, since the anti-terrorist provisions are more wide ranging and, subsequently, more accountable. For the sake of simplicity, the provisions of both sections will be covered concurrently.

The exercise of stop and search powers under ss 13A and 13B are contingent upon an authorisation being made by a police officer of at least the rank of assistant chief constable (outside London) or by a commander (in London) (see Figure 1). An authorisation, not exceeding 28 days, may be issued if it appears that this action is expedient in order to prevent acts of terrorism, and this may be given orally or in writing, although oral authorisations must be confirmed in writing as soon as is reasonably practicable. The authorisation should stipulate the place or locality where the stop and search powers may be exercised, which must be within the senior officer's police area.

Figure 7: police powers to stop/search under s 81 (as amended) of the Criminal Justice and Public Order Act 1994 and s 1 of the Prevention of Terrorism (Additional Powers) Act 1996

(Consolidated under ss 13A and 13B of the Prevention of Terrorism (Temporary Provisions) Act 1989)

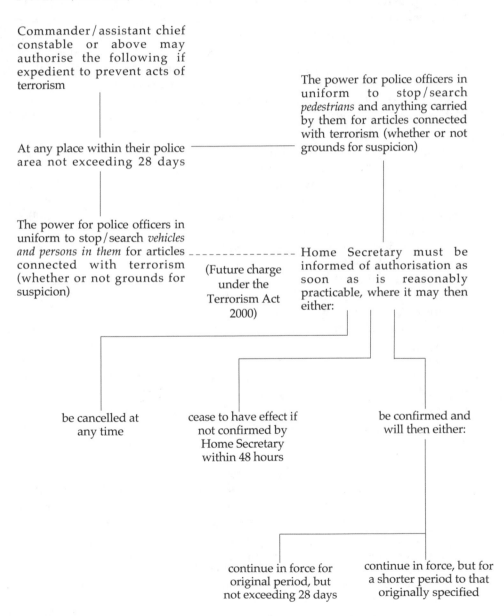

These constitute the rules which are common to both ss 13A and 13B. However, in the case of s 13B, which concerns the stopping and searching of pedestrians, there are additional procedures that must be followed. Whenever a s 13B authorisation has been made, the Home Secretary must be informed. He may then allow the authorisation to continue for its full duration (but not exceeding 28 days) or substitute a shorter period or cancel it at any time. If the Home Secretary does not confirm the authorisation within 48 hours of it being made, then it will automatically cease to have effect. Unlike an authorisation under s 13A, which can be renewed for a further 28 days by an officer of at least the rank of assistant chief constable or commander, a s 13B authorisation cannot be renewed, although there does not appear to be anything to prevent a new authorisation being made. Under the Terrorism Act 2000, it is intended that the powers will be amended so that s 13A authorisations will be subject to the same controls by the Home Secretary as those applicable to s 13B.

The effect of any of the above authorisations is that they confer on *uniformed* police officers the power to stop and search vehicles and persons in them and pedestrians, as well as anything carried by them, for articles that could be used in the commission, preparation or instigation of acts of terrorism. In common with the powers under s 60 of the 1994 Act, the police may conduct such searches without having any prerequisite reasonable suspicion. However, the Codes of Practice have also ameliorated the effects of what would otherwise be almost unfettered police powers to stop and search by largely applying the same general constraints on the exercise of these powers as in s 60. These include notes for guidance 1F and 1G (minimum periods of time and geographical areas to be set by authorising officers), note for guidance 1AA (objective and non-prejudicial grounds for stopping and searching) and para 2.4 (uniformed police officers to identify themselves, their station and the object and grounds for the search to be given). Since these powers are related to terrorist investigations, note that the officers are only required to give their warrant numbers, for instance, rather than their names. But, unlike the powers under s 60, para 3.5 of Code A does *not* apply in the case of ss 13A and 13B, because these powers enable uniformed police officers in public to remove headgear and footwear as well as outer coat, jacket and gloves. Removal of footwear and headgear in public does not apply to s 60 and is expressly excluded from the ambit of s 1 of PACE. One of the reasons why the removal of headgear in public is excluded from PACE is that certain religious groups would find this very offensive, such as Sikhs being required to remove their turbans. In recognition of this, note for guidance 3C states:

> Where there may be religious sensitivities about asking someone to remove headgear using a power under s 13A or 13B of the Prevention of Terrorism (Temporary Provisions) Act 1989, the police officer should offer to carry out the search out of public view (for example, in a police van or police station if there is one nearby).

Drivers of vehicles and also pedestrians stopped under these powers are entitled to a written statement covering the incident, provided any application is made within 12 months of its occurrence. Anyone who fails to stop for the police when required under s 13A or 13B, or who wilfully obstructs them in the exercise of such powers, commits a summary offence. The maximum penalty for each offence is six months' imprisonment and/or a fine not exceeding level 5 on the standard scale (currently £5,000). Note the significant difference in the maximum penalties between failing to stop under s 60 powers and those under ss 13A and 13B.[22]

As a conclusion to the discussion on ss 13A and 13B of the 1989 Act as well as s 60 of the 1994 Act, the following caveat under Code A has been made by note for guidance 1AA regarding the usage of these powers:

> It is important to ensure that powers of stop and search are used responsibly by those who exercise them and those who authorise their use. An officer should bear in mind that he may be required to justify the authorisation or use of the powers to a senior officer and in court, and that misuse of the powers is likely to be harmful to the police effort in the long term and can lead to mistrust of the police by the community ...

The Prevention of Terrorism (Additional Powers) Act 1996, which added many significant powers to the 1989 Act, has an interesting history. It was introduced as a Bill into the House of Commons on 1 April 1996 and was given the Royal Assent two days later. The Government who sponsored this Bill stated that the speed with which it had to be passed was due to an expected IRA bombing campaign that was anticipated during the forthcoming Easter weekend and these powers had to be available to the police in England and Wales before then. As a result, there was very little time for debate on these provisions. Since then, there has been much comment on police powers of stop and search under ss 13A and 13B (and also s 60 of the 1994 Act). One particular concern is that these powers may be used to achieve purposes other than those for which they are intended, such as drug swoops, for instance. Assurances have been made in Parliament and elsewhere that this will not occur.

Powers to stop and search for drugs

As mentioned above, in the introduction to PACE and the section entitled 'Other stop and search powers', a number of pre-existing police powers to stop and search were preserved by PACE. This includes s 23 of the Misuse of Drugs Act 1971, which provides the power for the police to stop, detain and search for controlled drugs.

It should be emphasised that this power is concerned with *controlled* drugs and not just drugs in general. Therefore, what is a controlled drug? These are

---

22 For further discussion on this point, see Jason-Lloyd, L, 'Some recent changes in police powers and their effect on road users' (1997) 2 Road Traffic Indicator 1, 27 May.

substances listed under the Misuse of Drugs Act, which are either addictive or otherwise socially harmful when misused. Most of them have medicinal properties and, when prescribed and used properly for that purpose, are designed to be therapeutic. However, when used for the wrong purpose, they can have the opposite effect. The Misuse of Drugs Act 1971 lists over 100 named substances (together with many chemical variations) which are classed as controlled drugs and places each substance under one of three classes. Class A controlled drugs are the most harmful when misused and these include heroin, cocaine, 'ecstasy', methadone, LSD, pethidine and dipipanone. Class B controlled drugs are less harmful compared to those under Class A, but are still subject to strict legal controls to prevent misuse. This class includes substances such as amphetamine, codeine, methylphenobarbitone and cannabis resin. Class C controlled drugs are largely mild sedatives which, although less potentially harmful than Class A or B drugs, can have addictive qualities. These include diazepam (valium), nitrazepam (mogadon), temazepam, and chlordiazepoxide (librium).[23]

Section 23(2) of the Misuse of Drugs Act provides that, where a police officer has reasonable grounds to suspect than any person is unlawfully in possession of a controlled drug, that officer may:

(a) search that person and detain him for the purpose of searching him;

(b) search any vehicle or vessel in which the constable suspects that the drug may be found and, for that purpose, require the person in control to stop it;

(c) seize and detain, for the purpose of proceedings under the Act, anything found in the course of the search which appears to the constable to be evidence of an offence under the Act.

The search should be conducted in accordance with the relevant rules and guidance under Code A, including the officer giving his or her name and police station, as well as stating the grounds and object of the search. If the officer is not in uniform, then he or she should produce some identification. The reason for the need for compliance with Code A is that para 1.3 states that:

This Code governs the exercise by police officers of statutory powers to search a person without first arresting him or to search a vehicle without making an arrest. The main stop and search powers to which this Code applies at the time the Code was prepared are set out in *Annex A*, but that list should not be regarded as definitive.

This illustrates the common link between certain stop and search powers enacted before (and after) PACE.

---

23 For further discussion, see Jason-Lloyd, L, *Drugs, Addiction and the Law*, 5th edn, 1999, Cambridgeshire: ELM; Fortson, R, *The Law on the Misuse of Drugs and Drug Trafficking Offences*, 3rd edn, 1996, London: Sweet & Maxwell; and Bucknell, P and Ghodse, H, *Bucknell and Ghodse on Misuse of Drugs*, 3rd edn, 1996, London: Sweet & Maxwell.

General points

It is important to note that if any of the procedures under any powers of stop and search, particularly under PACE or the Codes of Practice, are not conducted properly, then the relevant stop and search could be rendered unlawful (see *R v Fennelley* (1989), which is discussed in Chapter 3). Also, the police are not by any means totally reliant upon the stop and search powers covered in this chapter in order to detect crime. A variety of other search powers are available to the police once an arrest has been made, as well as certain other powers conferred on them under anti-terrorist legislation.

SOME MISCELLANEOUS POWERS OF STOP AND SEARCH

The powers of stop and search discussed above are among those most widely known and used within this sphere. A number of other powers exist, which may not be so well known, but are significant constituents within the battery of powers held by the police.

Powers to search unaccompanied goods

The Prevention of Terrorism (Additional Powers) Act 1996 has inserted a number of additional police powers of stop and search under the Prevention of Terrorism (Temporary Provisions) Act 1989, in addition to those discussed under ss 13A and 13B above. Section 3(1) of the 1996 Act has inserted a new para 4A into the 1989 Act, which enables the police (and others) to search unaccompanied goods in order to determine whether they are or have been involved in the commission, preparation or instigation of terrorist acts. Under these provisions, a police officer, immigration officer or customs and excise officer (classed as an 'examining officer' under the Act) may search any goods, such as baggage or stores, for instance, which have arrived in or are about to leave England, Scotland, Wales or Northern Ireland on any ship, aircraft or vehicle, and an examining officer may board any ship, aircraft or vehicle in pursuance of this power. Interestingly, an examining officer may delegate these powers to another person who is not a police, immigration or customs and excise officer, and all such persons may use reasonable force if necessary for such a purpose. These delegated search powers may be vested in ordinary citizens, including persons from the private security industry, although the bodies which appear to have been the main focus of this power include persons employed within organisations such as the Dover Harbour Board Police.[24]

---

24 See Jason-Lloyd, L, 'The Prevention of Terrorism (Additional Powers) Act 1996 – a commentary' (1996) 160 JP 503.

All persons entitled to exercise these search powers may detain anything found for up to seven days for the purpose of further examination. Should this later be required as evidence in criminal proceedings, the goods may be detained until no longer needed. Anyone who wilfully obstructs or seeks to frustrate the object of a search commits a summary offence, punishable by a maximum of three months' imprisonment and/or a level 4 fine on the standard scale (currently £2,500).

Police cordons

This is another power conferred on the police under the auspices of prevention of terrorism under the 1996 Act although, in this instance, it contains a mixture of provisions which include powers of entry into premises, as well as some search powers (see Figure 8). Section 4 of the 1996 Act inserted a new s 16C and Sched 6A into the 1989 Act, which enables a police superintendent or above to authorise the imposing of a cordon in a specified area, if it appears expedient to do so in connection with an investigation into the commission, preparation or instigation of a terrorist act. This may be given in written or oral form although verbal authorisations must be put into writing as soon as is reasonably practicable. A police officer below the rank of superintendent may make an authorisation, but only in matters of great urgency. In such circumstances, the officer must record this in writing and inform a superintendent or above of his or her action as soon as is reasonably practicable. The senior officer receiving this information may then either confirm or cancel the authorisation in writing.

Under this power, police cordons may be in force for up to 14 days initially, although a superintendent or above may renew it but, in aggregate, the total period for which an authorisation is in force must not exceed 28 days. Whilst an authorisation is operative, the area specified must be indicated as clearly as possible, involving the use of police tape or other means. *Uniformed* police officers have the power to order any person to leave the cordoned area immediately, including persons in premises within or adjacent to it, and persons in charge of vehicles within the cordoned area must remove them if ordered to do so by the police. Failure to comply with any of these orders without lawful authority or reasonable excuse constitutes a summary offence punishable by a maximum of three months' imprisonment and/or a fine not exceeding level 4 on the standard scale. This same maximum penalty also applies to persons who disobey directions by uniformed police officers whilst they are are exercising their power to prohibit or restrict access to the cordoned area to pedestrians or vehicles. Anyone who wilfully obstructs the police in the execution of any of these powers also commit an offence punishable by the same maxim.

Figure 8: police cordons

Superintendent or above may
authorise a cordon to be imposed
within a specified area if expedient to
do so in connection with an
investigation into terrorism

← Police officers below the rank of
superintendent may authorise a
cordon if the matter is of great
urgency, but must inform a
superintendent or above as soon
as is reasonably practicable, who
may either confirm or cancel it

Initial authorisation must not exceed 14 days (renewable
for overall period not exceeding 28 days)

Police officers at the scene have powers to:

order persons to
leave the cordoned
area, including
persons in
buildings

order persons in
charge of vehicles
to remove them

reposition any
vehicle

prohibit or restrict
any vehicular or
pedestrian access

Superintendent or above may authorise police officers
within the area of a cordon to do the following if reasonable
grounds for believing material likely to be of substantial
value to a terrorist investigation is likely to be found on
premises within the cordoned area (excluding items subject to
legal privilege, excluded or special procedure material)

Search premises specified in the
authorisation and any person found there

Seize and retain anything found if reasonable grounds for
believing it is likely to be of substantial value to the terrorist
investigation and it is necessary to prevent it from being
concealed, lost, damaged, altered or destroyed
(except items subject to legal privilege)

Written authority by a superintendent or above can extend police powers within cordoned areas even further. This will enable premises wholly or partly within that area to be searched, if the authorising officer has reasonable grounds to believe that material is to be found there that is likely to be of substantial value to a terrorist investigation, excluding items subject to legal privilege or excluded or special procedure material (see Chapter 4 for the definition of these terms). For as long as such premises are subject to a police cordon, entry may be effected at any time and on more than one occasion. In addition to the power to enter and search such premises, the police may also search any person found there and may seize anything which is reasonably believed to be of substantial value to the terrorist investigation (except items subject to legal privilege). Persons found in such premises who are subsequently searched *in public* may not be required to remove any of their clothing other than any headgear, footwear, outer coat, jacket or gloves. Anyone who wilfully obstructs or seeks to frustrate the object of such a search commits a summary offence punishable by the same maximum sentence as mentioned above.

The Terrorism Act 2000 was enacted in July 2000. Once it comes into force, it will repeal the Prevention of Terrorism (Temporary Provisions) Act 1989, although this is not anticipated until 2001. The provisions under the 1989 Act, which have been mentioned in this chapter, will be recast under the new legislation.

'Raves' and prohibited assemblies

Under ss 65 and 71 of the Criminal Justice and Public Order Act 1994, the police have been given powers to prevent persons going to certain gatherings, although this has provided them with powers to stop, but not search. Section 65 of the 1994 Act provides that police officers *in uniform* may stop persons who are reasonably believed to be travelling to a 'rave', where such a gathering has already been disbanded under the direction of a police superintendent or above. This power may only be exercised within a five mile radius of the gathering and the police have a further power to direct the persons stopped not to proceed in the direction of the 'rave'. The police may arrest without warrant anyone who disregards such a direction and that person will be liable on summary conviction to a fine not exceeding level 3 on the standard scale (£1,000). These powers may not be exercised on an 'exempt person', who is described under the Act as the occupier of the land where a 'rave' has been disbanded, any member of that person's family, any employee or agent of that person and any person whose home is on that land.

Section 71 of the 1994 Act is almost identical to s 65, except that it is applied in order to stop and turn back persons reasonably believed to be going to the venue of a prohibited assembly. As mentioned above, no power of search applies under the provisions of ss 65 or 71, although the police may draw upon search powers from other legal sources where appropriate. For example, if any persons are reasonably suspected of carrying stolen property or offensive weapons, the police may exercise their search powers under s 1 of PACE.

If, in the exercise of any of the search powers covered in this chapter, the police find any article which is suspected of being unlawfully carried, then they may arrest the suspect as well as seize the article. Police powers of arrest as well as arrest procedures will be covered in the following chapter, including police powers of seizure, which will be discussed in Chapter 5.

CHAPTER 3

POLICE POWERS OF ARREST

DEFINITION OF 'ARREST'

One of the most popularised conceptions of an arrest is the scenario whereby a police officer takes a suspect by the arm who is then led to a waiting police car having first been cautioned. In the American style, one would expect the suspect to be 'read his rights' whilst being handcuffed. These arrests usually occur in the street or other public places, or even in private property, but this is not the only situation under which a person may be arrested. A person may already be at a police station voluntarily, in order to 'assist the police with their enquiries', but could later be arrested. Under what other circumstances can a person be liable to arrest? What powers are available to the police? What are the correct arrest procedures? To what extent may ordinary citizens make arrests? These, among other questions, will be discussed throughout this chapter, but first it is necessary to define the word 'arrest'. An arrest may be defined as the lawful deprivation of a citizen's liberty, exercised to whatever degree of lawful force is reasonably necessary, in order to assist in the investigation and prevention of crime, to ensure that a citizen is brought before a court or to preserve a person's safety or others or their property. From this definition, an insight may already be gained regarding the complexity of this subject. This is not by chance, since it is a fundamental tenet of our basic rights and freedoms that no person shall be deprived of their liberty without lawful reason.[1]

An overview of police powers of arrest

As well as recognising the need to reform police powers of stop and search (see Chapter 2), the Philips Royal Commission were also aware of a similar need to rationalise police powers of arrest which, likewise, consisted of a patchwork of statutory and common law provisions:

> There is a lack of clarity and an uneasy and confused mixture of common law and statutory powers of arrest, the latter having grown piecemeal and without any consistent rationale.[2]

---

1   'The right to personal liberty as understood in England ... means, in substance, a person's right not to be subjected to imprisonment, arrest or other physical coercion in any manner that does not admit of legal justification.' Dicey, A, *An Introduction to the Study of the Law of the Constitution*, 10th edn, 1959, London: Macmillan, cited in Hood-Phillips, O, *Constitutional and Administrative Law*, 7th edn, 1987, London: Sweet & Maxwell, Chapter 25.

2   Philips Royal Commission, para 3.68.

The Government accepted this point in principle, but did not accept all of the Commission's proposals as to how this problem could be remedied.[3] In the end, the enactment of the Police and Criminal Evidence Act 1984 (PACE), among a number of other things, rationalised and preserved many statutory police powers of arrest that existed prior to its enactment. All such powers work through PACE, especially in terms of its procedures. These statutes include the Prison Act 1952, the Bail Act 1976, the Criminal Law Act 1977, the Public Order Act 1936, the Children and Young Persons Act 1969 and the Mental Health Act 1983 (see Sched 2 to PACE for the complete list). These were preserved basically because of the need to take certain vulnerable persons into police custody or to apprehend persons unlawfully at large. A substantial number of statutes conferring arrest powers on the police have been enacted since PACE. These include the Sporting Events (Control of Alcohol, etc) Act 1985, the Public Order Act 1986 and the Criminal Justice and Public Order Act 1994.

At this stage, it is important to distinguish between the different categories of arrest powers that are available to the police. The two *main* categories are arrests *without* warrant and arrest *with* warrant. Arrests with warrant are far less common than those which are made without; therefore, the former will be discussed later in this chapter.

Arrests *without* warrant

As far as arrests without warrant are concerned, these fall under five *main* subheadings as follows:

(1) offences where the police only are given an arrest power under the statutes which created these offences. This is known as a 'power of arrest'. A number of these, which existed before 1984, were preserved by PACE. For example, under s 1 of the Public Order Act 1936, it is an offence to wear a political uniform in public. Section 7(3) of the 1936 Act states:

> A constable may, without warrant, arrest any person reasonably suspected by him to be committing an offence under s 1 of this Act.

An example of a power of arrest conferred on the police for a specific offence since PACE was enacted is s 3 of the Public Order Act 1986, which created the offence of affray. Section 3(6) provides that:

> A constable may arrest without warrant anyone he reasonably suspects is committing affray.

A power of arrest actually created by PACE can be found under s 27. Under s 27(1), a person convicted of a 'recordable offence' (see Chapter 7, fn 21) who has not been in police detention for the offence and,

---

3   See Zander, M, *The Police and Criminal Evidence Act 1984*, 3rd edn, 1995, London: Sweet & Maxwell.

subsequently, has not been fingerprinted, may be required by a constable to attend a police station to have this done. Section 27(3) then states:

> Any constable may arrest without warrant a person who has failed to comply with a requirement under sub-s (1) above.

Also, s 63A(7) of PACE, which was inserted by s 56 of the Criminal Justice and Public Order Act 1994, has given the police a further power of arrest. This applies to persons who do not comply with a request to attend a police station to have a body sample taken (see Chapter 7).

The exercise of a 'power of arrest', as in all arrests made by the police, is subject to the general rules governing arrest procedures under PACE, as will be illustrated below;

(2) statutory powers of arrest without warrant conferred upon 'any person' for specific offences. These fall under a grey area and are, therefore, covered in the final part of this chapter, under s 3(4) of the Theft Act 1978;

(3) offences classed as 'arrestable offences', which are defined and listed under s 24 of PACE where the police and (subject to certain limitations) ordinary citizens may make an arrest (see Figure 9). Running alongside these provisions are those under s 116 and Sched 5 to PACE, which create 'serious arrestable offences', although these have greater significance to police powers of detention rather than arrest. Arrestable offences will be discussed in greater detail below;

(4) any offences to which there is no direct police power of arrest or which are not arrestable offences, but the circumstances surrounding their commission justify invoking 'general arrest conditions' under s 25 of PACE. These offences are normally dealt with by way of summons, such as nearly all motoring offences, but, under s 25, the police may arrest if certain adverse conditions or potential obstructions are present. Further coverage of this subject is included on p 68, below;

(5) the common law power to arrest for a breach of the peace. This is the only common law power that was not repealed by PACE and is available to both the police and ordinary citizens. The definition of what constitutes a breach of the peace, together with the relevant case law, will be discussed on p 71, below.

Arrestable offences

Arrestable offences are covered under s 24 of PACE, which is divided into seven sub-sections. Sub-sections (1) to (3) define arrestable offences and sub-ss (4)–(7) provide the conditions under which these arrest powers may be exercised. Section 24(1) provides that:

> (1) The powers of summary arrest conferred by the following sub-sections shall apply:

(a) to offences for which the sentence is fixed by law;

(b) to offences for which a person of 21 years of age or over (not previously convicted) may be sentenced to imprisonment for a term of five years (or might be so sentenced, but for the restrictions imposed by s 33 of the Magistrates' Courts Act 1980); and

(c) to the offences to which sub-s (2) below applies and, in this Act, 'arrestable offence' means any such offence.

Section 24(1)(a) simply means that murder is an arrestable offence because it is now the only offence for which the sentence is fixed by law. The only sentence that can be given on a murder conviction is mandatory life imprisonment (or its equivalent for offenders aged between 10 and 20 years inclusive). Up until 1998, technically at least, the offences of treason and piracy actually attracted the death sentence. However, s 36 of the Crime and Disorder Act 1998 has replaced this with discretionary (but not mandatory) life imprisonment; therefore, the sentences for these offences are no longer fixed by law.

Section 24(1)(b) is much wider in terms of the number of offences which fall under its provisions. It includes any offence which can attract at least a five year term of imprisonment if committed by a person aged 21 or over who has not been previously convicted. Examples of substantive offences which fall under this category, together with their maximum custodial terms, are: assault occasioning actual bodily harm (five years); wounding/grievous bodily harm (five years); blackmail (14 years); burglary of a dwelling (14 years); burglary of a non-dwelling (10 years); theft (seven years); obtaining property by deception (10 years); obtaining services by deception (five years); forgery (10 years); counterfeiting (10 years); simple criminal damage of more than £5,000 (10 years); rioting (10 years); violent disorder (five years); bomb hoax (seven years); contamination of goods (10 years); witness/juror intimidation (five years); perjury (seven years); possession of a Class A controlled drug (seven years); possession of a Class B controlled drug (five years) and many more.[4]

Section 24(2) is more complex than the preceding provisions. It specifically lists 19 categories of substantive offences which do not, themselves, attract the five year or more custodial sentences, as in sub-s (1)(b), but are considered serious enough to be classed as arrestable. This list has changed significantly since it was originally enacted in 1984 and has been subject to some deletions as well as many additions. The latest (under (r), below) came into force on 27 September 1999. Section 24(2) provides that the following are arrestable offences – the words in italics have been inserted for clarification where necessary:

---

4   A more complete list can be gained from authoritative works such as *Blackstone's Criminal Practice*, London: Blackstone and *Archbold's Criminal Pleadings, Evidence and Practice*, London: Sweet & Maxwell. See, also, Cape, E and Jawaid, L, *Defending Suspects at Police Stations*, 3rd edn, 1999, London: Legal Action Group, Appendix 4.

(a) offences for which a person may be arrested under the Customs and Excise Acts, as defined under the Customs and Excise Management Act 1979;

[This basically includes smuggling offences. Although enforcement of these provisions falls primarily on Customs and Excise officers, the police sometimes become involved in the enforcement of this aspect of the law.]

(b) offences under the Official Secrets Act 1920 that are not arrestable by virtue of the term of imprisonment for which a person may be sentenced in respect to them;

(bb) offences under any provisions of the Official Secrets Act 1989, except s 8(1), (4) or (5);

[Some offences under the 1920 Act attract terms of imprisonment which fall under s 24(1)(b) of PACE; therefore, they automatically become arrestable offences. Others do not, but are considered serious enough to justify making them arrestable under (b), above. The offences under (bb) cover the unauthorised disclosure of official information, but do not attract custodial sentences sufficient to place them under s 24(1)(b), they are nevertheless also considered serious enough to be classed as arrestable offences. Section 8(1), (4) and (5) of the 1989 Act covers offences which are triable summarily only and have been excluded from the ambit of arrestable offences.]

(c) offences under s 22 of the Sexual Offences Act 1956 (causing prostitution of a woman) or s 23 (procuration of girl under 21);

(d) offences under s 12(1) of the Theft Act 1968 (taking motor vehicle or other conveyance without authority, etc) or s 25(1) (going equipped for stealing, etc);

(e) any offence under the Football (Offences) Act 1991;

[These are the offences of throwing missiles, indecent or racialist chanting, or pitch invasion during designated football matches.]

(f) an offence under s 2 of the Obscene Publications Act 1959 (publication of obscene matter);

(g) an offence under s 1 of the Protection of Children Act 1978 (taking or making, etc, indecent photographs or pseudo-photographs of children);

(h) an offence under s 166 of the Criminal Justice and Public Order Act 1994 (football ticket-touting);

(i) an offence under s 19 of the Public Order Act 1986 (publishing, etc, material intended or likely to stir up racial hatred);

(j) an offence under s 167 of the Criminal Justice and Public Order Act 1994 (touting for hire car services);

(k) an offence under s 1(1) of the Prevention of Crime Act 1953 (prohibiting the carrying of offensive weapons without lawful authority or reasonable excuse in a public place);

(l) an offence under s 139(1) of the Criminal Justice Act 1988 (offence of having article with blade or point in public place);

(m) an offence under s 139A(1) or (2) of the Criminal Justice Act 1988 (offence of having article with blade or point (or offensive weapon) on school premises);

(n) an offence under s 2 of the Protection from Harassment Act 1997 (causing harassment);

(o) an offence under s 60(8)(b) of the Criminal Justice and Public Order Act 1994 (failure to comply with direction to remove a mask, etc);

(p) an offence under s 32(1)(a) of the Crime and Disorder Act 1998 (racially aggravated harassment);

(q) an offence under s 16(4) of the Football Spectators Act 1989 (failure to comply with a duty imposed by an international football banning order);

(r) an offence under s 32(3) of the Public Order Act 1986 (entering premises in breach of domestic football banning order).

In relation to the above list of arrestable offences under sub-s (2), s 24(3) of PACE provides:

Without prejudice to s 2 of the Criminal Attempts Act 1981, the powers of summary arrest conferred by the following sub-sections shall also apply to the offences of:

(a) conspiring to commit any of the offences mentioned in sub-s (2), above;

(b) attempting to commit any such offence [other than an offence under s 12(1) of the Theft Act 1968];

(c) inciting, aiding, abetting, counselling or procuring the commission of any such offence,

and such offences are also arrestable offences for the purposes of this Act.

These provisions mean that aiding, abetting, counselling or procuring any of the offences listed in s 24(2) of PACE (in other words, being an accomplice to any of them) are also arrestable offences. This also applies to the inchoate offences of inciting, conspiring or attempting to commit them, although there are some exceptions regarding attempts. Section 24(3)(b) states that an attempt does not apply to the offence under s 12(1) of the Theft Act 1968 (taking a motor vehicle or other conveyance without authority) under s 24(2)(d). This is because s 37 and para 98 of Sched 15 to the Criminal Justice Act 1988 downgraded this offence from being triable either way to a summary only offence. On the basis of the argument that s 1(4) of the Criminal Attempts Act 1981 provides that there is no such offence as attempting to commit an offence which is triable summarily only, it is submitted that offences under s 24(2)(e), (h), (j), (n), (o), (q) and (r), as well as the s 12(1) offence in (d), cannot be attempted and, therefore, fall outside the general scope of s 24(3)(b).[5]

An important point regarding the issue of arrestable offences is that certain wide investigative powers are available to the police where an offence is arrestable. These include powers of entry and search of premises without

---

5   For a full discussion, see Jason-Lloyd, L, 'Section 24(2) of the Police and Criminal Evidence Act 1984 – codification or complication?' (1999) 163 JP 944.

warrant, which will be covered in Chapter 4. This is one of the principal reasons for the inclusion of certain offences under s 24(2) of PACE. Whilst some of these are not particularly serious, several being triable summarily only, and a few are not even imprisonable, they can lead or be connected to more serious crimes.

Under what circumstances can an arrest be made for an arrestable offence? This is dealt with under s 24(4)–(7) of PACE, which provides:

(4) Any person may arrest without a warrant:

   (a) anyone who is in the act of committing an arrestable offence;

   (b) anyone whom he has reasonable grounds for suspecting to be committing such an offence.

(5) Where an arrestable offence has been committed, any person may arrest without a warrant:

   (a) anyone who is guilty of the offence;

   (b) anyone whom he has reasonable grounds for suspecting to be guilty of it.

(6) Where a constable has reasonable grounds for suspecting that an arrestable offence has been committed, he may arrest without a warrant anyone whom he has reasonable grounds for suspecting to be guilty of the offence.

(7) A constable may arrest without a warrant:

   (a) anyone who is about to commit an arrestable offence;

   (b) anyone whom he has reasonable grounds for suspecting to be about to commit an arrestable offence.

See Figure 9, which should assist in understanding the following discussion.

Figure 9: powers of arrest without warrant under ss 24 and 116 and Sched 5 to the Police and Criminal Evidence Act 1984

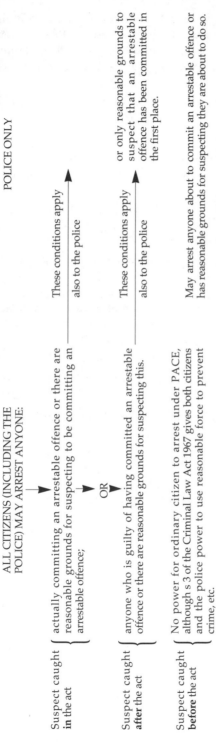

ALL CITIZENS (INCLUDING THE POLICE) MAY ARREST ANYONE:

POLICE ONLY

Suspect caught in the act { actually committing an arrestable offence or there are reasonable grounds for suspecting to be committing an arrestable offence;

These conditions apply also to the police

OR

Suspect caught after the act { anyone who is guilty of having committed an arrestable offence or there are reasonable grounds for suspecting this.

These conditions apply also to the police

or only reasonable grounds to suspect that an arrestable offence has been committed in the first place.

Suspect caught before the act { No power for ordinary citizen to arrest under PACE, although s 3 of the Criminal Law Act 1967 gives both citizens and the police power to use reasonable force to prevent crime, etc.

May arrest anyone about to commit an arrestable offence or has reasonable grounds for suspecting they are about to do so.

Arrestable offences (s 24)

Offences where sentence fixed by law, offences where a person 21 years or over may be given a five year term of imprisonment on a first conviction, offences under the Customs and Excise Acts, the Official Secrets Acts 1920 and 1989. Any offence under the Sexual Offences Act 1956, two offences under the Theft Act 1968. Any offence under the Football (Offences) Act 1991, publishing or distributing racially inflammatory material, possession of offensive weapon or article with blade or sharp point in a public place or school premises, ticket-touting, taxi-touting, causing harassment, racially aggravated harassment, failure to remove mask, etc, under s 60 of Criminal Justice and Public Order Act 1994, failure to report under an international football banning order and breach of a domestic football banning order. Also, conspiring, inciting, aiding, abetting, counselling or procuring any of the foregoing, and attempting, except football ticket-touting, taxi-touting, any offence under the Football (Offences) Act 1991, causing harassment, failure to remove mask, etc, failure to comply with conditions of an international football banning order, breach of a domestic football banning order and one offence under the Theft Act 1968.

Can be transformed into serious arrestable offences under s 116 if risk of: serious harm to State security or public order, death or serious injury to any person, serious interference with the administration of justice, or substantial financial gain or loss.

Crimes which are always classed as serious arrestable offences

Treason, murder, manslaughter, rape, kidnapping, incest with girl under 13, buggery with a person under 16, indecent assault in form of gross indecency, causing explosion likely to endanger life, intercourse with girl under 13, possession of firearm intending to commit criminal offences, causing death through dangerous driving, hostage taking, hijacking, torture, certain drug trafficking offences and offences under the Prevention of Terrorism (Temporary Provisions) Act 1989 – replaced by the Terrorism Act 2000. Also, obscenity offences and child pornography (except simple possession of material).

Section 24(4) of PACE

Under sub-s (a), any person, including the police, may arrest without a warrant anyone who is caught in the act of committing an arrestable offence. If a suspect is arrested on that basis and if he or she is not committing an arrestable offence, then the arrest is unlawful. However, if an arrest is made under sub-s (b) on the basis that the police or an ordinary citizen has reasonable grounds for suspecting a person to be committing an arrestable offence, the arrest will be lawful, even if the suspect was not committing such an offence. This is illustrated in *R v Brosch* (1988), where a store manager had lawfully arrested a man seen in the toilets who was looking dazed and had a syringe in his possession. The store manager asked him some questions about drugs and then took hold of him when he tried to leave and said 'You are not going anywhere'. In this case, the store manager had reasonable grounds for suspecting the defendant to be unlawfully in possession of controlled drugs which is an arrestable offence. But, if, for instance, the suspect did not unlawfully have drugs in his possession, the arrest would have still been lawful, because the store manager had reasonable grounds for suspecting that an arrestable offence *was being committed*. This constitutes the well known 'citizen's arrest power', which is often relied upon by security professionals, such as store detectives, since the focus of their attention is on theft, which is an arrestable offence, as it can attract a maximum seven year prison sentence. But such powers should always be exercised with care, since an arrest which is declared unlawful can result in civil or even criminal action being taken against the arrestor. If the police make an unlawful arrest, as far as the former is concerned, they are usually protected by the vicarious liability mentioned in Chapter 1. Others may not have the same legal protection and may suffer the punitive effects of being sued for making an unlawful arrest (see the coverage below regarding the consequences of such action).

Section 24(5) and (6) of PACE

This applies to situations where an arrestable offence *has been* committed, in contrast to s 24(4), where the offence *is being* committed. Under s 24(5)(a), any person may arrest anyone who is guilty of having committed an arrestable offence or, under sub-s (b), is reasonably suspected of being guilty of it. In both instances, the lawfulness of an arrest by an *ordinary citizen* under these provisions is contingent upon the suspect being found guilty in court. If not, then the arrest is unlawful. This is illustrated in *R v Self* (1992), where a store detective and a shop assistant allegedly saw the defendant take a bar of chocolate and leave the store without paying. He then threw it under a car and was challenged by the store detective. Following a scuffle, the defendant ran away and was pursued and later arrested by a man who had seen the earlier incident. The defendant was charged with theft (shoplifting) and assault with intent to resist arrest. He was acquitted of the shoplifting charge, but was found guilty of two counts of assault with intent to resist arrest. These two charges were overturned on appeal, because he had been acquitted of theft; therefore, no arrestable offence had been committed and this invalidated the arrest power that was used.[6] It should be noted that this was a scenario affecting just one defendant. There is one redeeming feature under these provisions where more than one suspect is allegedly involved. This is illustrated as follows:

> The legality of the arrest is not affected by the fact that the person arrested did not commit the arrestable offence if there were such reasonable grounds, provided that the offence was committed by someone. For example, security officers arrested three men reasonably suspected of theft from their employer. Two were subsequently acquitted; the third was convicted. The conviction made it clear than an arrestable offence had been committed; therefore, the arrest of those acquitted was lawful under s 24(5)(b). The acquittal of all three would not render the arrest unlawful.[7]

However, sub-s (6) significantly extends this arrest power to the *police only*, where they have reasonable grounds to suspect that an arrestable offence has been committed in the first place, even if it is later disclosed that one has not occurred. This may seem to militate somewhat harshly against public spirited citizens who make arrests when an arrestable offence has not been committed at the outset, but the rationale for this is that Parliament believed that wider powers are best left in the hands of trained police officers.

Section 24(7) of PACE

This arrest power applies only to the police, who may arrest a person about to commit an arrestable offence or anyone whom they have reasonable grounds for suspecting to be about to commit an arrestable offence. This would cover the situation where, for example, a police officer sees a person about to throw a brick through a window, but restrains the suspect at the last moment. In this case, the suspect is reasonably suspected of being about to commit criminal damage. This principle would also apply where a police officer sees a person about to stab someone, but manages to hold the suspect down before any harm is done to the intended victim. But what if an ordinary citizen sees the same things about to happen? It would be absurd to leave the general public with no legal provision for dealing with such situations; therefore, there is the power under s 3(1) of the Criminal Law Act 1967, which states:

---

6   See Stannard, J, 'The store detective's dilemma' (1994) 58 JCL 393, November.
7   Lidstone, K and Palmer, C, *Bevan and Lidstone's The Investigation of Crime: A Guide to Police Powers*, 2nd edn, 1996, London: Butterworths.

A person may use such force as is reasonable in the circumstances in the prevention of crime or in effecting or assisting in the lawful arrest of offenders or of persons unlawfully at large.

Note that this provision applies to 'a person', which includes all citizens, including the police. With regard to the latter, this empowers them to use reasonable force if necessary in the exercise of their powers outside of PACE (note that s 117 of PACE only empowers them to use reasonable force in the exercise of the coercive powers under that statute). Whether s 3(1) of the 1967 Act is used by the police or members of the public, it is essential that any force used must be reasonable and necessary. This is a question of fact which is left to the jury to decide. Another point which must be borne in mind is that any force used must be proportionate to the harm threatened. In the somewhat dramatic case of *Cockcroft v Smith* (1705), it was held that excessive violence should not be returned in response to a minor assault. Cockcroft, a clerk in a court, became involved in an altercation with Smith, an attorney. In the course of the scuffle, Cockcroft pointed his finger towards Smith's eye and Smith promptly bit it off. In this case, Holt CJ said:

> ... in a case of a small assault, [a man ought not to] give a violent or an unsuitable return. For hitting a man a little with a little stick is not a reason for him to draw a sword and cut and hew the other.

Serious arrestable offences

Certain offences are so grave that, by virtue of their nature and consequences, the Philips Royal Commission felt that these should attract additional police powers in order to enhance their chances of detection.[8] These include additional powers to detain those suspected of having committed such crimes, the authorising of road blocks and delaying a suspect's access to legal advice or notification to another of his or her arrest. The definition of serious arrestable offences is rather convoluted, as is the case with those which are simply arrestable. We therefore have a list of offences which are always classed as serious arrestable offences, as well as a formula for converting arrestable offences into the serious variety. The latter operates under s 116 of PACE, which provides that an arrestable offence becomes a serious arrestable offence where it has led to any of the following consequences or is intended or likely to lead to any of them, namely:

(a) serious harm to the security of the State or to public order;

(b) serious interference with the administration of justice or with the investigation of offences or of a particular offence;

---

8   Royal Commission on Criminal Procedure, 1981, para 3.5.

(c) the death of any person;

(d) serious injury to any person;

(e) substantial financial gain to any person; and

(f) serious financial loss to any person.

If an arrestable offence involves making a threat which, if carried out, would be likely to lead to any of the consequences in (a)–(f) above, that will also be classed as a serious arrestable offence (see Figure 9).

An example of where an arrestable offence may become serious can be illustrated in the following scenarios.

A person is caught whilst committing a burglary, which is an arrestable offence. However, this could be transformed into a serious arrestable offence if the premises constituted the home of an important government official and the suspect was about to break into a safe where secret documents were kept (see (a)). If the suspect was caught in official premises where important evidence was being held and was in the process of trying to destroy it, then the provisions under (b) may apply. Also, (e) may apply if the suspect was caught in premises whilst stealing valuable jewellery and art treasures, and (f) may apply if the burglar was caught stealing £1,000 from the home of a pensioner and this constituted the victim's life savings. But (f) may not apply if the same amount of money was stolen from a bank, as this would not constitute a great loss to it.

Crimes which are always classed as serious arrestable offences are listed under s 116 and Sched 5 to PACE. These include murder, manslaughter, causing death by dangerous driving, treason, rape, indecent assault which constitutes gross indecency, incest with a girl under 13, intercourse with a girl under 13, possession of firearms with intent to injure, use of firearms and imitation firearms to resist arrest, carrying of firearms with criminal intent, kidnapping, causing an explosion likely to endanger life or property, hostage taking, hijacking, torture, drug trafficking offences under the Drug Trafficking Act 1994, certain offences under the Prevention of Terrorism (Temporary Provisions) Act 1989, the publication of obscene matter and offences relating to indecent photographs and pseudo-photographs of children (except simple possession).

General arrest conditions

The provisions under s 25 of PACE were among some of the most controversial under the Police and Criminal Evidence Bill during its passage through Parliament. This is because it empowers the police to arrest persons who have committed offences which are not arrestable. At first sight, this would appear to be a rather draconian power, but deeper analysis into the purposes behind these provisions discloses sound practical reasons for this arrest power being conferred upon the police.

Non-arrestable offences include literally dozens of minor offences, which are usually dealt with at summary level before magistrates. The bulk of these constitute motoring offences, apart from some of the most serious, such as causing death by dangerous driving. However, there are also a substantial number of other offences which are non-arrestable, in view of their less serious nature, but which fall within the scope of law enforcement duties that fall upon the police. These include common assault, highway obstruction, litter dropping, unlawful street trading and many more. The usual procedure for prosecuting offences under this category is to issue a summons for the defendant to attend court. This procedure is known as 'reporting' rather than 'arresting'. The effectiveness of this method in bringing suspects to court is largely contingent upon the correct name and address being given. In the past, substantial numbers of summonses were 'unserved' on such persons, because of incorrect particulars being given to the police at the time, as well as other reasons.

Section 25 of PACE enables the police to arrest a person in connection with a non-arrestable offence which they have reasonable cause to suspect is being or has been committed or attempted, and where it appears that the service of a summons is impracticable or inappropriate 'because any of the general arrest conditions are satisfied'. Section 25(3) then defines what the general arrest conditions are (the words in italics have been added for clarification where appropriate):

(3) The general arrest conditions are:

(a) that the name of the relevant person in unknown to, and cannot be readily ascertained by, the constable;

[This includes situations where a suspect simply refuses to provide a police officer with his or her name, or gives an absurd name which is obviously not real, such as 'Donald Duck'.]

(b) that the constable has reasonable grounds for doubting whether a name furnished by the relevant person as his name is his real name;

[Sometimes, a name is given which does not sound quite as absurd as above, but the police officer has reasonable grounds for doubting that this is the suspect's real name.]

(c) that:

(i) the relevant person has failed to furnish a satisfactory address for service; or

(ii) the constable has reasonable grounds for doubting whether an address furnished by the relevant person is a satisfactory address for service;

[In both the above situations, a police officer may arrest a suspect who either refuses to give his or her address (or gives one which is obviously very doubtful, such as 10 Downing Street) or provides an address which would be unsatisfactory for the service of a summons. For instance, a large gypsy encampment.]

(d) that the constable has reasonable grounds for believing that arrest is necessary to prevent the relevant person:

　(i)　causing physical injury to himself or any other person;

　(ii)　suffering physical injury;

　(iii) causing loss of or damage to property;

　(iv) committing an offence against public decency; or

　(v)　causing an unlawful obstruction of the highway;

(e) that the constable has reasonable grounds for believing that arrest is necessary to protect a child or other vulnerable person from the relevant person.

[The above conditions may generally apply where a minor assault has been committed and the suspect is still in a very aggressive mood, despite the presence of the police, or if the suspect threatens self-harm or if that person is at risk of being harmed by others involved in the incident. Also, the suspect may threaten to damage property out of revenge or there may be a risk of evidence being destroyed. Where an offence involves generally indecent behaviour and the condition in sub-s (5) below applies, an arrest will be appropriate in order to remove such a person. If a person obstructs the highway and refuses to move the source of that obstruction, then an arrest may be a correct course of action. Finally, the protection of children and other vulnerable persons could apply where, for instance, a violent male commits a common assault against his female partner and there are children or very elderly people living in the same household.]

(4) For the purposes of sub-s (3) above, an address is a satisfactory address for service if it appears to the constable:

(a) that the relevant person will be at it for a sufficiently long period for it to be possible to serve him with a summons; or

(b) that some other person specified by the relevant person will accept service of a summons for the relevant person at it.

[Even if a suspect provides a correct address, if that abode happens to be an overnight hostel or a holiday address, for instance, and a more suitable alternative address is not given or the suspect is unable to specify someone living at a suitable address who is able to accept the summons on his or her behalf, that suspect will be arrested.]

(5) Nothing in sub-s (3)(d) above authorises the arrest of a person under sub-para (iv) of that paragraph, except where members of the public going about their normal business cannot reasonably be expected to avoid the person to be arrested.

In *Nicholas v DPP* (1987), it was held that the correct approach to arresting a person under s 25 is to inform the suspect of the offence for which he or she is being arrested and the general arrest condition which exists, such as failing to provide a name and address. As a matter of good practice, the police are advised that the suspect should be told the consequences of meeting the general arrest conditions before arresting that person, for example, by saying 'If you do not provide me with your name and address, then you will be arrested'. Under s 30(7) of PACE, there is a power to de-arrest a person before reaching a police station who co-operates and provides a name and address (see p 77, below, for further coverage of this power).

Common law power to arrest for a breach of the peace

This is a common law power of arrest that was preserved by PACE and is available to ordinary citizens as well as the police. As far as the police are concerned, it has not been widely used by them in more recent times because of the array of public order offences created by the Public Order Act 1986 and the Criminal Justice and Public Order Act 1994. Also, the police have specific powers under s 17 of PACE, for instance, to effect entry into premises in order to deal with incidents which can sometimes be placed under the heading of breaches of the peace (see Chapter 4). These have made the exercise of their powers more certain, in view of the availability of statutory provisions, rather than relying on the interpretation of the common law in individual cases.

What is a breach of the peace? It is important to note that a breach of the peace is not simply noisy or exuberant behaviour, but there must be violent conduct or the apprehension of it. In *R v Howell* (1981), a breach of the peace was defined by the Court of Appeal as follows:

> We are emboldened to say that there is a breach of the peace whenever harm is actually done or is likely to be done to a person or in his presence to his property, or a person is in fear of being so harmed through an assault, an affray, a riot, an unlawful assembly or other disturbance.

Any citizen (including the police) may arrest another where a breach of the peace has been committed in his or her presence, or where there is reasonable cause to believe that, unless a person is arrested, a breach will be committed in the immediate future, or where a breach has occurred and there are reasonable grounds to believe that it will be repeated if the person is not arrested (*R v Howell* (1981); see, also, *R v Kelbie* (1996)). The law permits the temporary restraint and detention of persons breaching or threatening to breach the peace, although this falls short of making an arrest. This is to enable the person to calm down, so that no further action will be necessary.[9] This was held in *Albert v Lavin* (1982), where Lord Diplock stated:

> Any person, in whose presence a breach of the peace is being or reasonably appears to be about to be committed, has the right to take reasonable steps to make the person who is breaking or threatening to break the peace refrain from doing so; and those reasonable steps in appropriate cases will include detaining him against his will. At common law, it is not only the right of every citizen, it is also his duty, although, except in the case of a citizen who is a constable, it is a duty of imperfect obligation.

This common law power also extends to the entering of premises, public or private, in order to deal with breaches of the peace. As far as the police are concerned, they have relied to a certain extent on the law as stated in *Thomas v Sawkins* (1935), which empowers them to enter and remain on any premises in

---

9   *Op cit*, Lidstone and Palmer, fn 7.

order to prevent a breach of the peace. In this case, two police officers were present during a meeting held on private premises, although the public were invited. The presence of these officers at the meeting was unwelcome and a steward attempted to eject one of them. Sergeant Sawkins prevented this and a private prosecution was brought against him. It was held by the Divisional Court, *inter alia*, that the police were entitled to enter and remain on premises if they reasonably anticipated a breach of the peace (see, also, *Lamb v DPP* (1990), regarding the power to enter premises where a breach of the peace is actually occurring).

Ordinary citizens should exercise great caution when intervening in matters concerning breaches of the peace, whether or not they enter premises for this purpose. It has been stated that even the police may be reluctant to use this power in private premises unless a breach of the peace is actually occurring.[10] The problems inherent when acting in anticipation of a breach of the peace are exemplified in *McLeod v Commissioner of Police for the Metropolis* (1994). In this case, in anticipation of a dispute, two police officers, together with a solicitor, accompanied a man to the home of his former wife in order to collect property under a court order. All four of them were admitted by the wife's mother in the absence of the wife and the property was duly removed. In later proceedings, the wife alleged that, although her mother opened the door, she had not given actual permission for them to enter; therefore, they were all trespassers. Whilst the Court of Appeal held that this applied to the husband and his solicitor, it did not apply to the two police officers whose presence was legitimised by s 17(6) of PACE, which preserved the common law power to deal with breaches of the peace. The court went on to issue a warning that police officers must be sure that, before they enter private premises against the will of the owner or occupier, a real and imminent risk of a breach of the peace exists. This case was later referred to the European Court of Human Rights (*McLeod v UK* (1997)), where it was held that the police officers should not have entered the applicant's home, as there were insufficient grounds to apprehend a breach of the peace. Subsequently, there had been a violation of Art 8 of the European Convention on Human Rights (the right to respect for private and family life, as discussed in Chapter 9).

In *Moss v McLachlan* (1985), discussed in Chapter 2, it was held that the police had correctly exercised their powers to prevent a breach of the peace by turning vehicles away four miles from a colliery. It was suspected that the occupants were intending to join fellow striking miners and that a breach of the peace was likely. The defendants were arrested for obstruction following refusal to comply with the direction to turn back.

---

10 Stone, R, *Entry, Search and Seizure: A Guide to Civil and Criminal Powers of Entry*, 2nd edn, 1989, London: Sweet & Maxwell.

ARREST PROCEDURE

Information that must be given on arrest

An arrest is the lawful deprivation of a person's liberty. In order for an arrest to be lawful, it must be based on a legal power to do so and must also be conducted in the correct manner. Part of the arrest procedure is that the suspect must be informed that he or she is under arrest and the correct grounds for the arrest must also be given. This was held in *Christie v Leachinsky* (1947), where it was stated, *inter alia*, that an arrest would be unlawful if such a procedure was not followed. The grounds for an arrest need not be in precise technical terms, but should be given in such a manner that the suspect 'knows in substance the reason why it is claimed that this restraint should be imposed'.[11] This common law principle was later enacted under s 28 of PACE (entitled 'information to be given on arrest'), which makes the following provisions:

28(1) Subject to sub-s (5) below, when a person is arrested otherwise than by being informed that he is under arrest, the arrest is not lawful, unless the person arrested is informed that he is under arrest as soon as is practicable after his arrest.

(2) Where a person is arrested by a constable, sub-s (1) above applies, regardless of whether the fact of the arrest is obvious.

(3) Subject to sub-s (5) below, no arrest is lawful unless the person arrested is informed of the ground for the arrest at the time of or, as soon as is practicable after, the arrest.

(4) Where a person is arrested by a constable, sub-s (3) above applies, regardless of whether the ground for the arrest is obvious.

(5) Nothing in this section is to be taken to require a person to be informed:

(a) that he is under arrest; or

(b) of the ground for the arrest,

if it was not reasonably practicable for him to be so informed, by reason of his having escaped from arrest before the information could be given.

The requirements under sub-ss (2) and (4) that the fact that an arrest is being made and the grounds for it must be conveyed to the suspect, even if those facts are obvious, only applies to the police. Sub-section (5) states, somewhat obviously, that this requirement does not apply where the suspect escapes before this information can be given. Sub-sections (1) and (3) cover the contingency where the suspect may be incapable of knowing what is happening, for example, where he or she is drunk, or may be violent to the extent that the police are compelled to immediately restrain the suspect. The police may later inform him or her of the arrest and the grounds for it when the person has either sobered up or calmed down at the police station.

---

11 *Per* Simon V in *Christie v Leachinsky* (1947).

It should be noted that the grounds for making an arrest as communicated to the suspect must constitute the correct reasons. If not, then the arrest is unlawful and a third party would also be legally entitled to intervene to prevent the arrest. This was confirmed in *Edwards v DPP* (1993), where Evans LJ stated:

> ... it has to be borne in mind that giving correct information as to the reason for an arrest is a matter of the utmost constitutional significance in a case where a reason can be and is given at the time.

Apart from the ethical implications of giving reasons for depriving a person of their liberty, there are also practical reasons for this course of action. An arrested suspect may be able to provide an explanation which could have the effect of reducing the charges against him or her (see *R v Fennelley* (1989), discussed on p 80, below).

In *Dhesi v Chief Constable of the West Midlands Police* (2000), it was held that the reason for an arrest does not necessarily have to be given by the arresting officer. An arrest is lawful, provided the suspect is given the reason at the time or as soon as is practicable thereafter, even if this is done by a police officer other than the one making the arrest.

The act of legal restraint

When an arrest is being made, it is necessary to convey to the suspect clear indication that he or she is under legal restraint. This may be done by words (see *Alderson v Booth* (1969)), although the suspect must submit to the arrest, which must then be followed by informing him or her of the reasons for it. If the suspect does not submit or circumstances militate against the use of mere words, an arrest may consist of taking hold of the suspect. In cases where a person about to be arrested is not showing any signs of hostility or likelihood of escaping, it is usual police procedure to take a firm hold of the suspect's arm whilst giving the reason for the arrest and administering the caution. In a more volatile situation, the police may use more physical force if necessary, but this must always be reasonable in all the circumstances (s 117 of PACE and s 3(1) of the Criminal Law Act 1967). It is largely for this reason, that the requirement to give certain information on arrest may be delayed until it is practicable to do so. It is not uncommon for the police to meet with such strong resistance when making arrests that this information cannot be conveyed until the suspect has ceased to behave in a violent and noisy manner or when other potential dangers have passed.

As a general rule, the use of handcuffs to effect restraint is confined to cases where the suspect may become violent or attempt to escape. This falls within the ambit of using reasonable force, as is the case where the police use batons or CS spray in accordance with police guidelines.

The caution

A further arrest procedure is the giving of the caution to the suspect. This is not covered under PACE, but under paras 10.3 and 10.4 of Code C, which provide:

> 10.3 A person must be cautioned upon arrest for an offence unless:
>
> (a) it is impracticable to do so by reason of his condition or behaviour at the time; or
>
> (b) he has already been cautioned immediately prior to arrest ...
>
> 10.4 The caution shall be in the following terms:
>
>> You do not have to say anything. But it may harm your defence if you do not mention when questioned something which you later rely on in court. Anything you do say may be given in evidence.
>
> Minor deviations do not constitute a breach of this requirement, provided that the sense of the caution is preserved.

Voluntary attendance at a police station

What is the position where a person is voluntarily at a police station and is 'helping the police with their inquiries'? This issue is covered under s 29 of PACE, but is a subject which has attracted much controversy. According to Professor Zander: 'The police frequently find it convenient to blur the line between freedom and arrest. The newspaper phrase "a man is helping the police with their inquiries" has become a polite euphemism to describe this shadowy area.' Professor Zander then goes on to make the following point: 'But, in law, the position is not in doubt. A person is either under arrest or he is not. If he is not technically under arrest, he is free to go.'[12] Section 29 of PACE makes the following provisions:

> 29 Where, for the purpose of assisting with an investigation, a person attends voluntarily at a police station or at any other place where a constable is present or accompanies a constable to a police station or any such other place without having been arrested:
>
> (a) he shall be entitled to leave at will, unless he is placed under arrest;
>
> (b) he shall be informed at once that he is under arrest if a decision is taken by a constable to prevent him from leaving at will.

During the passage of the Police and Criminal Evidence Bill through Parliament, it was suggested that such individuals should be protected by certain safeguards, such as expressly informing them that they were free to leave at any time or asking if they wished to have a solicitor. Lord Denning even described such attendance at a police station as 'half way to making an

---

12 *Op cit*, Zander, fn 3.

arrest'.[13] This was rejected by the Government on the grounds that so many people attend police stations for a variety of reasons that to introduce such a scheme would cause the police severe administrative burdens. There is one safeguard under para 10.2 of Code C, which states:

> Whenever a person who is not under arrest is initially cautioned or is reminded that he is under caution ... he must, at the same time, be told that he is not under arrest and is not obliged to remain with the officer ...

Further guidance is given under paras 3.15 and 3.16 of Code C, as follows:

> 3.15 Any person attending a police station voluntarily for the purpose of assisting with an investigation may leave at will, unless placed under arrest. If it is decided that he should not be allowed to leave, then he must be informed at once that he is under arrest and brought before the custody officer, who is responsible for ensuring that he is notified of his rights in the same way as other detained persons. If he is not placed under arrest, but is cautioned ... the officer who gives the caution must, at the same time, inform him that he is not under arrest, that he is not obliged to remain at the police station, but if he remains at the police station, he may obtain free and independent legal advice if he wishes. The officer shall point out that the right to legal advice includes the right to speak with a solicitor on the telephone and ask him if he wishes to do so.

> 3.16 If a person, who is attending the police station voluntarily (in accordance with para 3.15), asks about his entitlement to legal advice, he shall be given a copy of the notice explaining the arrangements for obtaining legal advice ...

But it will be observed that these safeguards only apply when a suspect is under caution and not before then. A suspect can, of course, be arrested at any time during his or her voluntary attendance at a police station once the police have the required grounds for making it.

Arrests made elsewhere than at police stations

Most arrests occur away from police stations and there is the *general* rule under s 30(1) of PACE that arrested persons shall be taken to a police station as soon as practicable following their arrest. Sub-section (10), however, provides that a constable may delay this procedure if the arrested person's presence is needed elsewhere in order to further the investigation, if it is reasonable to do this immediately. Sub-section (11) provides that, in the event of such a delay, the reasons for it must be recorded on arrival at the police station. Normally arrested persons should be taken to a 'designated' police station, namely, a station where there are facilities for the purpose of detaining arrested persons (s 35 of PACE), although there are exceptions to this general

---

13 House of Lords, *Hansard*, 5 July 1984, Col 502.

rule under sub-ss (3)–(6) inclusive. These provide that, unless the suspect will have to be detained for longer than six hours, police officers operating within an area covered by a non-designated police station may take an arrested person there. If it is necessary to keep that person for longer than six hours, that person must then be transferred to a designated police station. These rules also apply to constables employed by bodies which do not fall under the mainstream police forces, such as the British Transport Police. The other exception is where a police officer has arrested a suspect on his or her own (or taken charge of a person arrested by someone else, such as a store detective), no assistance is available from other officers and it appears to the arresting officer that the suspect may injure him or herself or anyone else (including the constable) if taken to a designated police station. This covers the contingency where a non-designated police station in proximity to an arrest may be closer than one which is designated, and the constable carrying out the arrest without police assistance is having difficulty restraining the suspect. This situation is more likely to occur in rural areas, where a local police station may be considerably closer than the nearest designated police station.

There is provision under s 30(7) for a police officer to de-arrest a suspect before arriving at a police station, where the constable is satisfied that there are no grounds for keeping that person under arrest. This can occur under a number of situations, but let us assume, for instance, that a man has been arrested under the general arrest conditions under s 25 of PACE because he has committed a minor road traffic offence and has refused to give the police officer his name and address. If the arrested person decides to co-operate before being taken to the police station or whilst en route and provides the police officer with the required details, that person may be released, as there are no grounds for keeping him or her under arrest. However, sub-ss (8) and (9) provide that a record must be made as soon as is practicable if this is done.

Arrest for one or more further offences

Section 31 of PACE provides that, where a person is at a police station as a result of being arrested and one or more further offences come to light, that person shall be arrested at the police station for those offences. This is to prevent an arrested person being released and then immediately re-arrested for further offences where this could have been done in the course of the original period of detention. In Chapter 6, the full significance of this procedure will be apparent; suffice it to say here that there are strict limitations on the times that an arrested suspect may be detained without being charged. Section 31, *inter alia*, prevents an arrested person being released without charge for one offence when the detention time becomes exhausted, and then being immediately re-arrested for another alleged crime, where fresh detention time will begin.

Searches on arrest

When a person has been arrested away from a police station under any arrest power, s 32 of PACE empowers the police to search the suspect and, if the arrest is for an offence, any premises the person was in at the time of the arrest or immediately before it, whether or not the premises are occupied or controlled by the suspect. The power of entry into premises must be confined to searching for evidence relating to the offence in question and can only be exercised if it is reasonably believed that such evidence will be found there. In *R v Beckford* (1991), it was stated that s 32 must not be used to initiate 'fishing expeditions'. The police must have genuine belief that the premises contain evidence of the offence for which the suspect has been arrested; this will be a matter of fact for the jury to decide. If a person is arrested in premises which consist of two or more separate dwellings, such as a block of flats, the police may only search the premises in which the suspect was arrested or was in immediately beforehand, as well as any common parts shared with others, such as stairways and balconies.

Section 32 of PACE shares certain similarities with s 18, in so far as both empower the police to search premises following the arrest of a suspect, although s 18 applies to premises occupied or controlled by the suspect, whether or not the suspect was in such places at the time of the arrest; also, s 18 is confined to arrestable offences only. Furthermore, the power to enter and search premises under s 32 has to be applied either immediately or very soon after the arrest. In *R v Badham* (1987), it was held that a lapse of four hours between an arrest and the subsequent entry and search of premises under s 32 was unacceptable. Section 18 is covered in more detail in Chapter 4, since all of it falls within the ambit of police powers of entry and search of premises. At this stage, it may be useful to mention s 17 of PACE, which is also covered in detail in Chapter 4. Part of this section empowers the police to, *inter alia*, enter and search premises in order to execute an arrest warrant issued in connection with criminal proceedings, as well as make an arrest for an arrestable offence or for certain other offences.

Under s 32, an arrested person may be searched on arrest if there are reasonable grounds for believing that the suspect may present a danger to him or herself, or to others. This will often be focused on the suspect carrying any weapons, as is the power to search an arrested person for anything which might be used to effect an escape from lawful custody. Section 32 also permits the searching of an arrested person for any evidence relating to an offence but, in all the foregoing circumstances, sub-ss (3) and (4) provide that a search must be confined to the extent that is reasonably required in order to find such objects. Where an arrested person is searched in public under these powers, sub-s (4) provides that such persons shall not be required to remove any clothing other than outer coat, jacket or gloves. Also, under s 59(2) of the

Criminal Justice and Public Order Act 1994, the mouth of an arrested suspect may be searched in public. Arrested suspects could be required to remove other clothing if there are reasonable grounds for this requirement, but this should not be done in public, although such items may be removed in public with the suspect's genuine consent.

Police discretion in making arrests

In *Holgate-Mohammed v Duke* (1984), a female was suspected of having stolen jewellery and was arrested by a detective on the basis that not only did he have reasonable grounds to suspect that she had committed this offence, but he also believed that she would be more ready to confess if she were arrested and questioned at the police station. This action was upheld by the House of Lords which, *inter alia*, held that a decision to arrest constitutes an executive discretion expressly conferred on the police, which can only be questioned in the courts on the grounds that no reasonable police officer would make such a decision. In other words, such an executive discretion can only be questioned if it was manifestly absurd (see *Associated Provincial Picture Houses Ltd v Wednesbury Corporation* (1948)).

Unlawful arrests

The consequences on the police in making unlawful arrests are varied. Such incidents can be the subject of formal complaints against the police (see Chapter 8) and may also involve civil and even criminal action being taken against those responsible. In *Holgate-Mohammed v Duke* (above), the arrest of the appellant was initially challenged before the county court and she was awarded £1,000 damages for false imprisonment. The chief constable for that police area appealed against this decision which, as already discussed above, resulted in the House of Lords finding in his favour. Although a civil action under the tort of false imprisonment is available in cases of wrongful arrest, sometimes, an action for assault and battery may also brought in the same case; this can apply where some degree of force was used in effecting that arrest (see Chapter 8 for further discussion of the consequences of unlawful police action). However, it should be noted that, in *Simpson v Chief Constable of South Yorkshire Police* (1991), it was held that the use of excessive force in making an arrest will not automatically render the arrest unlawful.

A further consequence of the police making wrongful arrests or otherwise unlawfully detaining a person can be the exclusion of any evidence obtained as a result of such improper conduct, thereby leading to the collapse of the case. Section 78 of PACE, headed 'exclusion of unfair evidence', makes the following provisions:

(1) In any proceedings, the court may refuse to allow evidence on which the prosecution proposes to rely to be given if it appears to the court that, having regard to all the circumstances, including the circumstances in which the evidence was obtained, the admission of the evidence would have such an adverse effect on the fairness of the proceedings that the court ought not to admit it.

(2) Nothing in this section shall prejudice any rule of law requiring a court to exclude evidence.

In *R v Fennelley* (1989), the defendant was stopped and searched in the street and then arrested. In the course of the searches, including a strip search at the police station, some jewellery was found and two packets of heroin were discovered in his underpants. Since the prosecution were unable to establish that the defendant was given reasons for the stop, search and subsequent arrest, the evidence of the search was excluded at the Crown Court trial under s 78 of PACE. This was done on the grounds that, had he been informed of the reasons for being stopped, he would have had the opportunity to provide an early explanation; it would therefore be unfair to admit evidence obtained in this matter where he was denied that opportunity. However, the decision in this case was criticised in *R v McCarthy* (1996), where the Court of Appeal stated that it was difficult to understand why the evidence was excluded in *Fennelley*. There was no denial by the defendant that the evidence was on him and the drugs would have been discovered by the police in any event, although the matter may be different where a confession is made. In *DPP v L and S* (1998), it was held by the Divisional Court that, even where an initial arrest is unlawful, it does not necessarily mean that everything which follows is also unlawful. An arrest which is flawed may be rectified later by complying with the relevant provisions of PACE. In this case, a person was arrested, but without being informed as such, despite the fact that it was reasonably practicable to do so. The arrest was therefore unlawful. However, the court took the view that it is well established that the custody officer (see Chapter 6) must comply with a set of procedures when a person is detained at a police station; therefore, at some stage after the arrested person's arrival, she must have been told the reason for the arrest. A custody officer receiving a prisoner at a police station may assume that the prisoner has been lawfully arrested. If that person then assaults the custody officer, this will constitute an assault on police, even though the initial arrest may have been unlawful.

Arrests *with* warrant

Arrests under warrant account for a minority of arrests and are applied in relatively limited circumstances. Under s 1 of the Magistrates' Courts Act 1980, an arrest warrant may be issued against any person aged 17 or above who is suspected of having, or has committed, an indictable offence or an offence which is otherwise punishable by imprisonment, or whose whereabouts are unknown. This method of arresting a suspect may be used, *inter alia*, where the suspect's identity is known, but not his or her location, or it may be too dangerous or otherwise inexpedient to make an arrest immediately. Section 13 of the 1980 Act enables 'Bench warrants' to be issued where a defendant fails to attend court when required to do so in answer to a summons or other official notification. Warrants under ss 1 and 13 of the Magistrates' Courts Act 1980 are issued by justices of the peace. Arrest warrants may also be issued in a number of other circumstances. These include instances where an offender has breached certain community sentences and has to be brought before the court to be re-sentenced, or where a member of Her Majesty's armed forces has deserted.

For a number of practical reasons, it is not essential for the arresting officer to be in actual possession of the warrant when executing it, although the arrested person must be shown the warrant as soon as is practicable if sight of it is requested. Where an arrest is made under a warrant, the procedure for making it is essentially the same as an arrest without one, although it seems that a suspect is entitled to be informed that he or she is being arrested under a warrant.[14] However, this should be done as a matter of good practice in view of the wording of s 28(3) of PACE (the giving of reasons for the arrest).

Under s 117 of the Magistrates' Courts Act 1980, arrest warrants are endorsed with or without bail. Where the latter applies, the arrested person must be held in custody until that person is brought before the court. If the former applies, the arrested person must be released from the police station as directed, although, if a warrant is endorsed for bail without sureties, that person need not be taken to a police station at all.[15] This could apply in cases where, for instance, the arrested person can be taken straight to the court. As will be discussed immediately below, some fairly recent provisions have been made regarding the cross-border enforcement of arrests, which includes those made under warrant.

Cross-border enforcement

Section 136 of the Criminal Justice and Public Order Act 1994 enables arrest warrants issued in England and Wales or Northern Ireland against persons charged with an offence to be executed in Scotland. Similarly, arrest warrants issued in Scotland or Northern Ireland may be executed in England and Wales, and warrants issued in England and Wales or Scotland may be

---

14 Levenson, H, Fairweather, F and Cape, E, *Police Powers: A Practitioner's Guide*, 3rd edn, 1996, London: Legal Action Group.

15 *Ibid.*

executed in Northern Ireland.[16] Warrants may be executed by any constable from within the country where the warrant was issued or the country where it is to be executed, or by any other person within the directions of the warrant.

Section 137 of the 1994 Act provides that any police officer in England and Wales who has reasonable grounds to suspect that an arrestable offence has been committed or attempted in England and Wales, where the suspect is in Scotland or Northern Ireland, may arrest that person within any of those countries without warrant. The same reciprocal measures will apply to police officers in Scotland and Northern Ireland. This power also applies to non-arrestable offences, provided the service of a summons would be impracticable or inappropriate.[17] In effect, the same conditions will apply as in s 25 of PACE (general arrest conditions).

Persons arrested should be taken by the arresting officer, as soon as is reasonably practicable, to the nearest convenient designated police station where the alleged offence is being investigated. Reasonable force may be used where necessary in the execution of the above powers, and s 139 of the 1994 Act provides almost the same search powers and procedures as those prescribed under s 32 of PACE on the arrest of a suspect, with or without warrant. However, s 139(1) and (5) provides that, in the case of suspects wanted in Northern Ireland or suspects from elsewhere in the UK being arrested in Northern Ireland, police powers to search such suspects in public may not extend beyond the removal of headgear and footwear as well as outer coat, jacket and gloves (but may include searching a person's mouth). Section 140 of the 1994 Act covers reciprocal powers of arrest and provides that police officers from one part of the UK who are exercising arrest powers under the above provisions in another part of the UK may conduct the arrest using the same powers applicable to that local jurisdiction.[18]

POWERS UNDER THE CRIME AND DISORDER ACT 1998

Sections 14, 15 and 16 of the Crime and Disorder Act 1998 confer two powers on the police which can be usefully be considered in this chapter, since they, technically at least, involve actions which come close to making arrests. These are powers to remove children from areas which are subject to local child curfews and the removal of truants from public places.

---

16 Jason-Lloyd, L, *The Criminal Justice and Public Order Act 1994: A Basic Guide for Practitioners*, 1996, London: Frank Cass.

17 *Ibid.*

18 *Ibid.*

Local child curfews

Under ss 14 and 15 of the 1998 Act, local authorities have the power to give notice of local child curfew schemes in certain areas. This will enable them to apply a ban on children under the age of 10 from being in specific public places between the hours of 9 pm and 6 am, unless under the effective control of a parent or a responsible person aged at least 18. These notices may specify different hours in relation to different age groups and the total period of such bans may not exceed 90 days. The curfew notices may be effected by posting them in one or more conspicuous places within the specified area and in any other such manner as the local authority considers to be desirable in order to publicise the notice. This could include distributing circulars through letter boxes or advertising in local newspapers. These curfews will be imposed if the relevant local authority considers it necessary for the purpose of maintaining order in response to complaints from local residents. These measures have been enacted because of increasing concerns regarding young children engaging in generally disruptive behaviour by being allowed to roam the streets unsupervised at night and placing themselves at risk. However, a rather protracted set of procedures and consultations have to be complied with before such curfews can be authorised.

Where a police officer has reasonable cause to believe that an unaccompanied child is contravening a ban imposed by a curfew notice, that officer may take the child to his or her place of residence, unless there is reasonable cause to believe that the child would be likely to suffer significant harm if taken there. In such circumstances, the officer may take the child into police protection, in order to be accommodated elsewhere. Where the child is returned home immediately after having been found in contravention of a curfew, the police have a duty to inform the relevant local authority as soon as is practicable. Although not expressly regarded as an arrest, the removal of a child from the street in this manner is technically a deprivation of that person's liberty and, therefore, reasonable force may be used where necessary. This matter is discussed further below when considering the power of the police to remove truants from public places.

So far, local child curfews have not been widely used and, subsequently, local authorities have been encouraged by central government to apply for them more readily. On the subject of police discretion in enforcing these curfews, the 1998 Act requires that they may only exercise their powers based on reasonable *belief* that a child is under the age of 10. Unless the officer actually knows each child's age, it may be extremely difficult to enforce this power, especially where a curfew notice specifies different age groups under the age of 10. It will also become very difficult to enforce where an officer has definite knowledge that one or more children are under the age of 10, but others in the group are not or the officer is unsure. It appears that, in such circumstances, the police will have to leave the others in the prohibited area, unless they have cause to exercise their powers under public order law, for instance.

Power to remove truants

In order to prevent under 16 year olds from committing criminal and anti-social acts whilst truanting from school, s 16 of the 1998 Act has empowered the police to remove them from public places and to take them to designated premises or back to their respective schools. A local authority may designate certain premises where children and young persons of compulsory school age who are caught truanting may be taken by the police. These premises may include offices in social services departments, for instance, or schools, although the Home Office has stressed that it is not appropriate to take such persons to police stations, unless they have committed an offence. The chief officer of police for that area should then be notified that such premises are available and a police officer of at least the rank of superintendent may authorise police officers to exercise their powers within specific areas and periods of time. Those powers are to remove a child or young person to designated premises, or return him or her to school if found in a public place within the geographical and time parameters mentioned above. The police may do this if they have reasonable cause to believe that the child or young person is of compulsory school age and is absent from school without lawful authority.

The provision of designated premises by a local authority (which are not intended to be permanent), plus the requirement of a police superintendent's authority, indicate that these powers are likely to be used following consultations with specific schools and other agencies. In other words, it appears that these powers may be intended to be used as part of an organised police 'swoop' on known trouble spots, involving truanters who are also known. The latter would seem necessary, since the police may only act on the grounds of reasonable belief that a child or young person is of compulsory school age and is absent from school without lawful authority.

Since the exercise of this power is not strictly an arrest, there has been some debate regarding the need to use reasonable force in the case of unco-operative youngsters. It has been suggested that the common law principles governing the use of force will apply here, but with the caveat that it is essential that anyone deprived of their liberty should be given the reasons for doing so (*Christie v Leachinsky* (1947)).[19] However, it has been suggested that the use of force in exercising this power should be less than that when making an arrest, because of the general rule that juveniles should be handled with

---

19 Card, R and Ward, R, *The Crime and Disorder Act 1998: A Practitioner's Guide*, 1998, Bristol: Jordans.

particular care wherever possible (including avoiding the use of handcuffs), plus the risk of endangering relations between the police and the younger community.[20] However, the possible long term consequences of allowing young people to 'cock a snook' at the police when exercising these powers could outweigh the utility of this argument, despite it being soundly based on the balance of social interest. Among other things, it could become common knowledge that a truanting youngster merely had to walk away from the police to avoid further action, thus rendering these powers useless.

ARREST POWER UNDER S 3(4) OF THE THEFT ACT 1978 AND SIMILAR POWERS

Section 3 of the Theft Act 1978 creates the offence of making off without payment. This covers activities described as 'bilking' where, for instance, a person arrives at their destination in a taxi, then runs off in order to avoid paying the fare or has a meal and then leaves the restaurant, intending to avoid paying the bill. Sub-section (4) states that:

> Any person may arrest without warrant anyone who is, or whom he, with reasonable cause, suspects to be, committing or attempting to commit an offence under this section.

Note the inclusion of the words 'any person', meaning that both the police and ordinary citizens have this power of arrest without warrant. Once again, it is suggested that ordinary citizens exercise great caution if considering using this power. Apart from the physical dangers inherent in making arrests, there may be potential legal traps, bearing in mind the instantaneous nature of this specific offence. A suspect may be able to convince magistrates or a jury that it was his or her intention to pay for the goods later, since it has to be proved beyond reasonable doubt that there was the intention never to pay the amount due. This offence is triable either way and, when tried on indictment, carries a maximum prison sentence of two years.

A number of other statutes have created arrest powers for specific offences where 'any person' or 'anyone' may arrest with warrant. For example, s 91 of the Criminal Justice Act 1967 (arrest of a person who is drunk and disorderly in a public place) and s 41 of the Sexual Offences Act 1956 (arrest of a man soliciting or importuning for an immoral purpose in a public place). See, also, s 1 of the Licensing Act 1902, s 11 of the Prevention of Offences Act 1851 and s 6 of the Vagrancy Act 1824. According to some commentators,[21] these arrest

---

20 Leng, R, Taylor, R and Wasik, M, *Blackstone's Guide to the Crime and Disorder Act 1998*, 1998, London: Blackstone.

21 *Op cit*, Lidstone and Palmer, fn 7 and, also, *op cit*, Zander, fn 3.

powers have not strictly been removed from the police by s 26(1) of PACE, which repealed all statutory powers of arrest without warrant previously held by them, except those re-cast under Sched 2. The general line of argument is that, since the above arrest powers may be exercised by any person, this also includes the police (although, with specific reference to s 3 of the Theft Act 1978, a contrary view has been expressed).[22] However, it has been suggested in Home Office guidance, *inter alia*, that it may be prudent for the police to take into account the criteria in the general arrest conditions under s 25 of PACE before exercising such powers of arrest.

---

22 *Op cit*, Levenson, Fairweather and Cape, fn 14, p 116. See, also, *op cit*, Cape and Jawaid, fn 4, p 45.

CHAPTER 4

POLICE POWERS OF ENTRY
AND SEARCH OF PREMISES

INTRODUCTION

As discussed in Chapters 2 and 3, the Royal Commission on Criminal Procedure recognised that police powers of stop and search, as well as those affecting arrests, were both fragmented and unclear. This also applies to the Commission's findings regarding police powers of entry and search of premises, and the seizure of any evidence found there. A number of recommendations were made, some of which, but by no means all, were later enacted under the Police and Criminal Evidence Act 1984 (PACE).

The relevant provisions under s 8 of PACE, described below, constitute a *general* power to obtain search warrants. Sections 17 and 18 of PACE also include certain powers to enter and search premises, but without warrant, as well as s 32 (entry and search of premises which an arrested person was in at the time of their arrest or immediately before it, as considered in the previous chapter).

It should be noted that PACE is not the only legal source enabling the police to enter and search premises. A number of statutes conferring specific police powers to obtain search warrants also exist, although the procedures involved in issuing search warrants and executing them must comply with the standard procedures and safeguards contained in PACE and Code of Practice B. Some examples of these specific powers are included under the following statutes: s 26 of the Theft Act 1968 (warrant to enter premises to search for stolen goods); s 23(3) of the Misuse of Drugs Act 1971 (warrant to enter and search premises for controlled drugs or documents relating to unlawful drug transactions); s 2(4) of the Criminal Justice Act 1987 (warrant to enter and search for evidence of serious fraud); s 142 of the Criminal Justice Act 1988 (warrant to enter and search for certain offensive weapons) and many more.[1]

There are also specific statutory powers of entry and search without warrant included under the following examples: s 23(1) of the Misuse of Drugs Act 1971 (power of entry into premises of a person carrying on business as a producer or supplier of controlled drugs in order to examine records and stocks of drugs); s 13 of the Aviation Security Act 1982 (power to enter any building, etc, at airports to search for firearms, explosives or other dangerous

---

1   Stone, R, *Entry, Search and Seizure: A Guide to Civil and Criminal Powers of Entry*, 3rd edn, 1997, London: Sweet & Maxwell.

articles).[2] More recently, the Prevention of Terrorism (Additional Powers) Act 1996, which substantially included more police powers under the Prevention of Terrorism (Temporary Provisions) Act 1989, has given them further powers of entry and search in order to combat terrorism. These will be discussed later in this chapter. Mention should be made at this stage of powers under ss 4(7) and 6(6) and the Road Traffic Act 1988. These empower the police to enter premises in order to arrest persons for drink-drive offences or for the purpose of making breath tests where road traffic accidents involving personal injury have occurred.

There is also a common law power of entry into premises which has been unchanged by PACE and that is the power to enter premises to deal with or prevent a breach of the peace. However, as discussed earlier (see p 71, above), this common law power is largely superseded by s 17 of PACE. A more clandestine and, in many ways, controversial power to enter premises can be found under the relevant provisions of the Police Act 1997 covering intrusive surveillance. These provisions will be discussed separately in this chapter (see below, p 112).

Definition of 'premises'

For the purposes of the exercise of police powers of entry and search, the word 'premises' applies to a wide variety of public and private places. Section 23 of PACE provides only a partial definition by stating:

> 23   In this Act – 'premises' includes any place and, in particular, includes:
>
>   (a) any vehicle, vessel, aircraft or hovercraft;
>
>   (b) any offshore installation; and
>
>   (c) any tent or movable structure; ...
>
>   'Offshore installation' has the meaning given to it by s 1 of the Mineral Workings (Offshore Installations) Act 1971.

Apart from those specific examples mentioned above, what constitutes 'any place'? Using case law, the term 'premises' has also been held to include buildings, caravans, houseboats, non-residential premises, such as unattended garages, and land. In *Palmer v Bugler* (1988), it was held that a field used on a regular basis for car boot sales constituted 'a place'.[3]

---

2   *Op cit*, Stone, fn 1.

3   Levenson, H, Fairweather, F and Cape, E, *Police Powers: A Practitioner's Guide*, 3rd edn, 1996, London: Legal Action Group.

ENTRY AND SEARCH BY WARRANT

As already discussed, s 8 of PACE has introduced a general power under which magistrates may issue warrants enabling the police to enter premises and search for items not covered by the specific Acts mentioned above. However, according to Professor Stone:

> There is no evidence that these more specific powers are used any less now that the police have the general power to obtain a search warrant under s 8 of PACE. This power only applies to 'serious arrestable offences' and, in some cases (perhaps where it is proposed to use other procedures under an Act, for example, the forfeiture procedures under the Obscene Publications Act 1959), the specific powers may anyway be thought more appropriate.[4]

Section 8 provides that a police officer may apply in writing for a warrant from a justice of the peace if there are reasonable grounds for believing that there is material on premises relating to the committing of a serious arrestable offence which is likely to be of substantial value to the investigation and admissible as evidence in court, and that this is the only means to obtain such evidence. In other words, where it would be impracticable to try to gain entry without a search warrant. This will include instances where the purpose of the search may be frustrated or seriously prejudiced unless the police effect immediate entry. It will also include circumstances where no one can be contacted who has the authority to grant access to the premises or to the required material on those premises, or where consent to enter those premises has already been refused. It therefore follows that a justice of the peace should not issue a search warrant if entry can be gained through the consent of the occupier. Certain items may not be obtained by a search warrant under s 8, but may be obtained through other provisions. These are items subject to legal privilege, excluded material or special procedure material.

Meaning of 'items subject to legal privilege'

This is defined under s 10 of PACE as follows, with explanations in italics where appropriate:

(1) Subject to sub-s (2) below, in this Act, 'items subject to legal privilege' means:

(a) communications between a professional legal adviser and his client or any person representing his client made in connection with the giving of legal advice to the client;

[First, what is meant by the term 'professional legal adviser'? This includes qualified barristers and solicitors. A solicitor in this context does not have to be employed by a

---

4   *Op cit*, Stone, fn 1.

solicitors' practice. This will therefore include a solicitor working from an advice centre, for instance. Solicitors' clerks are also included, since they act under the direction of solicitors. Unqualified advisers may possibly claim that communications fall under this heading if acting as agents for barristers or solicitors, but generally the advice from unqualified persons does not fall under legally privileged material, although it could receive some protection as 'excluded material' (see below, p 91). Communications subject to legal privilege can be written or verbal, including tape recordings of interviews.][5]

    (b) communications between a professional legal adviser and his client or any person representing his client or between such an adviser or his client or any such representative and any other person made in connection with or in contemplation of legal proceedings and for the purposes of such proceedings; and

    (c) items enclosed with or referred to in such communications and made:

        (i) in connection with the giving of legal advice; or

        (ii) in connection with or in contemplation of legal proceedings and for the purpose of such proceedings,

    when they are in the possession of a person who is entitled to possession of them.

(2) Items held with the intention of furthering a criminal purpose are not items subject to legal privilege.

What is meant by 'the intention of furthering a criminal purpose'? Within the context of sub-s (2), this can perhaps be illustrated by the following scenarios.

Mr X is thinking of committing a crime and writes a letter to his solicitor, asking what the consequences would be. His solicitor writes and tells him that he could go to prison, say, for five years if convicted. These letters would be subject to legal privilege. However, if Mr Y writes to his solicitor and tells him of a crime he intends to commit and asks how he can avoid being detected and his solicitor replies and gives him this information, this would not be subject to legal privilege, as this constitutes furthering a criminal purpose.

In *R v Central Criminal Court ex p Francis and Francis* (1989), the exclusion of legal privilege immunity was given a broad interpretation by the House of Lords which excludes from such immunity not only the criminal intentions of legal advisers or their clients, but also anyone using a client as an innocent agent.[6] Material which is legally privileged cannot be subject to a search, except under rare circumstances, where it can be obtained under written authority other than a warrant. Examples include the powers under s 73 of the Explosives Act 1875 and s 9(2) of the Official Secrets Act 1911, where a police superintendent may, in extremely urgent cases, make a written order to enter and search specified premises for explosives or for certain material in the

---

5   *Op cit*, Levenson, Fairweather and Cape, fn 3

6   Cited in Jason-Lloyd, L, *The Law on Money-Laundering: Statutes and Commentary*, 1997, London: Frank Cass.

interests of State security. Legally privileged material is therefore highly protected and in *R v Guildhall Magistrates' Court ex p Primlaks Holdings Co* (1989), it was stressed that great care should be exercised by those applying for search warrants to ensure that the material sought after did not include anything that was subject to legal privilege. However, in *R v Chesterfield Justices ex p Bramley* (1999), it was held that the police will not be acting unlawfully if they seize items subject to legal privilege, providing they do not have reasonable grounds for believing that the material is privileged; however, 'violation of the legal privilege by making use of the privileged information would be unlawful'.

Meaning of 'excluded material'

The term 'excluded material' is defined under s 11 of PACE as follows, with explanations included in italics where appropriate. Such material falls under three categories, namely, personal records, human tissue or tissue fluid and journalistic material. It is important to note that there must always be an element of confidentiality in the holding of excluded material, whichever category it falls under:

(1) Subject to the following provisions of this section, in this Act, 'excluded material' means:

   (a) personal records which a person has acquired or created in the course of any trade, business or profession or other occupation or for the purposes of any paid or unpaid office and which he holds in confidence;

['Personal records' are defined under s 12 of PACE and consist of documents and other records regarding a person, whether living or dead, which relate to the following: (1) documentary or other records regarding physical and mental health (this also includes dental records);[7] (2) personal records in relation to spiritual counselling or assistance, which includes information kept by members of the clergy and other religious ministers; (3) personal records regarding counselling or assistance given to a person for personal welfare purposes by any voluntary organisation or by any person who, 'by reason of his office or occupation, has responsibilities for his personal welfare'. This may include careers advice records in educational establishments, records of social workers, records in advice centres and so on.[8]

Also included are personal records regarding counselling or assistance given to a person for his or her welfare by any voluntary organisation or individual who, 'by reason of an order of a court, has responsibilities for his supervision'. This was originally designed to protect personal records held by probation officers, but this must now clearly extend to local authority social workers and, more recently, to members of Youth Offending Teams and, when Pt I of the Youth Justice and Criminal Evidence Act 1999 comes into force, members of Youth Offender Panels.]

---

7   *R v Singleton* [1995] Crim LR 236, cited in Levenson, Fairweather and Cape, *op cit*, fn 3.
8   *Ibid.*

(b) human tissue or tissue fluid which has been taken for the purposes of diagnosis or medical treatment and which a person holds in confidence;

[This category of excluded material is not defined in PACE, but such material will include blood samples, for instance.]

(c) journalistic material which a person holds in confidence and which consists:

(i) of documents; or

(ii) of records other than documents.

(2) A person holds material other than journalistic material in confidence for the purposes of this section if he holds it subject:

(a) to an express or implied undertaking to hold it in confidence; or

(b) to a restriction on disclosure or an obligation of secrecy contained in any enactment, including an enactment contained in an Act passed after this Act.

(3) A person holds journalistic material in confidence for the purposes of this section if:

(a) he holds it subject to such an undertaking, restriction or obligation; and

(b) it has been continuously held (by one or more persons) subject to such an undertaking, restriction or obligation since it was first acquired or created for the purposes of journalism.

[The protections afforded to journalistic material apply to the media generally and not exclusively to professional journalists. The material may be in the form of maps, plans, photographs, discs, tapes, films or microfilms. If journalistic material is not continuously held in confidence, then it does not constitute excluded material, but falls under 'special procedure material', which will be discussed on p 93, below. Media coverage of certain public demonstrations involving the photographing or filming of those events has been regarded as special procedure material, since this material, although journalistic, was not held in confidence. See, for example, R v Bristol Crown Court ex p Bristol Press and Picture Agency Ltd *(1987).]*

Unless they are able to gain access to such evidence with the appropriate co-operation and consent from the person concerned, if the police need access to excluded material, they must apply to a circuit judge for a 'production order'. This avoids the police having to search premises to find and obtain such evidence because a production order requires the person in possession of this material to either give it to the police or allow them access to it. In exceptional circumstances, such as where this evidence is likely to be tampered with, a circuit judge may issue a warrant instead of a production order or may even issue both.

Meaning of 'special procedure material'

The provisions regarding the definition of special procedure material are contained under s 14 of PACE. As mentioned above, such material includes that of a journalistic nature, but which is not continuously held in confidence (or the material may not be in the prescribed form required under the Act). The second type of special procedure material is that which is not legally privileged or excluded material, but which is in 'the possession of a person who acquired or created it in the course of any trade, business, profession, or other occupation or for the purposes of any paid or unpaid office' and holds it in confidence.

Examples of special procedure material include bank accounts, stock records, the accounts of a youth association, conveyancing documents and photographs held by the media (see *R v Bristol Crown Court ex p Bristol Press and Picture Agency Ltd* (1986)). The most important sources of special procedure material are banks and building societies, as well as accountants, estate agents, financial brokers, insurance brokers, telecommunications organisations, journalists and solicitors (excluding legally privileged material, such as conveyancing matters).[9] Access of the police to special procedure material can be gained in several ways. First, such access can be voluntarily given by the person who holds this material. However, where such consent cannot be obtained, the police may apply for a search warrant from a justice of the peace or, depending on the nature of the material in question, they may apply for a production order from a circuit judge. In the exceptional circumstances mentioned above (see p 92), a judge may grant a search warrant instead of a production order or may issue both.

The importance of the provisions under PACE regarding such material is illustrated by the following:

> In England and Wales, more than 2,000 orders for the production of special procedure material or warrants to search for and seize such material were granted in the first three years of PACE 1984. These have enabled the police to investigate crimes which they were previously unable to investigate and to obtain evidence in respect of other crimes which they were previously unable to obtain, or were able to obtain only after a charge had been laid under the Bankers' Books Evidence Act 1879.[10]

Section 9 of PACE, in conjunction with Sched 1, makes detailed provision regarding special procedures when applying for production orders or search warrants from circuit judges in respect of excluded or special procedure material. These finer points will not be covered in detail within this chapter, as they are largely applicable to those working within specialist areas of criminal

---

9   Lidstone, K and Palmer, C, *Bevan and Lidstone's The Investigation of Crime: A Guide to Police Powers*, 2nd edn, 1996, London: Butterworths.

10   *Ibid*.

investigation. It is also for this reason that not all police powers pertaining to the prevention of terrorism are included either, except those which are likely to be enforced by the police in the course of routine duties, rather than by specialised squads. However, mention should be made at this stage of the methods of obtaining evidence in cases connected with terrorism. Provision is made under Sched 7 to the Prevention of Terrorism (Temporary Provisions) Act 1989, whereby magistrates may issue search warrants and circuit judges may issue production orders and warrants in such cases. These are very similar to the provisions under s 9 and Sched 1 to PACE, although, in terrorist investigations, only a police officer of at least the rank of superintendent may authorise the application and an officer of the rank of inspector or above shall be in charge of the actual search (this latter provision also applies to warrants issued under Sched 1 to PACE). Also, with regard to Scheds 1 and 7, para 2.7 of Code B states that, in both cases, an application for a search warrant shall indicate why it is believed that the service of the relevant notice of application for a production order may seriously prejudice the investigation.

General search provisions

Notwithstanding the multiplicity of legal powers enabling the police to enter and search premises, whether enacted before or after 1984, PACE has established a common procedure regarding applications for all search warrants, as well as establishing a uniform set of procedures in respect of the conduct of such searches. This is in addition to applications for search warrants under PACE itself, whether obtained from circuit judges or justices of the peace, and the subsequent searches. These procedures are covered under ss 15 and 16 of PACE which, if breached, will render the entry and search unlawful. These provisions are supplemented by Code B, although, under para 1.3(a), this Code does not apply to police searches of premises following bomb threats or when answering alarm or fire calls, or when making investigations at the scenes of crimes, including burglaries. Neither do they apply where it is unnecessary to seek the consent of a person entitled to grant entry, because this would cause disproportionate inconvenience to that person, or where there is a statutory power to enter premises to inspect goods, equipment or procedures where no offence is suspected. It is submitted that the latter may apply to s 23(1) of the Misuse of Drugs Act 1971, where the police may routinely examine the records and stocks of a person carrying on the business of producing or supplying controlled drugs such as pharmaceutical manufacturers and distributors. Any breaches of the Codes of Practice, whilst not necessarily rendering police action unlawful, may constitute evidence in civil or even criminal proceedings and also in internal disciplinary proceedings.

Paragraph 2 of Code B, entitled 'Search warrants and production orders. Action to be taken before an application is made', states that the following must be complied with prior to any action under s 15 of PACE. First, any information which appears to justify an application for a search warrant must be checked for accuracy and that it is not out of date. Reasonable steps must also be taken to ensure that the information has not been provided maliciously or irresponsibly. Corroboration must also be sought in cases where the information comes from an anonymous source. Note for guidance 2A to Code B states the following with regard to such information:

> 2A The identity of an informant need not be disclosed when making an application, but the officer concerned should be prepared to deal with any questions the magistrate of judge may have about the accuracy of previous information provided by that source or any other related matters.

Secondly, the officer concerned in the application must ascertain, as specifically as possible, the nature of the articles sought and their location. Thirdly, the officer shall be expected to make reasonable inquiries to see if anything is known about the likely occupier of the premises in question, as well as the nature of the premises, and to obtain any other information which may be relevant to the application. This will include whether the premises have been searched before and, if so, how recently. Fourthly, no application for a search warrant may be made without the authority of a police officer of at least the rank of inspector although, in urgent cases, the senior officer on duty may do this. However, as mentioned earlier, applications for production orders or search warrants under Sched 7 to the Prevention of Terrorism (Temporary Provisions) Act 1989 must be made on the authority of a police officer of at least the rank of superintendent. Finally, if there is reason to believe that the execution of a search warrant might have an adverse effect on relations between the police and the community, the local police/community liaison officer must be consulted beforehand. The exception to this rule is in cases of urgency where such persons should be informed of the search as soon as practicable after the event. Note for guidance 2B to Code B states:

> 2B The local police/community consultative group, where it exists, or its equivalent, should be informed, as soon as practicable after a search has taken place, where there is reason to believe that it might have had an adverse effect on relations between the police and the community.

Safeguards regarding applications for search warrants

The provisions governing applications for search warrants are contained under s 15 of PACE, which are augmented by Code B. Section 15 will now be reproduced, with annotations in italics where appropriate, accompanied by the relevant information and guidance under Code B in each instance:

Search warrants – safeguards

15(1)This section and s 16 below have effect in relation to the issue to constables under any enactment, including an enactment contained in an Act passed after this Act of warrants to enter and search premises, and an entry on or search of premises under a warrant is unlawful, unless it complies with this section and s 16 below.

[Sub-section (1) states that the provisions under this section and s 16 apply to applications for warrants under any enactment, whether it was passed before or after PACE, including applications made under PACE itself. It also provides that any non-compliance with these provisions will render the entry and search unlawful.]

(2) Where a constable applies for any such warrant, it shall be his duty:

    (a) to state:

        (i) the ground on which he makes the application; and

        (ii) the enactment under which the warrant would be issued;

    (b) to specify the premises which it is desired to enter and search; and

    (c) to identify, so far as is practicable, the articles or persons to be sought.

[Code B, under the subheading 'making an application', reiterates much of what is already stated in sub-s (2), although para 2.8 makes the following statement which is absent from the above provisions: 'If an application is refused, no further application may be made for a warrant to search those premises unless supported by additional grounds.']

(3) An application for such a warrant shall be made *ex parte* and supported by an information in writing.

(4) The constable shall answer on oath any question that the justice of the peace or judge hearing the application asks him.

[See, also, note for guidance 2A to Code B (see above, p 95, with regard to sub-s (4).]

(5) A warrant shall authorise an entry on one occasion only.

[The reason for this safeguard will be obvious. Unlimited entry to premises in this context would be viewed as too draconian and challengable on constitutional grounds. This rule is also repeated in para 5.3 of Code B. There are, however, exceptions under prevention of terrorism legislation, which will be discussed later in this chapter.]

(6) A warrant:

    (a) shall specify:

        (i) the name of the person who applies for it;

        (ii) the date on which it is issued;

        (iii) the enactment under which it is issued; and

        (iv) the premises to be searched; and

    (b) shall identify, so far as is practicable, the articles or person to be sought.

[In R v South Western Magistrates' Court and Metropolitan Police Commissioner ex p Cofie *(1996), it was held that, where a property is in multi-occupancy, the warrant should state to which part of those premises the search should*

be directed. In this case, a search warrant was obtained in which the number of the house was 78. The police did not make it clear that they only needed to search Flat 78F and the common parts of the building. The court held that the warrant was unlawful, as it did not comply with s 15(6)(a)(iv) of PACE.]

(7) Two copies shall be made of a warrant.

(8) The copies shall be clearly certified as copies.

The execution of search warrants

Section 16 of PACE, together with the relevant provisions under Code B, cover the important issue of the conduct of entry and search of premises. The provisions under s 16 are as follows, together with appropriate annotations and quotations from the Code of Practice:

Execution of warrants

16(1) A warrant to enter and search premises may be executed by any constable.

[This means that any constable may execute a search warrant, in so far as that officer need not be the person named in it. It also means that the constable may be of any rank, although note the provisions mentioned above, whereby an inspector or above must take charge and be present during a search under Sched 1 to PACE and Sched 7 to the 1989 Act.]

(2) Such a warrant may authorise persons to accompany any constable who is executing it.

[Occasionally, other persons may accompany the police during the search of premises. This may include an expert witness,[11] a social worker, a community leader where the search may adversely affect police/community relations or even a carpenter to lift floorboards.[12] But, in R v Reading Justices ex p South West Meats Ltd (1992), it was held, inter alia, that the police must exercise care in order to avoid delegating their authority to non-police officers who may accompany them.]

(3) Entry and search under a warrant must be within one month from the date of its issue.

(4) Entry and search under a warrant must be at a reasonable hour, unless it appears to the constable executing it that the purpose of a search may be frustrated on an entry at a reasonable hour.

[The provisions under sub-ss (3) and (4) are repeated in paras 5.1 and 5.2 of Code B. These are designed to prevent warrants lasting indefinitely and to ensure that 'dawn raids' on premises are restricted to cases where this is essential. The latter is reinforced under note for guidance 5A to Code B, which is cited as follows:]

5A In determining at what time to make a search, the officer in charge should have regard, among other considerations, to the time of day at which the occupier of the premises is likely to be present, and should

---

11 *Op cit*, Levenson, Fairweather and Cape, fn 3.
12 *Op cit*, Lidstone and Palmer, fn 9.

not search at a time when he, or any other person on the premises, is likely to be asleep, unless not doing so is likely to frustrate the purpose of the search.

(5) Where the occupier of premises which are to be entered and searched is present at the time when a constable seeks to execute a warrant to enter and search them, the constable:

(a) shall identify himself to the occupier and, if not in uniform, shall produce to him documentary evidence that he is a constable;

(b) shall produce the warrant to him; and

(c) shall supply him with a copy of it.

[In R v Chief Constable of Lancashire ex p Parker and Magrath (1993), the police executed search warrants to which a schedule listing the articles sought was attached when the application was made. Following the search and subsequent seizure of documents, the police supplied the applicants with a copy of the authorisation, but not the schedule. The court held that, since there had been a breach of s 16(5)(c) of PACE, the police had no legal right to retain the documents seized in the course of this unlawful entry and search.]

(6) Where:

(a) the occupier of such premises is not present at the time when a constable seeks to execute such a warrant; but

(b) some other person who appears to the constable to be in charge of the premises is present,

sub-s (5) above shall have effect as if any reference to the occupier were a reference to that other person.

(7) If there is no person present who appears to the constable to be in charge of the premises, he shall leave a copy of the warrant in a prominent place on the premises.

[Paragraphs 5.4 to 5.6 of Code B cover 'Entry other than with consent' and fill certain gaps uncovered by s 16 of PACE by making the following provisions:]

5.4 The officer in charge shall first attempt to communicate with the occupier or any other person entitled to grant access to the premises by explaining the authority under which he seeks entry to the premises and ask the occupier to allow him to enter, unless:

(i) the premises to be searched are known to be unoccupied;

(ii) the occupier and any other person entitled to grant access are known to be absent; or

(iii) there are reasonable grounds for believing that to alert the occupier or any other person entitled to grant access by attempting to communicate with him would frustrate the object of the search or endanger the officers concerned or other people.

5.5 Where the premises are occupied, the officer shall identify himself (by warrant or other identification number in the case of inquiries linked to the investigation of terrorism) and, if not in uniform, show his warrant card (but, in so doing in the case of inquiries linked to the investigation of terrorism, the officer need not reveal his name); and state the purpose of the search and the grounds for undertaking it, before a search begins, unless sub-para 5.4(iii) applies.

[In R v Longman (1988), police officers obtained a search warrant under s 23(3) of the Misuse of Drugs Act 1971 and went to the defendant's address in plain clothes. One of them posed as a delivery lady, since there had been difficulty executing a warrant there in the past. Once the door was opened by the defendant, the police entered the premises and one of them shouted who they were and that they had a warrant. In the course of the search, the defendant lunged at a police officer with a knife and was subsequently convicted of attempted wounding, and obstructing the police. During his appeal, it was contended that, under ss 15 and 16 of PACE, the police officer should have announced his identity and produced his warrant card as well as the search warrant prior to entry. The Court of Appeal held that these procedures could be bypassed if there were reasonable grounds for believing that this would frustrate the object of the search or endanger the police or others.

However, in R v Linehan (1999), the police attended the defendant's address, intending to conduct a search under s 18 of PACE, having previously arrested his son (this power to enter and search premises is covered below, p 104). When they identified themselves and requested entry, he responded by asking them to push their warrant under the door; instead, the police offered to display it at the window, but this offer was rejected. The defendant was then warned by the police that the door would be forced, which they subsequently did, and he then threw liquid through the door, which struck two of the officers in the face. The defendant was later convicted of two charges of assault on police. In allowing his appeal against conviction, the Divisional Court held that, as it was unclear as to whether the police had given a proper explanation regarding the reason for their intention to enter and search the premises, the officers were not acting in the execution of their duty.]

5.6 Reasonable force may be used if necessary to enter premises if the officer in charge is satisfied that the premises are those specified in the warrant, or in exercise of the powers described in 3.1 to 3.3, above,[13] and where:

   (i) the occupier or any other person entitled to grant access has refused a request to allow entry to his premises;

   (ii) it is impossible to communicate with the occupier or any other person entitled to grant access; or

   (iii) any of the provisions of 5.4(i) to (iii) apply.

Apart from specific mention of the use of reasonable force in the Codes of Practice, it should also be remembered that s 117 of PACE applies this to all the coercive powers under PACE; also, the provisions of s 3(1) of the Criminal Law Act 1967 should be borne in mind in the exercise of other powers.

Section 16 of PACE continues as follows:

(8) A search under a warrant may only be a search to the extent required for the purpose for which the warrant was issued.

---

13 Code B, paras 3.1 to 3.3 refer to entry without warrant under PACE, ss 17, 18 and 32.

[This is a safeguard which prevents unfettered search powers being exercised by the police. If, for instance, a warrant is issued to search for a large power drill suspected of being used to break into a bank, police officers executing a search warrant would not be justified in sifting through clothing in a small drawer in a dressing table, unless they were also seeking documents relating to ownership of the drill. This is confirmed in para 5.9 of Code B, which states:]

> 5.9 Premises may be searched only to the extent necessary to achieve the object of the search, having regard to the size and nature of whatever is sought. A search under warrant may not continue under the authority of that warrant once all the things specified in it have been found or the officer in charge of the search is satisfied that they are not on the premises.

[But, in the other extreme, it does not mean that the police should ignore the presence of a dead body when looking for something else! (See sub-s (9)(b), below, which covers such eventualities.) Sub-section (8) should also be read in conjunction with s 15(2)(c) and (6)(b), which states that the warrant should state, as far as is practicable, the articles or persons to be sought. In R v Reading Justices ex p South West Meats Ltd *(1992), cited above, a search warrant was applied for by the police at the request of the Intervention Board for Agricultural Produce. However, the warrant was not executed correctly, as the actual search was conducted by members of the Board, instead of the police, and the warrant did not identify the persons likely to enter the premises with the police. Also, the objects and documents sought were not described in sufficient detail and an inappropriate enactment was cited. The Divisional Court held the warrant to be invalid and the subsequent entry and search unlawful to the extent that exemplary damages were awarded against the police and the Board.*

Also relevant to sub-s (8) is R v Chesterfield Justices ex p Bramley *(1999), where it was held that, when executing warrants under s 8(1) of PACE, the police are not entitled to remove items from the premises in order to 'sift through' them for the purpose of ascertaining whether or not they fall within the scope of the warrant. Items seized unlawfully during a search must be returned, although the search remains valid regarding any items that were properly seized. Law enforcement bodies are now in a difficult position, especially those who need to sift through large quantities of materials, such as during a fraud investigation. According to Mr Justice Turner, whilst expressing reluctance in making his judgment: '... I agree that further statutory power has to be provided to cover the situation which I have considered above. For my part, I doubt whether anything short of primary legislation would suffice to meet the stringency of the requirements of the European Convention. Having regard to the practical implications of the result of this case, it may be thought that the authorities should consider this matter with a degree of urgency.' In other words, an Act of Parliament may have to be passed in order to resolve this difficult situation. In limited circumstances, the removal of disputed legally privileged material for sifting may be permissible, unless the police have reasonable belief that it is legally privileged (s 19(6) of PACE).]*

(9) A constable executing a warrant shall make an endorsement on it, stating:

    (a) whether the articles or persons sought were found; and

    (b) whether any articles were seized other than articles which were sought.

(10) A warrant which:

    (a) has been executed; or

    (b) has not been executed within the time authorised for its execution, shall be returned:

        (i) if it was issued by a justice of the peace, to the clerk to the justices for the petty sessions area for which he acts; and

        (ii) if it was issued by a judge, to the appropriate officer of the court from which he issued it.

(11) A warrant which is returned under sub-s (10) above shall be retained for 12 months from its return:

    (a) by the clerk to the justices, if it was returned under para (i) of that sub-section; and

    (b) by the appropriate officer, if it was returned under para (ii).

(12) If, during the period for which a warrant is to be retained, the occupier of the premises to which it relates asks to inspect it, he shall be allowed to do so.

ENTRY AND SEARCH WITHOUT WARRANT

Introduction

At the beginning of this chapter, it was stated that there are a number of statutory powers available to the police enabling them to enter and search premises without warrant (apart from executing arrest warrants). One of those cited was s 23(1) of the Misuse of Drugs Act 1971, which empowers the police to enter premises where a person is carrying on business as a producer or supplier of controlled drugs, in order to examine their records and stocks of drugs. Others include s 13 of the Aviation Security Act 1982, s 15(3) of the Theatres Act 1968 and s 2 of the Performing Animals (Regulation) Act 1925, to name but a few.[14] Many of these provisions are essentially regulatory by nature and often specialised in their enforcement since, *inter alia*, certain premises are excluded from their ambit.

The three *main* statutory sources of police powers to enter and search premises without warrant are to be found under ss 17, 18 and 32 of PACE, although the search powers in these instances are limited. There is also a common law power which has been preserved by PACE, namely, the power for the police to enter premises in order to deal with or prevent a breach of the peace. Finally, there are a number of specific entry and search powers conferred on the police in order to prevent acts of terrorism, following the

---

14   For a comprehensive list of such statutory powers, refer to *op cit*, Levenson, Fairweather and Cape, fn 3, Appendix 6.

enactment of the Prevention of Terrorism (Additional Powers) Act 1996, and also powers to enter school premises in order to search those premises and any person on them for knives and any offensive weapons. The latter provisions are to be found in the Offensive Weapons Act 1996. All the statutory sources of police powers to enter and search premises mentioned in this paragraph will now be discussed.

Section 17 of PACE – entry for purpose of arrest, etc

Section 17 applies to any premises (which includes vehicles for this purpose) and permits entry for a number of purposes, including making arrests. As far as the latter is concerned, a constable may enter and search premises in order to execute a warrant for an arrest in connection with or arising out of criminal proceedings, or to execute a warrant of commitment (these are issued in response to non-payment of fines, compensation orders or maintenance orders). The police may also enter and search premises in order to arrest a person for an arrestable offence or for the following offences:

(a) s 1 of the Public Order Act 1936 – prohibiting the wearing of uniforms in connection with political objects;

(b) any enactment under ss 6–8 or 10 of the Criminal Law Act 1977 – offences relating to entering and remaining on property (squatting);

(c) s 4 of the Public Order Act 1986 – causing fear or provocation of violence;

(d) s 76 of the Criminal Justice and Public Order Act 1994 – failure to comply with interim possession order (squatters failing to leave).

Note that, with regard to (b) and (d), these police powers of entry and search may only be exercised by officers in uniform.

Section 17 also empowers the police to enter and search premises for the purposes of recapturing persons unlawfully at large. Under sub-ss (1)(ca) and (cb), this includes any child or young person remanded or committed to local authority accommodation under s 23(1) of the Children and Young Persons Act 1969 and persons unlawfully at large from a prison, remand centre, young offender institution or secure training centre. Also included are children or young persons guilty of 'grave crimes' who are unlawfully at large from any place designated by the Home Secretary for their detention. 'Grave crimes' are defined under s 53 of the Children and Young Persons Act 1933, which refers to particularly serious offences which, if committed by any 10–17 year old, can justify long term detention.

Persons unlawfully at large who do not fall under any of the aforementioned categories are covered under sub-s (1)(d), which provides that the police may enter and search premises in order to recapture any person 'whatever' who is unlawfully at large. This appears to include those who escape from such places as police stations, court cells and police vehicles, and compulsory patients who abscond from psychiatric hospitals. However, it is important to note that, with regard to this miscellaneous category under sub-s (1)(d), the police may only exercise these powers when in actual pursuit of the person unlawfully at large.

The meaning of the word 'pursuing' means actually 'chasing' or being in 'hot pursuit', according to the House of Lords in *D'Souza v Director of Public Prosecutions* (1992). In this case, Mrs D'Souza was compulsorily admitted to a psychiatric unit, but absconded shortly afterwards. Three police officers, acting on information received, later arrived at her home, together with two nurses, intending to return her to hospital, although they did not have a warrant. Other members of the family refused to admit the police to the premises; therefore, they forced entry. A struggle ensued between the family and the police, and subsequently the daughter, Miss D'Souza, was charged and later convicted of assault on police. Her conviction was quashed by the House of Lords on the grounds that, whilst her mother was unlawfully at large, the police had no legal right to enter her home, since they were not actively pursuing her at the time and, therefore, they were not acting in the course of their duty. Subsequently, there could be no assault on police. In this decision, Lord Lowry stated:

> There must be an act of pursuit – a chase – however short in time and distance. It was not enough for the police to form an intention to arrest, which they put into practice by resorting to the premises where they believed the person whom they sought might be found. Entry without warrant under s 17(1)(d) of PACE could be made for the purpose of recapturing a person who was unlawfully at large, but could be made only if the constables were 'pursuing' that person and not in any other circumstances. Therefore, a constable, acting on information received, but not being in possession of a warrant, who simply goes to a house where he reasonably (and correctly) believes that the person he is seeking can be found, cannot conceivably say that he is 'pursuing' that person. To do so would empty the word 'pursuing' of all meaning.[15]

Up until the passing of the Prisoners (Return to Custody) Act 1995, the recapture of all persons unlawfully at large was subject to the 'hot pursuit' requirement. This no longer applies to those mentioned above in sub-ss (1)(ca) and (cb), although it is still an essential requirement regarding those who fall under sub-s (1)(d), which includes formally detained psychiatric patients who abscond, as illustrated in the above case.[16]

---

15 (1992) *The Guardian*, 17 November.

16 The legal situation, however, is not entirely clear on this issue. See Jason-Lloyd, L, 'Prisoners (Return to Custody) Act 1995 – a review' (1995) 159 JP 754 and, also, Jason-Lloyd, L, 'Escape from lawful custody and the Prisoners (Return to Custody) Act 1995 – are they reconcilable?' (1997) 161 JP 354.

Section 17 further empowers the police to enter and search premises without warrant in order to save life or limb or to prevent serious damage to property (sub-s (1)(e)). A number of situations which may fall under this broad heading could also constitute a breach of the peace for which a common law power of entry exists and has been preserved under sub-s (6). In addition to this overlapping of powers, it has been suggested that the potential for intervention under sub-s (1)(e) can create even further inroads into other police powers. For example, entry in order to deal with or prevent a child or wife being battered by a violent partner, entry into the premises of a terrorist organisation where it is believed that weapons are being kept for imminent use and entry into premises where it is alleged that a drunken brawl is taking place.[17] In view of the infinite variety of dangerous situations that sub-s (1)(e) is designed to prevent or alleviate, it may come as no surprise that this is not subject to the following procedural requirements under sub-s (2), which restrict all the other entry and search powers under s 17. These are that they are only exercisable if the police have reasonable grounds for believing that the person being sought is on the premises, and confining the entry and search to communal parts of premises where they consist of more than one dwelling. Since this limitation does not apply to sub-s (1)(e), the scope for its application is even wider, as illustrated in the following statement:

> Furthermore, there is no requirement that the threat to life, limb and property should concern the premises in question, for example, the police can enter if they believe that the premises contain material such as burglary or arson equipment which may be used against other premises or if a person who has planted a bomb elsewhere is on the premises.[18]

Section 17 goes on to state that all search powers within its ambit must be confined to searching premises to the extent that is reasonably required to find who or what the police are seeking. Since most of this section applies to searching for persons, this means, *inter alia*, that it would not be permissible to search a dressing table for a fully grown adult, although it may be permissible to open a wardrobe which could be large enough to conceal such a person. Section 17 ends by abolishing all the earlier common law rules governing entry of premises without warrant but, at the same time, it preserves the common law power of entry to deal with or prevent a breach of the peace (see sub-s (6), mentioned above).

Section 18 of PACE – entry and search after arrest

Section 18 provides that the police may enter and search premises occupied or controlled by a person who has been arrested for an arrestable offence. This is

---

17 *Op cit*, Lidstone and Palmer, fn 9.
18 *Op cit*, Lidstone and Palmer, fn 9.

contingent upon them having reasonable grounds for suspecting that there is evidence on those premises which relates to the offence in question or some other arrestable offence connected with, or similar to it, although this excludes items subject to legal privilege. The power to search premises under this section may only be exercised to the extent that is reasonably required to discover any evidence just mentioned. If the arrested suspect is already at the police station, a police officer of at least the rank of inspector must make written authorisation before these entry and search powers are exercised. In *R v Badham* (1987), it was held that this authorisation must be made on an independent document and not a mere entry in a notebook as confirmation of verbal instructions. On this issue, para 3.3 of Code B states that, unless wholly impracticable, that authority shall be given on the notice of powers and rights (see below).

If the presence of the arrested person is necessary for the effective investigation of the offence, the police may exercise their powers under s 18 *before* the suspect is taken to the police station and without an inspector or above giving prior written authorisation. Where this is done, the officer conducting the search must inform the inspector as soon as practicable following its completion. Where an inspector or above either authorises a search under s 18 or has been informed that one has been conducted prior to the suspect being brought to the police station, that officer shall record, in writing, the grounds for the search and the nature of evidence that was sought. This will be part of the custody record if the person who was in occupation or control of the premises during the search is under police detention at the time the record is being made.

Section 32 of PACE – search upon arrest

The provisions under s 32 were discussed in Chapter 3, since searches under this section can apply to suspects themselves as well as premises they were in at the time of the arrest or immediately beforehand (see above, p 78).

Notice of powers and rights

Whenever a search of premises is made under Code B, para 5.7 states that, unless it is impracticable to do so, the occupier shall be given a copy of a notice in a standard format, which contains the following information:

(a) whether the search is made under a warrant or with the occupier's consent, or under s 17, 18 or 32 of PACE;

(b) a summary of the extent of the powers of search and seizure conferred under PACE;

(c) an explanation of the occupier's rights and those of the owner of any property seized;

(d) notification that compensation may be available in appropriate cases where damage has been caused by entering and searching premises, together with the address to which such claims may be directed;

(e) a statement that a copy of this Code may be consulted at any police station.

Paragraph 5.8 provides that copies of the notice of powers and rights shall be given to the occupier and any warrant, where applicable, if he or she is present. This shall, if practicable, be given to the occupier prior to the commencement of the search, unless the officer in charge reasonably believes that this would frustrate the object of the search or endanger police officers present or other people. Where the occupier is not present, a copy of the notice and warrant, where appropriate, shall be left in a prominent place on the premises. This shall be endorsed with the name of the officer in charge (or warrant number, where the search is linked to a terrorist investigation), the name of the police station where that officer is attached and the date and time of the search. Any warrant shall be endorsed to the effect that this has been done.

Consensual entry and search of premises

Paragraph 5.4 to Code B provides that, wherever possible, the police are obliged to seek the co-operation of the occupier to enter premises, even where they have the power to enter without his or her consent. The exceptions to this rule are where the premises are known to be unoccupied or the occupier or any other person entitled to grant access are absent, or where attempting to communicate with such persons would frustrate the object of the search or endanger police officers or others present. Paragraph 5.6 states that reasonable force may be used if necessary to enter premises under the authority of a warrant or where entry is required under s 17, 18 or 32 of PACE. This may be done where any of the foregoing conditions are present or where the occupier or other person entitled to grant access has refused to allow entry to the premises, or where it is not possible to communicate with such persons.

Searches with consent are covered under paras 4.1–4.4 of Code B, together with notes for guidance 4A, 4B and 4C as follows. Unless it would cause disproportionate inconvenience to the person concerned,[19] the police should seek the consent of that person in the following manner. First, the officer in

---

19 Note for guidance 4C states that this applies where it is reasonable to assume that innocent occupiers would not object to the police taking action where, eg, a suspect is fleeing from the police and they need to quickly check surrounding gardens and readily accessible places to see if that person is hiding there or the police have arrested someone and wish to briefly check gardens nearby for any discarded evidence.

charge should make necessary inquiries to ensure that the person is in a position to give consent. Secondly, the officer should state the purpose of the search and inform the person that he or she is not obliged to co-operate and that anything seized may be produced in evidence. If the person is not suspected of an offence at the time, the officer shall tell that person when stating the purpose of the search. Thirdly, where consent is given, this should be put into writing if practicable on the notice of powers and rights before the search takes place. The police cannot enter and search premises, or continue to do so once a search has started, if the consent has been given under duress or the person withdraws their consent before completion of the search.

Searches of lodging houses or similar accommodation should not be made solely on the basis of the landlord's consent, unless the matter is urgent and the tenant, lodger or occupier is not available.

Powers of entry and search in the prevention of terrorism

Terrorism in its general sense falls within the definition of a number of different offences, including firearms and explosives offences to name but a few. These will often necessitate the use of entry and search powers of premises, since many of them fall under the heading of serious arrestable offences. The Prevention of Terrorism (Additional Powers) Act 1996, which substantially amended the Prevention of Terrorism (Temporary Provisions) Act 1989, conferred wide ranging powers on the police in order to deal with and prevent acts of terrorism. These provisions augment the more general powers already held by the police in England and Wales to deal with terrorist activities. The powers under ss 1, 3 and 4 of the 1996 Act have already been discussed in Chapter 2, since the bulk of these provisions involve the stopping and searching of vehicles and persons, although entry and search of premises within police cordons under s 4 should also be noted for the purposes of this chapter.

Section 2 of the 1996 Act makes provision for the police to search non-residential premises where an officer of at least the rank of superintendent may apply to a magistrate for a warrant to search one or more premises named in the application. This may be done where a terrorist investigation is taking place and there are reasonable grounds for believing that it is likely that material of substantial value to this investigation will be found there (although this excludes items subject to legal privilege or excluded or special procedure material).

A search warrant issued under s 2 must be executed within 24 hours and empowers the police to enter and search any of the premises named in it and anyone found there. Anything found on the premises or found on anyone discovered there may be seized and retained if there are reasonable grounds for believing that it is likely to be of substantial value to the investigation and it is necessary to prevent it from being concealed, lost, damaged, altered or destroyed. The provisions under s 2 enable the police to search any number of non-residential premises specified under the warrant, whereas, under the earlier provisions, separate warrants would have to be issued for each of them. It is important to note that s 2 does not apply to premises which the applicant has reasonable cause to believe are used wholly or mainly as a dwelling. An example of the type of premises to which s 2 may apply would be a block of lock-up garages. Instead of applying for a warrant, a police superintendent or above may make a written order for the entry and search of one or more unattended premises if there are reasonable grounds for believing that this is a case of great emergency and immediate action is necessary in the interests of the State.[20]

Police powers of entry and search of school premises[21]

In response to a series of incidents involving the use of knives and similar weapons both in and around school premises, the Offensive Weapons Act 1996 was passed, in order to combat the increasing knife culture that has been particularly prevalent among teenagers in recent times. One of the provisions under the 1996 Act is the power under s 4, enabling the police to enter school premises in order to search such places and any person in them for any article with a blade or point, or any offensive weapon. The definition and general search powers to find such dangerous articles have been covered in Chapter 2, although it should be noted that these apply to public places. Prior to the passing of the Offensive Weapons Act, there was some contention as to whether these general stop and search powers applied to school premises. This was subsequently resolved when s 4 made express provision for school premises to be included within the ambit of police powers to search for articles such as knives (except folding pocket knives with cutting edges of no more than three inches) and offensive weapons.

In addition, s 1 of the 1996 Act created the new offences of unlawful possession of an offensive weapon or an article with a blade or point in school premises, and made them arrestable offences under s 24 of PACE (see Chapter 3). This is subject to a number of defences, which include instances where the person in possession of such an article has it with good reason, with lawful authority or where it was for use at work or for educational purposes, religious reasons or as part of a national costume. 'School premises', for the

---

20 For a complete commentary on all the provisions of the 1996 Act, see Jason-Lloyd, L, 'The Prevention of Terrorism (Additional Powers) Act 1996 – a commentary' (1996) 160 JP 503.

21 For further discussion on this subject, as well as other issues arising from the enactment of the Offensive Weapons Act 1996, see Jason-Lloyd, L, 'The Offensive Weapons Act 1996 – an overview' (1996) 160 JP 931; and 'The Offensive Weapons Act 1996 and the Knives Act 1997 – how effective will they be?' (1997) 161 JP 572, p 599.

purposes of the 1996 Act, include main and secondary buildings, playgrounds, sports fields, and even extend to school buses.[22] However, dwellings used by persons employed at schools are excluded from these provisions. This will include the homes of caretakers and groundsmen, for instance.

Entry by the police in school premises for the purposes of searching for such dangerous articles is contingent upon them having reasonable grounds to believe that someone is in unlawful possession of them. The requirement of reasonable belief, rather than reasonable suspicion, seems rather anomalous. If a police officer has reasonable *suspicion* that someone on school premises is unlawfully in possession of a prohibited article under the 1996 Act, that officer has the power to enter those premises in order to make an arrest under s 17 of PACE and may then search the premises and that individual under s 32. This is possible because such offences are arrestable. Also, subject to the constraints mentioned above under the coverage of s 18 of PACE, the police may then search the suspect's home. Why rely on the much higher requirement of reasonable *belief* to enter and search school premises or any person there for weapons when the lesser requirement of reasonable *suspicion* avails the police far greater powers? The position is even more puzzling when considering that the 1996 Act, as applied in Scotland, requires police officers there to have only reasonable suspicion in this context.

Where any suspected person in school premises is below the age of criminal responsibility (10 years), the police cannot exercise this arrest power, because those under 10 years old are not criminally liable; therefore, they cannot commit this or any other offence. In such cases, the police may even have difficulty in relying on their entry and search powers conferred under the 1996 Act where *any* person may be searched, because, according the wording of the Act, an offence has to be involved. Primary schools, therefore, appear to be excluded from the ambit of the 1996 Act. It could be argued, however, that weapons offences are more likely to be committed in secondary schools; therefore, these potential legal difficulties may not present a serious problem.

Further anomalies seem apparent under the 1996 Act. First, it enables the police to use reasonable force where necessary in order to effect entry into school premises, but makes no express provision regarding force in order to search persons. However, it is submitted that the courts may imply such a power, notwithstanding the absence of any precise provision under the Act. Secondly, there is no mention of the extent to which searches in school premises can take place. The Codes of Practice make no precise mention of the conduct of searches in school premises or of persons within such places. In the former instance, this would not have been possible, since the latest Code B

---

22 *Hansard*, Parliamentary Debates, HC Standing Committee C, 6 March 1996, p 15.

was published over a year before the passing of the Offensive Weapons Act, but the most recent Code A took effect nearly two years after the Act received the royal assent. Will the proposed new Codes of Practice include the necessary guidance for the 1996 Act? In the meantime, perhaps some reliance may be placed on the provisions under para 1.3A of Code B, which states: 'Any search of a person who has not been arrested which is carried out during a search of premises shall be carried out in accordance with Code A.'

General provisions under Code B

Some remaining provisions under Code B that have not been discussed above will now be mentioned. Paragraphs 5.10 and 5.11 make provision regarding certain aspects of the conduct of searches and para 5.12 covers police conduct when leaving premises that have been searched. These are cited as follows, with annotations in italics where appropriate:

5.10 Searches must be conducted with due consideration for the property and privacy of the occupier of the premises searched, and with no more disturbance than necessary. Reasonable force may be used only where this is necessary, because the co-operation of the occupier cannot be obtained or is insufficient for the purpose.

5.11 If the occupier wishes to ask a friend, neighbour or other person to witness the search, then he must be allowed to do so, unless the officer in charge has reasonable grounds for believing that this would seriously hinder the investigation or endanger the officers concerned or other people. A search need not be unreasonably delayed for this purpose.

[This provision exists for a number of reasons, including reducing fears of evidence being 'planted' in the course of a search, as well as having a witness to any damage done to property.]

5.12 If premises have been entered by force, the officer in charge shall, before leaving them, satisfy himself that they are secure, either by arranging for the occupier or his agent to be present or by any other appropriate means.

Note for guidance 5C gives the following important advice when errors have been made:

5C If the wrong premises are searched by mistake, everything possible should be done at the earliest opportunity to allay any sense of grievance. In appropriate cases, assistance should be given to obtain compensation.

Paragraphs 7.1 to 7.3 and 8.1 provide the action to be taken after police searches and the maintenance of search registers at police stations as follows:

7.1 Where premises have been searched in circumstances to which this Code applies, other than in the circumstances covered by the exceptions to para 1.3(a) *[note that these exceptions cover scenes of routine crime searches, calls to fires or burglaries, bomb threat calls and searches where it would cause disproportionate inconvenience if consent was sought]*, the officer in charge of the search shall, on arrival at a police station, make or have made a record of the search. The record shall include:

(i) the address of the premises searched;

(ii) the date, time and duration of the search;

(iii) the authority under which the search was made. Where the search was made in the exercise of a statutory power to search premises without warrant, the record shall include the power under which the search was made and, where the search was made under warrant or with written consent, a copy of the warrant or consent shall be appended to the record or kept in a place identified in the record;

(iv) the names of all the officers who conducted the search (except in the case of inquiries linked to the investigation of terrorism, in which case, the record shall state the warrant or other identification number and duty station of each officer concerned);

(v) the names of any people on the premises, if they are known;

(vi) either a list of any articles seized or a note of where such a list is kept and, if not covered by a warrant, the reason for their seizure;

(vii) whether force was used and, if so, the reason why it was used;

(viii) details of any damage caused during the search and the circumstances in which it was caused.

7.2 Where premises have been searched under warrant, the warrant shall be endorsed to show:

(i) whether any articles specified in the warrant were found;

(ii) whether any other articles were seized;

(iii) the date and time at which it was executed;

(iv) the names of the officers who executed it (except in the case of inquiries linked to the investigation of terrorism, in which case, the warrant or other identification number and duty station of each officer concerned shall be shown);

(v) whether a copy, together with a copy of the notice of powers and rights was handed to the occupier, or whether it was endorsed, as required by para 5.8 [see above, p 106], and left on the premises, together with the copy notice and, if so, where.

7.3 Any warrant which has been executed or which has not been executed within one calendar month of its issue shall be returned, if it was issued by a justice of the peace, to the clerk to the justices for the petty sessions area concerned or, if issued by a judge, to the appropriate officer of the court from which he issued it ...

[Note that para 7.2 constitutes an extension of the provisions contained under s 16(9) of PACE, and para 7.3 is identical to s 16(10).]

8.1 A search register shall be maintained at each sub-divisional police station. All records which are required to be made by this code shall be made, copied or referred to in the register.

Common law power of entry to prevent or deal with a breach of the peace

This was the only common law power to enter premises which survived PACE. The power to arrest in order to deal with or prevent a breach of the peace has been discussed in Chapter 3, along with the power to enter public and private premises to do this.

CLANDESTINE POWERS OF ENTRY INTO PREMISES

Part III of the Police Act 1997 is focused on a particularly specialised aspect of police operations, namely covert surveillance, which includes entry into premises and the planting of 'bugging' or listening devices. Such activities by law enforcement bodies have been part of their function for many years and the targeting of certain suspects in this manner is often the only way to further certain criminal investigations. But how far can the police go in such investigations and what are the safeguards regarding intrusive surveillance in premises?

Prior to the passing of the 1997 Act, apart from statutory rules governing telephone and mail interception, intrusive surveillance by the police was not subject to statutory regulations. Instead, such activities were subject to Home Office guidelines. In *R v Khan* (1995), police officers placed a listening device in premises occupied by the defendant, who was suspected of importing heroin. During his trial for this offence, it was submitted that the incriminating conversation recorded on tape as a result of police 'bugging' the premises should be ruled inadmissible, since this had been obtained as a result of trespass and criminal damage. Whilst admitting the lack of statutory guidance governing police action in this respect, the trial judge proceeded to admit this evidence. The Court of Appeal upheld this decision, but also commented on the lack of statutory regulation regarding this form of intrusive surveillance by the police. This view was later upheld by the House of Lords.

The case of *Khan*, together with the human rights implications surrounding this matter, were major contributory factors in the later enactment of Pt III of the Police Act 1997, which now provides a statutory scheme regulating the authorisation of entry into premises for, *inter alia*, the purposes of planting listening devices in private property. It should be noted that this does not include other forms of surveillance that do not require entry into property, such as long range listening devices. It has therefore been suggested that:

The setting up of a Police Information Technology Organisation under Pt IV of the 1997 Act signals the importance of new technology in crime prevention. In years to come, the surveillance capability of the police is likely to develop to such an extent that the current provisions will become pedestrian and obsolete.[23]

In the meantime, the relevant provisions under the 1997 Act are as follows. First, ss 93 and 94 of the Act make provision for the actual authorisation of entry into premises in order to carry out covert surveillance, which also covers interference with property for this purpose. But, before discussion of these provisions, s 92 of the 1997 Act needs to be mentioned, since it makes such actions lawful, but only where such authorisation has been given; otherwise, the police could be guilty of burglary and possibly other offences, apart from liability under the civil law. The wide parameters applicable to s 92 have attracted the following comment:

> This section is very broadly drawn – it will make lawful any entry or interference with property where the necessary authorisation has been given under s 93 or s 94. 'Property' includes both real and personal property and 'interference' must involve any form of dealing with that property. The 'interference with property' is not constrained to the property of the person directly under surveillance – the section encompasses the bugging of a person who happens to employ a suspected criminal or even give him or her a bed for the night ... The section clearly encompasses such straightforward bugging, but also can embrace placing a tracking device on a car, cloning a mobile phone or committing a burglary to download the contents of a suspect's hard disk. *Authorising a literal reading of the section means that it would be possible to circumvent the procedures for the search of premises under Pt II of the Police and Criminal Evidence Act 1984.*[24]

The authorisation of such actions under ss 93 and 94 is contingent upon the rank of the officer concerned and the justifications for this form of intrusive surveillance. With regard to the former, s 93 states that the following may authorise entry and interference with property: a chief constable from any of

---

23 Emmerson, B and Friedman, D, *A Guide to the Police Act 1997*, 1998, London: Butterworths, but see the final paragraph of this chapter, regarding the Regulation of Investigatory Powers Bill. Also, the application under *Khan v UK* was declared admissible by a section of the European Court of Human Rights on 20 April 1999. The matters later heard before the full Court were whether the placement of the listening device infringed Art 8 of the European Convention on Human Rights (the right to respect for private life) and whether the admission of this evidence contravened Art 6 (the right to a fair trial). Also, a complaint was made of a violation of Art 13 (the right to an effective remedy). The Court ruled that the applicant's right to respect for private and family life had been violated, since there was no statutory scheme at the relevant time to regulate the use of covert listening devices; as the applicant did not have an effective remedy regarding this claim, there was a breach of Art 13. However, the use of the secretly recorded tape at the applicant's trial did not go against the requirements of fairness under Art 6.1.

24 Uglow, S and Telford, V, *The Police Act 1997*, 1997, Bristol: Jordans. Emphasis has been added to the final sentence to indicate material for further discussion, although there are numerous safeguards under the 1997 Act which would prevent this (see further commentary).

the 41 police forces in England and Wales outside London that are maintained under s 2 of the Police Act 1996; the Commissioner or an Assistant Commissioner in the Metropolitan Police; the Commissioner of the City of London Police; a chief constable of any Scottish police force; the chief constable or deputy chief constable of the Royal Ulster Constabulary; the Director General of the National Criminal Intelligence Service; the Director General of the National Crime Squad; or a customs officer designated for this purpose by the Commissioners of Customs and Excise. However, s 94 makes the following provisions as to who may make authorisations in the absence of an authorising officer. Where a case is urgent or it is not reasonably practicable for a designated deputy of any of those persons listed under s 93 to consider an application for an authorisation, those powers may be exercised by the following: an assistant chief constable in any police force in England, Wales and Scotland; a commander in the Metropolitan or City of London Police; an assistant chief constable in the Royal Ulster Constabulary; or by persons designated to act in such a capacity by the Director General of the National Criminal Intelligence Service or the National Crime Squad or the Commissioners of Customs and Excise.

The justifications for taking such action are specified under s 93(2) and (4), which state:

(2) This sub-section applies where the authorising officer believes:

(a) that it is necessary for the action specified to be taken on the ground that it is likely to be of substantial value in the prevention or detection of serious crime; and

(b) that what the action seeks to achieve cannot reasonably be achieved by other means.

(4) For the purposes of sub-s (2), conduct which constitutes one or more offences shall be regarded as serious crime if, and only if:

(a) it involves the use of violence, results in substantial financial gain or is conduct by a large number of persons in pursuit of a common purpose; or

(b) the offence or one of the offences is an offence for which a person who has attained the age of 21 and has no previous convictions could reasonably be expected to be sentenced to imprisonment for a term of three years or more ...

Authorisations should be in writing, except in cases of urgency where they may be given orally although, if given by a person listed under s 94, this must always be in writing. Authorisations given orally by authorising officers under s 93 or in writing by senior officers under s 94 are valid for 72 hours, during which they may be renewed for a period up to three months, but only by an authorising officer specified under s 93. The latter are also empowered to cancel an authorisation, whether or not made by themselves, where they feel it is no longer needed. In any event, no authorisation may last for longer than three months.

What are the safeguards in terms of scrutinising the actions of the police under these powers of intrusive surveillance? These can be found under the provisions regarding the role of the 'commissioners', who should not be confused with police commissioners. Under s 91 of the 1997 Act, the commissioners in this context are senior judges, headed by a chief commissioner, who are appointed by the Prime Minister and who hold such office for three years, which may be subject to renewal. Under s 96, whenever an authorising officer makes, renews or cancels an authorisation regarding intrusive surveillance, a written notification must be given, as soon as is reasonably practicable, to a commissioner. But, under s 97, there are certain cases where a commissioner must first be consulted before an authorisation is given, unless in cases of emergency. These are: where the property is used wholly or mainly as a dwelling or as a bedroom in a hotel; where the property constitutes office premises; and where it is likely that any person may acquire knowledge of matters subject to legal privilege, confidential personal information or confidential journalistic material. The commissioner must then give written notice to the authorising officer, as soon as is reasonably practicable, as to whether the authorisation has been approved or refused. This also applies in cases of renewals. Where a refusal has been made, the commissioner must report his or her findings to the authorising officer, who may make an appeal against this decision to the chief commissioner. Where an authorising officer alone makes an authorisation in an emergency and bypasses the prior scrutiny of a commissioner, that officer must inform the commissioner of the reasons for believing the case was one of emergency. If the commissioner disagrees that there were sufficient grounds for such belief, the authorisation may be quashed.

Under s 103 of the 1997 Act, a commissioner may quash any authorisation or a renewal. This may include an authorisation to which the commissioner gave prior approval. The basis on which such a decision can be made is: (1) where there are no reasonable grounds for believing that the provisions under s 93(2)(a) and (b) existed (see above); (2) where prior authorisation should have been obtained; or (3) where there has been a change in the circumstances of the case and intrusive surveillance is no longer justified. The cancellation of any authorisation or renewal by a commissioner does not necessarily mean that the police immediately abort any further action. Sufficient time may be allowed where necessary for the police to dismantle and remove any equipment from the property in question.

Schedule 7 to the 1997 Act makes provision for a complaints procedure regarding persons who believe that they have been subjected to intrusive surveillance. Of course, this can only take effect if they have some awareness of such activity. Where a complaint is made, a commissioner will assess whether the authorisation was justified or if prior approval should have been obtained, or if the intrusive surveillance should have been discontinued due to a change of circumstances. If the commissioner finds in favour of the complainant, compensation may be awarded to the person affected, although the authorising officer may appeal against this decision to the chief commissioner, who is also responsible for deciding appeals from unsuccessful complainants.

Under s 101 of the 1997 Act, the Home Secretary is under a duty to issue a Code of Practice for the guidance of authorising officers as well as all those involved in the process of intrusive surveillance. This excludes the commissioners who are not expected to have regard to the provisions of the Code in the course of their duties.

The Regulation of Investigatory Powers Act 2000

The Regulation of Investigatory Powers Act 2000 endeavours to regulate police surveillance even further, in anticipation of the implementation of the Human Rights Act 1998 (see Chapter 9). The Act, *inter alia*, replaces the provisions of the Interception of Communications Act 1985 with extended powers to intercept computer communications systems, including e-mails. The location of persons using mobile telephones[25] may be ascertained by the police power to demand from telecommunications companies information obtained whilst calls are actually being made. Whilst the Act introduces other new measures, it does not consolidate all the law regarding police surveillance. According to a leading commentator when the Bill was introduced in Parliament:

> Missing an opportunity to simplify the law, the Bill will not repeal Pt III of the Police Act 1997, which regulates 'bugging' achieved by entry on to or interference with property, but sets up a parallel regulatory structure for other forms of intrusive surveillance and also for other forms of covert surveillance and the use of informants and undercover officers.[26]

---

25 See *R v Effik* (1995), where the House of Lords held that mobile telephones do not fall within the ambit of the Interception of Communications Act 1985, since they do not constitute part of the public telecommunications system (see further comment in Chapter 9).

26 Cape, E, 'Regulating police surveillance' (2000) 150 NLJ 452.

CHAPTER 5

THE SEIZURE OF EVIDENCE AND DUTIES OF DISCLOSURE

POLICE POWERS OF SEIZURE

Introduction

A number of sections under the Police and Criminal Evidence Act 1984 (PACE) have given the police specific and general powers to seize evidence, and a number of other statutes passed before and after PACE provide the police with a variety of powers of seizure in respect of certain categories of property. These include the Betting, Gaming and Lotteries Act 1963, the Biological Weapons Act 1974, the Criminal Damage Act 1971, the Misuse of Drugs Act 1971, the Theft Act 1968, the Financial Services Act 1986, the Criminal Justice (International Co-operation) Act 1990 and the Drug Trafficking Act 1994, to name but a few. Some examples of specific police powers of seizure under statutes enacted since PACE will be illustrated towards the end of this chapter.

General powers of seizure under PACE, other statutes and the common law

Under s 19 of PACE, a constable may seize anything if he or she has reasonable grounds for believing that it constitutes evidence in relation to any offence or that it has been obtained as a result of an offence being committed, and that it is necessary to seize such items to prevent them being concealed, lost, altered or destroyed. The general power of seizure only applies when the constable is on premises lawfully, namely, where the officer is executing a search warrant or any other search under written authority, is dealing with or preventing a breach of the peace, entering premises under s 17, 18 or 32 of PACE or has entered premises with the consent of a person entitled to give it. It is submitted that this may also apply where the police are on premises under the authority of any statutory power to enter premises without a warrant.[1]

It is irrelevant that the police did not have the express authority to search for a particular item which is seized. This will include situations where the

---

1   In *Cowan v Metropolitan Police Commissioner* (1999), it was held that ss 18(2) and 19(2) of PACE 1984 include the power to seize everything, even the premises themselves! In this case, a car, which was held to constitute 'premises', was seized by the police, since it was alleged that a number of indecent assaults had taken place in it and the car was needed as evidence.

police may be searching premises for a murder weapon, for instance, but find illicit drugs in the course of the search. It will be for the trial judge to decide whether such articles should be admitted as evidence in accordance with s 78 of PACE.

Paragraph 6.3 of Code of Practice B makes provision for the scenario where a constable has entered premises and has reasonable grounds for believing that property there has been obtained as a result of the commission of a criminal offence, but decides that it is inappropriate to seize that property, because of an explanation by the person holding it. In those circumstances, that officer shall inform the holder of his suspicions and explain that he may be liable to civil or criminal proceedings if he or she disposes of that property.

It should be noted at this stage that, whilst excluded or special procedure may be seized under these provisions, material subject to legal privilege may not be seized under any power under PACE or any other statute.

Specific powers of seizure under PACE

Property may be seized by the police under the following circumstances:

- articles obtained as a result of a search under s 1 of PACE which are reasonably suspected to be stolen or prohibited;
- anything obtained as a result of a warrant issued by magistrates under s 8 regarding evidence of a serious arrestable offence, or anything obtained in the execution of a search warrant authorised by a circuit judge under Sched 1 to PACE;
- any object found as a result of searches under ss 18 and 32; and
- anything found under ss 54 and 55 as a result of the search of a suspect while detained by the police.

Information held on computer

Section 19(4) of PACE makes provision for access to information held on computer. This is put into more simplified form under para 6.5 of Code B, which states:

> 6.5 Where an officer considers that a computer may contain information which could be used in evidence, he may require the information to be produced in a form which can be taken away and in which it is visible and legible.

This, for example, will cover the police obtaining a print out, as opposed to a disk,[2] and such procedures may be applied under the following powers:

---

2   Levenson, H, Fairweather, F and Cape, E, *Police Powers: A Practitioner's Guide*, 3rd edn, 1996, London: Legal Action Group.

powers of seizure under any enactment before or after PACE; powers of seizure under s 8 of PACE; powers of entry and search under s 18 of PACE; searches under Sched 1 of PACE; and the power under s 19 of PACE to seize evidence discovered when the police are lawfully on premises, but which is not the object of the search. It has been stated that, in order to avoid a computer being destroyed or tampered with, the police may secure it in order to ensure the production of a print out.[3]

Access to and the copying of seized articles

Access to all property seized and subsequently held by the police under any power of seizure is provided for under s 21 of PACE. Where a person can show that he or she was the occupier of the premises from which the police have seized property, or had custody or control of the property immediately before it was seized, that person may request a record of the items taken, which must be provided within reasonable time. Such a person, or someone acting on their behalf, may be granted supervised access to the property by the investigating officer and may photograph or copy it; alternatively, this may be done by the police and given to the person concerned. However, these provisions will not apply where there are reasonable grounds for believing that this would prejudice that or any other criminal investigation or proceedings.

Retention of articles seized

Under s 22 of PACE, the police may retain any property seized (including information obtained from a computer) for as long as is necessary in all the circumstances. This will include retaining it for use as evidence at a trial, for forensic examination, for investigation into any criminal offence or to establish the rightful owner of the property where applicable. However, the police should not retain any property which can be photographed or otherwise copied for their purposes. In some circumstances, the police may not be under an obligation to return the property at all, for example, drugs which have been unlawfully possessed.[4] But they should return anything seized from a person where it may have been used to cause physical injury or damage to property, to interfere with evidence, or to assist in escape from police detention or lawful custody, if that person is no longer in police detention or the custody of a court or is in the custody of a court, but has been released on bail.

At this stage, further mention should be made of *R v Chesterfield Justices ex p Bramley* (1999), discussed in Chapter 4, p 100, above, where it was held,

---

3   Zander, M, *The Police and Criminal Evidence Act 1984*, 3rd edn, 1995, London: Sweet & Maxwell.

4   *Op cit*, Levenson, Fairweather and Cape, fn 2.

inter alia, that it is unlawful to remove items from premises in order to 'sift through' them, so as to find out if they fall within the scope of the search warrant. In this case, it was stated that:

> ... if the material is taken from the premises searched other than by agreement, it is 'seized' ... and the only right to seize is that to be found in s 8(2) of the [1984] Act which, subject to s 19(2)(iii) and (iv),[5] is restricted to items for which a search has been authorised by the warrant. If a constable executing a warrant seizes items which, when examined, are found to be outside the scope of the warrant and not covered by s 19, even if he acts in good faith, I find in the statute no defence to an action for trespass to goods based on that unjustified seizure ...

Any items that have been seized unlawfully during a search must be returned, although this will not invalidate the search regarding any other items that were properly seized.

Seizure of suspected drug trafficking cash

Under Pt II of the Drug Trafficking Act 1994, provision has been made to prevent the import or export of cash being used as part of the drug trafficking process. If a police (or customs) officer has reasonable grounds for suspecting that at least £10,000 cash in coins or notes of any currency is being brought into this country or exported from it, and it directly or indirectly represents the proceeds of drug trafficking, that officer is empowered to seize and detain that cash for up to 48 hours. Once this time limit has been reached, the money must be either returned or an application may be made to a magistrate for it to be retained for up to a further three months. This is subject to the police or customs officer continuing to have reasonable grounds to suspect that the cash represents the proceeds of drug trafficking, that the source of the cash is under investigation or that criminal proceedings are being considered against anyone connected with the cash, regardless of whether they are in the UK or abroad.

Further court orders may be issued which can result in the cash being detained for up to two years, although an appeal may be made to the magistrates' court for the money to be released, unless legal proceedings linked to this money are pending, whether in the UK or abroad. If it is proven, on the balance of probabilities, that the cash constitutes the proceeds of drug trafficking, a prosecutor may apply to the magistrates' court for a forfeiture order. If this is granted or criminal proceedings are instituted, the two year time limit will be extended and the cash will be detained until those

---

5   It is respectfully submitted that this should have been quoted as s 19(2)(a) and (b).

proceedings have been completed. An appeal may be made to the Crown Court within 30 days against the making of the forfeiture order by the magistrates' court.[6]

SPECIFIC POWERS OF SEIZURE UNDER OTHER STATUTES

Some examples of specific police powers of seizure will be provided below. These will include provisions under the Criminal Justice and Public Order Act 1994, the Prevention of Terrorism (Additional Powers) Act 1996, the Offensive Weapons Act 1996 and the Confiscation of Alcohol (Young Persons) Act 1997.

The Criminal Justice and Public Order Act 1994

Section 60(6) of the 1994 Act provides the police with the power to seize any offensive or dangerous weapons found in the course of a search under written authority in anticipation of serious violence (see Chapter 2); and s 60(4A)(b), inserted by s 25 of the Crime and Disorder Act 1998, empowers the police to seize any item which it is reasonably believed any person intends to wear wholly or mainly to conceal his or her identity whilst such a written authority is in force. Under s 64(4) of the 1994 Act, the police may seize vehicles and/or sound equipment used for 'raves' under specific circumstances, and s 62 provides them with the power to seize vehicles which have not been removed from land in accordance with a direction under s 61 (power to remove trespassers on land).

The Prevention of Terrorism (Additional Powers) Act 1996

The police are provided with the power to seize and retain items (except those subject to legal privilege) which are found in non-residential premises and on persons within them, in the course of a search under s 2 (see Chapter 4). This may be done where any item is reasonably believed to be of substantial value to a terrorist investigation and that it is necessary to prevent it from being concealed, lost, damaged, altered or destroyed.

Under Sched 6A to the 1996 Act, which is linked with s 4, the police may seize and retain anything found on premises or on any person found there

---

6　Jason-Lloyd, L, *The Law on Money-Laundering: Statutes and Commentary*, 1997, London: Frank Cass. Under the Terrorism Act 2000, very similar powers and procedures will apply to the seizure and detention of cash suspected of being used to finance terrorism. However, this will only apply to cash in transit from Northern Ireland to Great Britain and vice versa. Also, this power may be exercised by immigration officers, as well as customs officers and the police.

which are within a police cordon and are subject to a search under the written authority of a superintendent or above (see Chapter 4). Any property seized must not be subject to legal privilege and it must be reasonably believed that it is likely to be of substantial value to a terrorist investigation and that seizure is necessary to prevent its concealment, loss, damage, alteration or destruction.

The Offensive Weapons Act 1996

Police officers, using their powers to search school premises and persons on them for offensive weapons and articles with blades or points, may seize and retain such articles if found in the course of a search under the Offensive Weapons Act. This same power of seizure will also apply, of course, where such items have been discovered as a result of a stop and search in a public place under s 1 of PACE.

The Confiscation of Alcohol (Young Persons) Act 1997

Although there is no direct power of seizure under this statute, the 1997 Act is considered here because it empowers the police to require under 18 year olds to surrender any intoxicating liquor in their possession when in a public place, other than in licensed premises. Failure to do so without reasonable excuse and to state name and address when requested constitutes a summary only offence and confers a power of arrest on the police, which is a powerful inducement for the youngster to hand over the alcoholic drink.[7]

POLICE DUTIES OF DISCLOSURE OF EVIDENCE

The Criminal Procedure and Investigations Act 1996 was passed in the wake of a number of miscarriage of justice cases which attracted widespread public attention and contains, *inter alia*, provisions regarding the disclosure of evidence. Parts I and II of this Act are of prime importance to the police, although this part of the current chapter will be confined to a brief discussion of the Code of Practice regarding the disclosure rules under Pt II.

As far as the police are concerned, the two key participants governed by the Code of Practice are the 'officer in charge' of the case and the 'disclosure officer'. The officer in charge has the responsibility for preserving and recording all materials and records which constitute evidence, whether

---

7 For a full commentary on the 1997 Act, see Jason-Lloyd, L, 'The Confiscation of Alcohol (Young Persons) Act 1997 – an overview' (1997) 161 JP 871; and, also, Jason-Lloyd, L, 'The Confiscation of Alcohol (Young Persons) Act 1997: implications for the police service' (1997) LXX(4) Police Journal 287, October–December.

positive or otherwise. A close liaison must be maintained between the officer in charge and the disclosure officer, in order to ensure that all such material is made available to the latter. The disclosure officer may be a civilian and not necessarily a police officer; however, the officer in charge of the case, who will be a constable or above, may also perform the disclosure officer's role. Whatever the case, an investigating officer is now required by the Code of Practice to pursue every reasonable avenue of investigation, regardless as to whether or not this works to the advantage of the suspect.

The disclosure officer is the link between the Crown Prosecution Service and those involved in the criminal investigation. In essence, the disclosure officer has the overall duty to record and identify any material which should be disclosed under the provisions of the 1996 Act. In addition to complying with any request made by the prosecution, he has a number of other duties, which include responsibility for preparing schedules of the material regarding the investigation, identifying any material which may undermine the prosecution's case and making available any material which may create doubt regarding the reliability of a witness or a confession, as well as making the prosecution aware of any material which the defence will need to inspect under the requirements of primary disclosure.[8]

The 'general responsibilities' under the Code of Practice are reproduced below, followed by the main headings of the remaining provisions, in order to provide the reader with a broad outline of their overall direction. Those requiring in-depth knowledge of the complex provisions of the Code should consult this document in its entirety:

3.1 The functions of the investigator, the officer in charge of an investigation and the disclosure officer are separate. Whether they are undertaken by one, two or more persons will depend on the complexity of the case and the administrative arrangements within each police force. Where they are undertaken by more than one person, close consultation between them is essential to the effective performance of the duties imposed by this Code.

3.2 The chief officer of police for each police force is responsible for putting in place arrangements to ensure that, in every investigation, the identity of the officer in charge of an investigation and the disclosure officer is recorded.

3.3 The officer in charge of an investigation may delegate tasks to another investigator or to civilians employed by the police force, but he remains responsible for ensuring that these have been carried out and for accounting for any general policies followed in the investigation. In particular, it is an essential part of his duties to ensure that all material which may be relevant to an investigation is retained and either made

---

8 English, J and Card, R, *Butterworths Police Law*, 6th edn, 1999, London: Butterworths. See, also, Card, R and Ward, R, *The Criminal Procedure and Investigations Act 1996*, 1996, Bristol: Jordans; and Leng, R and Taylor, R, *Blackstone's Guide to the Criminal Procedure and Investigations Act 1996*, 1996, London: Blackstone.

available to the disclosure officer or (in exceptional circumstances) revealed directly to the prosecutor.

3.4 In conducting an investigation, the investigator should pursue all reasonable lines of inquiry, whether these point towards or away from the suspect. What is reasonable in each case will depend on the particular circumstances.

3.5 If the officer in charge of an investigation believes that other persons may be in possession of material that may be relevant to the investigation, and if this has not been obtained under para 3.4 above, he should ask the disclosure officer to inform them of the existence of the investigation and invite them to retain the material, in case they receive a request for its disclosure. The disclosure officer should inform the prosecutor that they may have such material. However, the officer in charge of an investigation is not required to make speculative inquiries of other persons; there must be some reason to believe that they may have relevant material. That reason may come from information provided to the police by the accused or from other inquiries made or from some other source.

3.6 If, during a criminal investigation, the officer in charge of an investigation or disclosure officer for any reason no longer has responsibility for the functions falling to him, either his supervisor or the police officer in charge of criminal investigations for the police force concerned must assign someone else to assume that responsibility. That person's identity must be recorded, as with those initially responsible for these functions in each investigation.

The Code of Practice then provides detailed procedures that fall under the following main headings: the recording of information; retention of material; preparation of material for the prosecutor; revelation of material to the prosecutor; subsequent action by the disclosure officer; certification by the disclosure officer; and disclosure of material to the accused.

CHAPTER 6

POLICE POWERS OF DETENTION

INTRODUCTION

Section 30 of the Police and Criminal Evidence Act 1984 (PACE) (already discussed above, Chapter 3, p 76) provides that, following the arrest of a person by the police away from a police station or the taking into custody of a suspect arrested by a non-police officer (a store detective, for example), there is a duty to convey the suspect to a police station as soon as practicable. *Normally*, that police station will be one designated for the purposes of detaining suspects, although there are exceptions, as discussed earlier. What is a designated police station, as distinct from one which is not?

Designated police stations

Section 35 of PACE places a statutory duty on all chief officers of police to provide designated police stations within their respective police areas. These may not necessarily function in that capacity all the time. For instance, a designated police station may operate as such for certain days of the week, although they may not be restricted to just certain times of the day.[1] Police stations falling within this category are places where custody areas are provided for the detention and subsequent questioning of suspects, and where at least one 'custody officer' is present.

The custody officer

Under s 36(3) of PACE, a custody officer must be a sergeant or above, although, under s 36(4), if a custody officer is not readily available at a designated police station, a police officer of any rank may perform this duty. However, in any event, such an officer must not be involved in the investigation of the case. A person appointed as a custody officer may not necessarily perform such duties all the time and may be assigned to other tasks although, in particularly busy police stations, custody officers are invariably full time. Under s 36(7) of PACE, where a suspect is taken to a non-designated police station, any police officer may assume the role of custody

---

1   Zander, M, *The Police and Criminal Evidence Act 1984*, 3rd edn, 1995, London: Sweet & Maxwell.

officer although, wherever possible, it should not be done by the officer investigating the case. If this cannot be avoided, due to shortage of manpower, for instance, then the officer who took the suspect to the police station or any other police officer may assume the role of custody officer; however, the arresting officer must, under s 36(9) and (10), inform an officer of at least the rank of inspector at a designated police station, as soon as practicable, that this is being done.

The custody officer, including anyone acting in that capacity under any of the circumstances mentioned above, is the person primarily responsible for ensuring the proper treatment of persons held in police detention (s 36(8)). This is in accordance with the relevant provisions of PACE and the Codes of Practice (s 39(1)). Custody officers are also under a duty to record all relevant matters which have to be included in the 'custody record' (see Figure 10, which depicts a simplified format of this document). Where it is necessary to transfer the suspect to the investigating officer or to an officer who has charge of that person outside the police station, the responsibilities of the custody officer are then incumbent upon them (s 39(2)). Where a suspect is subsequently returned by the investigating officer, he or she must account to the custody officer for the proper treatment of that person whilst in their charge. Section 39(6) deals with the potentially difficult situation where a higher ranking officer than the custody officer gives directions which are at a variance with those of the custody officer. In such circumstances, the custody officer must immediately refer the matter to a police officer of at least the rank of superintendent who is responsible for that police station.

Section 34(1) to (5) of PACE contains important provisions regarding the overall responsibilities of custody officers towards detained suspects, whether arrested at the police station or elsewhere. However, para 1.10 of Code C makes the important point that the Code also applies to persons in custody at police stations, whether or not they have been arrested for an offence, as well as those removed to police stations as a place of safety under ss 135 and 136 of the Mental Health Act 1983 (mentally ill persons removed to police stations as an interim measure, prior to examination by medical practitioners); but para 1.12 excludes the following from the ambit of the Code, whilst providing that they should still be subject to the same minimum standards on conditions and treatment as other detainees (see, also, Chapter 7): persons arrested by police officers from Scotland exercising their detention powers under cross-border powers of arrest (see Chapter 3); persons arrested under s 3(5) of the Asylum and Immigration Appeals Act 1993 for fingerprinting (due to be replaced by s 141 of the Immigration and Asylum Act 1999 when in force) or those served a notice advising them of their detention under certain immigration laws; or convicted or remanded prisoners held in police cells on behalf of the Prison Service.

Figure 10: custody record

BARCHESTER POLICE

POLICE STATION: **CUSTODY NO:**

REASON FOR ARREST: CONDITION ON ARRIVAL AT POLICE STATION:

A notice of my rights has been read to me and I have also been provided with a written notice.

REASON FOR DETENTION:

Signature of person detained:_____

Time:_____ Date:_____

Surname:
(Mr/Mrs/Miss/Ms):_____

Signature of appropriate
adult/interpreter:_____

First name: _____

Time:_____ Date:_____

Notification of detention to named person
requested/not requested

Address: _____

Named person:_____

Time:_____ Date:_____

Occupation: _____

'I want a solicitor as soon as is practicable'

Age:_____ DoB:_____ /_____/_____

Place of birth: _____

Signature:_____

Ident code: _____ Height: _____ Sex: M/F

Time:_____ Date:_____

Signature of appropriate
adult/interpreter:_____

Arrested by
Name:_____

Time:_____ Date:_____

(block capitals)

'I do not want a solicitor at this time'

Rank: _____ No:_____ Station:_____

Signature:_____

Arrested at (place):_____

Time:_____ Date:_____

Signature of appropriate
adult/interpreter:_____

Time:_____ Date:_____

	Time	Date
Arrested at:		
Arrival at station:		

CUSTODY OFFICER
Signature:_____

Name, rank and no: _____

PROPERTY (FOUND ON PERSON OR ELSEWHERE)

	YES	NO	RETAINED BY POLICE REASON
1 CASH £			
2			
3			
4			
5			

SIGNATURE OF PRISONER AGREEING WITH ABOVE [any refusal to sign should be recorded]:

Rank and no of officer searching: _____ Signature:_____

	DATE	TIME		REVIEW OF DETENTION DUE AT		
RELEVANT TIME				1st	2nd	3rd
				4th	5th	6th

Date	Time	Details of any action/occurrence involving the detained person

For the sake of simplicity, the remainder of this chapter will concentrate on arrested persons.

The provisions under s 34(1) to (5) of PACE are as follows:

(1) A person arrested for an offence shall not be kept in police detention except in accordance with the provisions of this Part of this Act.

(2) Subject to sub-s (3) below, if, at any time, a custody officer:

    (a) becomes aware, in relation to any person in police detention, that the grounds for the detention of that person have ceased to apply; and

    (b) is not aware of any other grounds on which the continued detention of that person could be justified under the provisions of this Part of this Act,

it shall be the duty of the custody officer, subject to sub-s (4) below, to order his immediate release from custody.[2]

(3) No person in police detention shall be released, except on the authority of a custody officer at the police station where his detention was authorised or, if it was authorised at more than one station, a custody officer at the station where it was last authorised.

(4) A person who appears to the custody officer to have been unlawfully at large when he was arrested is not to be released under sub-s (2) above.

Sub-section (5) states that where a suspect is released from police detention, this must be unconditional, except where there is the need to impose bail because it appears to the custody officer that proceedings may be taken against the suspect in respect of the case or that further investigation is needed into the matter. But what are the provisions for holding suspects before any of these circumstances may apply? These will now be discussed.

THE FIRST STAGES AT THE POLICE STATION

The custody record

On arrival at a police station, an arrested person has the benefit of a considerable number of rights and safeguards, many of which either did not exist or were not clearly defined before the enactment of PACE. These provisions also apply to persons already at the police station prior to being arrested. Once an arrested person has arrived at the police station (or once a person has been arrested at the police station), that person should be brought before the custody officer, who will normally open a custody record for each

---

2   Code C, para 1.1 reinforces this duty by stating that: 'All persons in custody must be dealt with expeditiously and released as soon as the need for detention has ceased to apply.'

individual. In strict accordance with procedure, the custody officer should do this once he or she has decided whether or not to authorise the detention of the suspect having heard the reasons for the arrest from the arresting officer.

Under s 37 of PACE, the custody officer must determine if there is enough evidence to charge the suspect and, if so, may detain that person for as long as is necessary for that purpose. If not, the suspect must be released either on bail or without bail,[3] or the custody officer may authorise the suspect being detained without charge if there are reasonable grounds for believing that this is necessary to secure or preserve evidence relating to the offence in question, or to obtain such evidence by questioning the suspect. However, since custody officers rarely refuse to authorise detention, the custody record for the arrested suspect is usually opened on their arrival at the police station or very soon afterwards.

Where detention without charge is authorised, the grounds must be noted on the custody record and the suspect informed accordingly, unless incapable of understanding what is said, or is violent or likely to be so, or is in urgent need of medical attention. According to para 2.1 of Code C: '... any audio or video recording made in the custody area is not part of the custody record.' Paragraphs 2.3, 2.6 and 2.7 provide that the custody officer is responsible for the accuracy and completeness of the custody record. All of its entries must be signed and timed by the persons making them, together with their appropriate identification. If any person refuses to sign an entry in the custody record when required to do so, this must be recorded, including the reasons and the time of the refusal. When a detained person is transferred to another police station, it is the duty of the custody officer to ensure that the custody record or a copy of it accompanies the suspect.

THE INITIAL AND CONTINUING THREE RIGHTS OF ARRESTED PERSONS

Under para 3.1 of Code C, the custody officer must inform the arrested person of the following rights which may be exercised at any stage throughout his or her detention, although this is subject to certain exceptions under Annex B, which is discussed on p 143, below. In practice, unless those exceptions apply, arrested persons are usually notified of them at a very early stage in the detention process. These rights are to have someone informed of the arrest; to consult privately with a solicitor who may, if required, provide independent legal advice free of charge under the duty solicitor scheme; and to consult the

---

3   If a person is arrested on warrant which is endorsed for bail, that person must be released on bail accordingly.

Codes of Practice. Under para 3.2, the arrested person should then be served with a written notice, setting out these rights, together with the entitlement to a copy of the custody record, an explanation of the caution and the arrangements for obtaining legal advice. A further written notice must also be given to that person, which briefly sets out his or her entitlements whilst being held in custody. The arrested person should then be asked to sign the relevant part of the custody record which acknowledges receipt of these notices and any refusal to sign should be noted on it. In the case of the right to legal advice, posters advertising this right should be displayed in prominent places within police stations and in different languages where it is practicable and likely to be helpful.

Legal advice

The provisions regarding access to legal advice are contained under s 58 of PACE, augmented by procedures covered under Section 6 of Code C. Apart from the exceptions already mentioned above, arrested persons held in police custody (whether or not they have been arrested for an offence) have the fundamental right to consult a solicitor in private at any time. This may be in person, in writing or by telephone, unless the design and layout of the custody area or the positioning of the telephones make the latter impracticable. In *Roques v Metropolitan Police Commissioner* (1997), a successful action for breach of statutory duty was brought where the police had insisted on being present during the time that a suspect was speaking on the telephone to his solicitor.

Persons voluntarily attending police stations ('helping police with their inquiries') also have the same right and this cannot be subject to any delay as long as they remain unarrested. Persons detained under prevention of terrorism legislation may have access to legal advice (subject to any postponement), although they may not consult with a solicitor privately if the provisions of s 58(14)–(18) of PACE apply. In such cases, an assistant chief constable (or a commander in London) may give a direction authorising a uniformed officer of at least the rank of inspector to be within the sight and hearing of a solicitor giving legal advice to a person detained under the relevant terrorism provisions.

As previously stated, arrested persons are usually informed of the right to legal advice at an early stage during their detention (or voluntary attendance at a police station), but this right must also be notified to them at other stages during the detention period where appropriate. This includes: the stage before a review of detention is made; the stage just prior to the commencement of any interview or continuation of an interview; where further questions are put to, or answers are invited from, a person already charged or notified of possible prosecution; where a person is asked to provide an intimate sample; and the stage before an identification parade or a group identification or video identification is arranged. If the presence of a solicitor is declined, the detained person should be informed that he or she may consult with a solicitor on the telephone. If this is also declined, that person must be asked to state the reason which, if given, must then be recorded in the custody or interview record. If this is not given, the detained person should not be pressed to explain any reasons for declining legal advice, but no police officer shall do or say anything intended to dissuade a person from obtaining legal advice. It should be noted that, in *Rixon and Others v Chief Constable of Kent* (2000), it was held, *inter alia*, that, if a detained person has the right to legal advice, a solicitor does not automatically have the right to see his or her client. This right only applies if the detained client is entitled to legal advice and requests it.

How may a solicitor be obtained? It is important that the detained person be informed that he or she has the right to free legal advice and of the availability of the Duty Solicitor Scheme for this purpose. This scheme operates in each locality where a 24 hour rota system is organised by local legal practitioners who attend police stations on a 'call out' basis. However, detained persons who request legal advice should be given the opportunity to consult with a specific solicitor of their choice or another solicitor from the same firm. If legal advice is not available by these means or the services of the duty solicitor are declined, a list may be provided, containing solicitors willing to provide legal advice, from which the detained person may select a legal adviser and up to two alternatives if the first choice is not available. Even then, the custody officer has a discretion to make further efforts to obtain a solicitor if these attempts to secure legal advice are unsuccessful, although specific advice by the police about particular firms of solicitors must be avoided. In *R v Vernon* (1988), the defendant, who was arrested for assault, nominated a solicitor of her choice who was not available, due to the lateness of the hour. She was not informed of the Duty Solicitor Scheme and agreed to be interviewed without legal representation, which she would not have done had she known that a solicitor would have attended. The record of the interview was subsequently excluded under s 78 of PACE.

Can only fully qualified solicitors provide this service? Paragraph 6.12 of Code C clarifies the position as follows:

> In Codes of Practice issued under the Police and Criminal Evidence Act 1984, 'solicitor' means a solicitor who holds a current practising certificate, a trainee solicitor, a duty solicitor representative or an accredited representative included on the register of representatives maintained by the Legal Aid Board. If a solicitor wishes to send a non-accredited or probationary representative to provide advice on his behalf, then that person shall be admitted to the police station for this purpose, unless an officer of the rank of inspector or above considers that such a visit will hinder the investigation of crime and directs otherwise.

Paragraph 6.14 states that any refusal of access to a non-accredited or probationary representative must be followed by the inspector notifying the solicitor who sent such a person, in order that alternative arrangements may be made and the custody record noted accordingly. Note for guidance 6F provides that, if a police officer of at least the rank of inspector considers that a particular solicitor or firm is persistently sending non-accredited or probationary representatives who are not suited to provide legal advice, that officer should make this known to a superintendent or above for consideration as to whether this matter should be taken up with the Law Society.

The above provisions clarify the position arising from *R v Chief Constable of Avon and Somerset ex p Robinson* (1989). In this case, an instruction was issued by the deputy chief constable to police officers in that area regarding the suitability of certain solicitors clerks, with particular reference to some unqualified clerks who were employed by a solicitor to be present during the interviewing of clients in police stations. This related to their background and conduct, with particular reference to four of them. The Divisional Court held that a police inspector or above is entitled to deny access if that officer knew or believed that a clerk was not capable of providing legal advice. This would not apply if such a person was capable of giving advice, even though it was of poor quality, and that a clerk could be denied entry if that person had a criminal record or was criminally orientated.

Paragraph 6.12 then goes on to make the important point that hindering the investigation of crime does not include giving proper legal advice to a detained person in accordance with the provisions under note for guidance 6D. This stresses the right of a detained person to free legal advice and to be represented by a solicitor, and goes on to state what constitutes acceptable and non-acceptable conduct on the part of a solicitor during the questioning of a suspect. This, and other relevant provisions relating to the interviewing of suspects, will be covered in detail in Chapter 7.

Notification to another of a person's detention

Paragraph 5 of Code C sets out the basic right for detained persons not to be held incommunicado. This applies whether or not they have been arrested for an offence; for example, they might have been arrested to prevent a breach of the peace. Anyone arrested may request that one person be informed of his or her whereabouts as soon as is practicable. This will be done at public expense. Up to two alternatives may be contacted if the first attempt does not succeed and any further attempts are at the discretion of the person in charge of detention or the investigation. The detained person may also receive visits at the discretion of the custody officer. Any friend, relative or other person interested in the suspect's welfare who contacts the police station inquiring if that person is there should be informed as such, provided the suspect agrees and that the exceptions under Annex B to Code C do not apply.

There is a difference between having a person informed by the police of a suspect's whereabouts and allowing the suspect direct contact with such persons for this purpose. Whilst a suspect may be supplied with writing materials on request and allowed to speak on the telephone for a reasonable time to one person, an inspector or above may deny or delay either or both of these privileges. This will apply where an arrestable or a serious arrestable offence is involved and the consequences laid down in Annex B apply. This does not affect the right of having a person informed of the suspect's whereabouts or the suspect's entitlement to legal advice, provided these do not run contrary to Annex B. Before the suspect sends any letter or message, that person must be warned that any of these may be read and given in evidence; where the suspect makes a telephone call, he or she must be warned that the conversation may be listened to and also given in evidence. This does not apply to communications with a solicitor. The cost of such telephone calls can be at public expense, but this will be at the custody officer's discretion. This will take into account factors such as the distance at which a call is being made and the time involved. A telephone call may be terminated if the right is being abused.

Paragraph 5 of Code C provides that a record must be kept of all requests made under these rights and privileges, and the action taken, including any letters, messages or telephone calls made or received, or of any visits to the suspect. A record must also be kept of any refusal on the part of the suspect to have any information or the whereabouts regarding him or herself disclosed to an outside inquirer. The suspect must be asked to countersign the record to this effect and a record should be made of any refusal to sign.

Unco-operative detainees

It should be mentioned that the conduct of persons as a whole can vary considerably when confronted by the police at any point in the execution of their duties. Whether a police officer is exercising stop and search powers or effecting an arrest or detaining a suspect at a police station, it is often the case that such actions are met with verbal abuse, physical resistance and violent behaviour directed towards the police themselves. In many cases, such conduct is drink or drug related. Also, arrested persons may not always be in the best physical condition when brought to the police station, for example, they might have been injured in a fight. Paragraph 1.8 of Code C, therefore, makes the following provisions:

1.8 Whenever this Code requires a person to be given certain information he does not have to be given it if he is incapable at the time of understanding what is said to him or is violent or likely to become violent or is in urgent need of medical attention, but he must be given it as soon as practicable.

General search provisions

Under s 54 of PACE, a person brought to a police station following an arrest or under other circumstances may be searched where necessary if the custody officer needs to do this in order to fulfil the duty to ascertain and record everything that such persons have with them. This especially includes anything which could be used to: (a) cause physical injury; (b) cause damage to property; (c) interfere with evidence; (d) assist in an escape; or (e) where there are reasonable grounds for believing that it constitutes evidence of an offence. Anything which falls within any of these categories may be seized by the custody officer (except items subject to legal privilege), who must list them in the custody record, together with all property that the person has when brought to the police station or when arrested at the police station. This includes anything found as a result of a search under ss 18 and 32 of PACE if the person was arrested away from the police station. Anyone searched at a police station should be informed of the reasons, unless this is unnecessary or impracticable; this provision could, therefore, render 'automatic' searches unlawful (see *Brazil v Chief Constable of Surrey* (1983)).

A detained person's clothes and any personal property, such as watches and spectacles, for example, may only be seized if the custody officer believes that the conditions mentioned in (a)–(e) above apply. If *any* property is seized, whether clothes, personal effects or otherwise, the custody officer is under a duty to give reasons to the suspect, unless that person is violent or likely to be so, or is incapable of understanding what is being said. Any cash and valuables should be removed from a detained person and held in safe custody after being recorded in the custody record. A search under s 54 must be carried out by police officers of the same sex as the individual being searched, using reasonable force if necessary (s 117), and this may be conducted to the extent that the custody officer considers necessary. This could include a strip search, but *not* an intimate search, which has to be authorised under the provisions of s 55.

Strip searches

The rules governing strip searches are to be found under Annex A to Code C. These were explained in Chapter 2, since a strip search involves more than the removal of outer clothing, but any search requiring exposure of intimate parts of the body must not be conducted in a police van. The legal source of the power to strip search detained suspects can be found under the relevant part of s 54 of PACE. This provides that, in the exercise of a custody officer's duty to ascertain and record everything which a suspect has in his or her possession following arrest, the suspect may be searched 'to the extent that the custody officer considers necessary for that purpose'. However, para 10 of Annex A to Code C states that:

> A strip search may take place only if it is considered necessary to remove an article which a person would not be allowed to keep, and the officer reasonably considers that the person might have concealed such an article. Strip searches shall not be routinely carried out where there is no reason to consider that articles have been concealed.

Intimate searches

Section 55 of PACE provides that a police superintendent or above may authorise the intimate search of an arrested suspect if that officer has reasonable grounds to believe that the suspect may have concealed on him or herself any of the following: anything which the suspect could use to cause physical self-injury or injury to others while lawfully detained; or any Class A drug being smuggled in or out of this country, or possessed with intent to supply to another. It is important to emphasise that the drugs in question must be Class A controlled drugs listed under the Misuse of Drugs Act 1971 – the most socially harmful substances when misused. These include heroin (diamorphine), cocaine, 'ecstasy', LSD, pethidine, methadone, dipipanone and at least another 100 named substances, including numerous chemical variations. These do not include cannabis resin or amphetamine, which are both Class B controlled drugs, or temazepam, which is under Class C.[4]

Such authorisations must ultimately be put into written form if initially given orally and may not be given if the object can be obtained in some other way. Therefore, the suspect should be given the opportunity to voluntarily hand over the object and, if there is a refusal, then an intimate search may be authorised. An intimate search for a drug offence must be carried out by a registered medical practitioner or a registered nurse and may only be conducted at a hospital, a doctor's surgery or other place used for medical purposes, but not at a police station. Intimate searches for other objects covered under s 55 (which can generally be headed 'weapons') may be made at any of these premises, including police stations, and by a registered medical practitioner or nurse. However, if a police superintendent or above considers this impracticable, then the search may be carried out by a constable of the same sex as the suspect. Apart from medical practitioners and nurses, no person of the opposite sex shall be present or anyone whose presence is not necessary. However, a minimum of two people must be present during an

---

4   For further reading on the law on controlled drugs, see Jason-Lloyd, L, *Drugs, Addiction and the Law*, 5th edn, 1999, Cambridgeshire: Elm.

intimate search, which should be conducted with due regard to the sensitivity and vulnerability of the suspect under these conditions.

Where an intimate search involves a juvenile or a person who is mentally disordered or handicapped, this may only take place in the presence of an 'appropriate adult' (see p 150, below) who is of the same sex, unless the suspect requests a particular adult of the opposite sex who is readily available. An intimate search of a juvenile may only take place in the absence of the appropriate adult if the juvenile states that he or she prefers the search to be done in this way and the appropriate adult agrees. A record shall be made of the juvenile's decision, and this should then be signed by the appropriate adult.

An intimate search involves the examination of the bodily orifices, except the mouth;[5] in other words, the ears, nasal passages, rectum and vagina. Where such a search is carried out, the custody record must state which parts of the suspect's body were searched and why. Anything found in the course of an intimate search may be seized and retained by the custody officer where it is believed that it may be used to cause physical injury to the suspect or anyone else, cause damage to property, interfere with evidence or assist the suspect to escape. The custody officer may also seize and retain an article obtained in this way which, it is reasonably believed, may constitute evidence relating to an offence. The suspect must be informed of the reason for the seizure, unless he or she is violent or likely to be so, or is incapable of understanding what is being said.

The average layperson may be amazed at the number of items falling under the above description which can be concealed in the body orifices in question. Fairly substantial quantities of drugs in appropriate packaging can sometimes be concealed in a vagina or rectum and so may certain weapons:

> The types of weapon which may be concealed in a body orifice include a penknife in the mouth (*no longer an intimate search*),[6] a wrapped razor blade concealed in the vagina, a detonator or radio transmitter designed to detonate explosives elsewhere concealed in the rectum ... and a phial of poison concealed in the nose.[7]

The very intrusive nature of an intimate search justifies careful scrutiny; therefore, s 55 requires that annual reports to the Home Secretary from chief officers of police must contain details of all intimate searches carried out within their police area. However, such searches are used infrequently:

---

5   The examination of a suspect's mouth was excluded from the ambit of an intimate search by the Criminal Justice and Public Order Act 1994, s 59.

6   Emphasis added.

7   Lidstone, K and Palmer, C, *Bevan and Lidstone's The Investigation of Crime: A Guide to Police Powers*, 2nd edn, 1996, London: Butterworths.

... only 77 were recorded in England and Wales in 1994. Indeed, in 18 police forces, no intimate searches were carried out in 1994. Of the 77 searches made, 42 were for drugs and 36 for harmful articles. In eight cases, Class A drugs were found and, in one case, a harmful article was found.[8]

DETENTION WITHOUT CHARGE

Introduction

As mentioned above, p 129, if the custody officer authorises the detention of a suspect in order to secure or preserve evidence relating to the offence in question or to obtain such evidence by questioning the suspect, the custody officer may authorise that the suspect be detained without charge. The suspect must then be informed of the grounds for detention, unless incapable of understanding what is being said or is violent, or likely to be so, or in urgent need of medical attention. The grounds for detention should be recorded in the custody record as soon as is practicable. If a suspect is not in a fit state to be either charged or released, that person may be kept in police detention until fit. However, whether the suspect is fit or otherwise once the appropriate time limit has been reached, that person must either be released on bail, released unconditionally or charged. If released without charge, that person cannot be re-arrested unless new evidence is discovered which justifies arresting the suspect again or unless a warrant is issued for the same offence. The exception to this rule is where, under s 46A of PACE, a person fails to surrender to police bail and is subsequently arrested without warrant and taken to the police station where the suspect should have reported at the due time and date. This is to be treated as an arrest for an offence.

Time limits

The general rules

Section 41 of PACE imposes strict limits on the period of detention without charge. This is normally 24 hours, but is subject to certain exceptions, discussed below. The 24 hour maximum starts from the 'relevant time', which, in most cases, is either the time that an arrested person arrives at the first police station he or she is taken to, or the time that a person already at the police station is actually arrested. If a person is arrested outside England and Wales, the relevant time operates from when the suspect arrives at the first police station within the area where the alleged crime is being investigated or 24 hours after the suspect's arrival in England and Wales. It is the earlier of the

---

8   *Op cit*, Lidstone and Palmer, fn 7.

two which is calculated as the relevant time. If a suspect is arrested in a different police area to the one where the alleged offence is being investigated, but within England and Wales, much depends on whether the arrested person is questioned regarding the offence at the time. If so, the relevant time operates from when the suspect arrived at the first police station following arrest. If not, the relevant time is calculated from either 24 hours after the arrest or the time of arrival at the police station where the alleged offence is being investigated, whichever is the earlier.

If a person returns to a police station in response to police bail and is detained on arrival, the relevant time is calculated from that applicable to the initial detention, and that person may be detained without charge up to the maximum of any unused detention time left from the previous occasion. If a suspect in police detention is taken to hospital, the detention clock stops running whilst he or she is in hospital and in the course of the journey, unless the suspect is being questioned during this time. No account is taken under PACE where a suspect is taken directly to hospital following arrest and then to the police station.

The reader may find it useful to consult Figure 11 in order to follow the main stages in the detention of a suspect from arrest until eventual release from the police station.

Periodic reviews of detention

In order to ensure that no person arrested for an offence is detained any longer than can be legally justified, s 40 of PACE provides a system of periodic reviews of persons in police detention. These rules do not apply where a person is voluntarily attending a police station, but will, of course, apply if that person is later arrested for an offence. The general rule is that arrested suspects detained *without charge* are reviewed by a police officer of at least the rank of inspector who is not directly involved with the investigation of the alleged offence. These reviews must be carried out periodically from the time that the suspect's detention was authorised by the custody officer. This will be later than the relevant time which, in most cases, applies when an arrested suspect arrives at the police station. It therefore follows that two 'clocks' run alongside each other when a person is in police detention, namely, the detention clock and the review clock (see Figure 11).

Figure 11: police detention – the basic rules

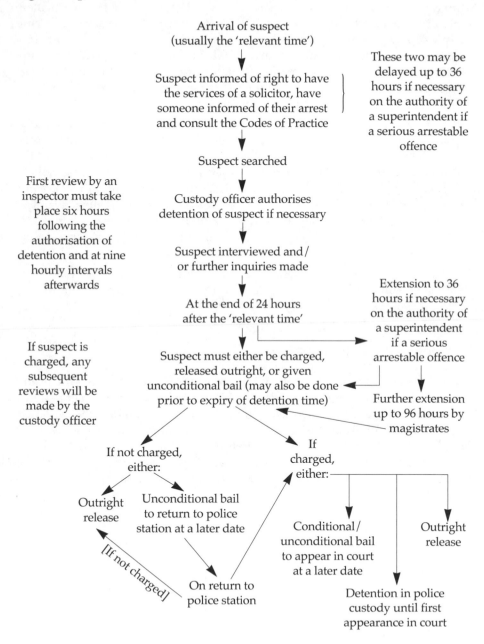

Arrival of suspect
(usually the 'relevant time')

These two may be delayed up to 36 hours if necessary on the authority of a superintendent if a serious arrestable offence

Suspect informed of right to have the services of a solicitor, have someone informed of their arrest and consult the Codes of Practice

Suspect searched

First review by an inspector must take place six hours following the authorisation of detention and at nine hourly intervals afterwards

Custody officer authorises detention of suspect if necessary

Suspect interviewed and/or further inquiries made

At the end of 24 hours after the 'relevant time'

Extension to 36 hours if necessary on the authority of a superintendent if a serious arrestable offence

If suspect is charged, any subsequent reviews will be made by the custody officer

Suspect must either be charged, released outright, or given unconditional bail (may also be done prior to expiry of detention time)

Further extension up to 96 hours by magistrates

If not charged, either:

If charged, either:

Outright release

Unconditional bail to return to police station at a later date

[If not charged]

On return to police station

Conditional/unconditional bail to appear in court at a later date

Outright release

Detention in police custody until first appearance in court

It should be noted at this stage that periodic reviews are applicable to persons in 'police detention', namely, suspects who have been arrested for an offence and have been taken to a police station (including arrests made under s 14 and Sched 5, para 6 of the Prevention of Terrorism (Temporary Provisions) Act 1989) or those subsequently arrested after initially attending a police station voluntarily. Therefore, they do not apply to arrested persons who have not been arrested for an offence (for example, persons arrested to prevent a breach of the peace or to be fingerprinted, or mentally disordered persons arrested under s 136 of the Mental Health Act 1983 in order to be taken to a place of safety). Neither do they apply to persons held by the police who are awaiting extradition or deportation.

Where a person in police detention *has been charged*, it is then the *custody officer* who is responsible for carrying out the periodic reviews. Whether the reviews are conducted by an inspector or the custody officer, either is regarded as the 'review officer'. The first review must be carried out no later than six hours following the authorisation of the suspect's detention and then at intervals of no more than nine hours. Reviews may be postponed where necessary, but must be resumed as soon as practicable; this takes into account the wide and often unpredictable nature of police duties. This will include instances where the criminal investigation would be prejudiced if the questioning of the suspect were interrupted or where a review officer is not readily available, due to a serious incident requiring his or her urgent attention. The review officer must record the reasons for any postponement in the custody record; however, a review may be conducted over the telephone if this is the only practicable means by which it can be conducted (see note for guidance 15C to Code C).

Prior to authorising a suspect's further detention, the review officer must give the suspect or the solicitor representing that person the opportunity to make any representations. Other people may be involved in this process, at the review officer's discretion. These will be persons having an interest in the suspect's welfare, including the appropriate adult, if available. These representations may be given orally or in writing and may include such matters as whether detention without charge is necessary in order to secure or preserve evidence, or whether there is sufficient evidence for the police to charge the suspect. Any dispute between the review officer and someone of higher rank regarding a suspect's detention in police custody should be referred to an officer of at least the rank of superintendent.

The review officer is under a duty to remind the suspect of the entitlement to free legal advice prior to conducting a review and to ensure that all such reminders are entered in the custody record. Other matters should also be recorded in the custody record, including the reasons for any delay in conducting a review and the extent of the delay, as well as the result of each review and any application for a warrant of further detention and any extension of it (see below). Any representations made in writing must be retained. Note for guidance 15A to Code C states that, if the suspect is likely to be sleeping at the latest time when either a review of detention or an authorisation of continued detention may occur, any of these actions may be brought forward, in order that the detained person will have the opportunity to make representations without being disturbed.

In *Roberts v Chief Constable of Cheshire* (1999), the claimant sued for damages for false imprisonment. Having been arrested on suspicion of burglary, he arrived at a police station at 11.25 pm, where his detention without charge was authorised. The first review should have been made at 5.25 am, but did not take place until 7.45 am. The court held that the detention was unlawful after 5.25 am, until some event occurred to make it lawful.

Extensions to normal detention periods

As mentioned above, the general time limit for detention without charge is 24 hours, but this is subject to the following exceptions. Sections 42, 43 and 44 of PACE make provision for the authorisation of continued detention by the police and warrants of further detention by magistrates and their extension.

The provisions under s 42 regarding continued detention by the police apply only where it is reasonably believed that the criminal investigation is concerned with a *serious* arrestable offence (as defined in Chapter 3), where the investigation is being conducted diligently and expeditiously, and where continued detention without charge is necessary to secure or preserve evidence or to obtain evidence by questioning the suspect. The authorisation for continued police detention *without charge* must be given before the expiry of the 24 hour detention period and by an officer of at least the rank of superintendent if the above criteria are met. Under note for guidance 15C to Code C, this must be done in person and not over the telephone. The period of detention *without charge* may then be extended up to 36 hours from the relevant time; in other words, up to another 12 hours beyond the initial 24 hours that normally apply. Representations may be made by the suspect or any solicitor representing that person on grounds such as whether the investigation is proceeding with due diligence, the length of the continued detention or whether the alleged crime constitutes a serious arrestable offence. Representations may also be made by other persons having an interest in the welfare of the suspect, including the appropriate adult where applicable.

Where continued detention has been authorised, the suspect must be informed by that officer of the grounds for the decision which, in turn, must be recorded in the custody record. Unless a warrant for further detention has been granted by magistrates (see below, p 146), if at the end of the 36 hour time limit the suspect has not been charged, that person must be released on bail or released unconditionally. The suspect must not be re-arrested for the same offence without a warrant, except where new evidence has been discovered.

Delay in access to legal advice and notification of arrest to another

It is important to mention at this stage that access to legal advice, as well as the right for a suspect to have a person informed of their detention, can be postponed in the case of a serious arrestable offence where the suspect has *not been charged*. The following provisions, under ss 56 and 58 of PACE and Annex B to Code C, constitute the exceptions to the general rules discussed above, p 130.

Section 58 and Annex B provide that a police superintendent or above may delay access to a solicitor for up to 36 hours if there are reasonable grounds for believing that such access would lead to: interference with or harm to evidence connected with any serious arrestable offence; interference with or physical injury to other persons; alerting other persons not yet arrested, but suspected of having committed a serious arrestable offence; or hindering the recovery of any property obtained as a result of such an offence.

Section 58 provides two further grounds under which a superintendent or above may postpone access to legal advice. The first is where the above conditions are present and the serious arrestable offence is a drug trafficking offence;[9] the police superintendent must also have reasonable grounds for believing that the suspect has benefited from this activity and that the recovery of those drug trafficking proceeds will be obstructed if legal access is granted. The second ground, inserted into PACE by s 99 of the Criminal

---

9   Drug trafficking offences under the Drug Trafficking Act 1994, s 1, can broadly be defined as follows: the unlawful production and supply of controlled drugs, and possession of controlled drugs with intent to supply; assisting in or inducing the commission outside the UK of a drug offence punishable under a corresponding law; illegal drug importation or exportation; the unlawful supply or offer to supply of articles for use in the administration or preparation of controlled drugs; contravention of the law regarding the manufacture, transportation or distribution of substances which can be used to unlawfully produce controlled drugs; persons possessing or knowingly carrying or concealing controlled drugs on ships. Drug trafficking offences also include the following money-laundering activities: drug traffickers who conceal or transfer their proceeds to avoid a confiscation order and/or prosecution; persons who assist drug traffickers to do the aforementioned or assist them to retain the benefit of drug trafficking; and recipients of the proceeds of drug trafficking who know that they have been derived from another's drug trafficking activities. A drug trafficking offence also includes incitement, conspiracy or attempt to commit any of the foregoing, as well as being an accomplice, namely aiding, abetting, counselling or procuring the commission of any of them.

For further reading, see *op cit*, Jason-Lloyd, fn 4. Also, it should be noted that this amendment to PACE was made under the Drug Trafficking Offences Act 1986, s 32.

Justice Act 1988, is where a serious arrestable offence, to which Pt VI of that Act is applicable, has been committed[10] and a police superintendent or above reasonably believes that the detained suspect has benefited from such activity, and that access to legal advice will hinder the recovery of the value of the property in question. The reason for such a postponement is to enable sufficient time for a restraint order to be applied for, as well as to enable the suspect's assets to be frozen.[11]

The rules governing the postponement of the right for a detained suspect to have a person informed of his or her detention are the same as those applicable to delaying access to legal advice. These are to be found under s 56 of PACE and Annex B to Code C. However, it should be noted that if one right can be delayed, it does not mean that the other can be denied automatically (see note for guidance B5 to Code C).

If the authorisation for a delay in giving access to legal advice or informing a person of a suspect's detention is given orally, it must be put into writing as soon as is practicable and the suspect must be informed of the postponement, together with the reasons, which must be noted in the custody record. If the grounds for the postponement cease to exist before the 36 hour time limit, the detained person must be asked if he or she requires the presence of a solicitor and sign the custody record to this effect. This will also apply where the suspect is charged during this period.

In *R v Samuel* (1987), two important points were established regarding the power to delay access to legal advice under s 58 of PACE. In this case, the defendant was arrested for armed robbery and was subsequently detained for questioning. In the course of the second interview with the police, he requested access to legal advice, but this was denied on the ground that this might inadvertently alert other suspects. He later confessed to two burglary offences, one of which constituted a serious arrestable offence, since firearms were allegedly used, and he was duly charged with both these offences. About 15 minutes later, the defendant's solicitor telephoned and was informed of this, but was still denied access to the defendant. Shortly afterwards, during the final interview, the defendant confessed to the robbery

---

10 These offences have been termed 'general criminal conduct' and include indictable offences, except those which fall within the ambit of drug trafficking. Also included are a number of summary only offences listed under the Criminal Justice Act 1988, Sched 4, which are: offences relating to sex establishments; supplying video recordings of unclassified work; possession of video recordings of unclassified work for the purposes of supply; and the use of unlicensed premises for exhibition which requires a licence. The following offences have been added to Sched 4 since the original enactment of the 1988 Act: offences under the Copyright, Designs and Patents Act 1988 and the Trade Marks Act 1994; criminal liability for making or dealing with infringing articles and making, dealing with or using illicit recordings, offences relating to the unauthorised use of trade marks in relation to goods. The Criminal Justice Act 1988, Pt VI, is concerned with the confiscation of the proceeds of such crimes.

11 Levenson, H, Fairweather, F and Cape, E, *Police Powers: A Practitioner's Guide*, 3rd edn, 1996, London: Legal Action Group.

and was later charged. Eventually, he was allowed access to his solicitor 29 hours after his arrest. The Court of Appeal held that the trial judge should have ruled the evidence regarding the final interview inadmissible, since the denial of access to the solicitor was not justified. His conviction for robbery was therefore quashed. The two important points held by the Court of Appeal were that, once the suspect is charged with any offence, especially if it is a serious arrestable offence, the right to legal advice cannot be delayed thereafter. Secondly, an authorising officer must believe that such access will lead to alerting other suspects and not just *may* lead to this consequence, even if this could occur inadvertently or unwittingly, and that due regard should be had as to whether legal advice could be given by another solicitor where there is such a risk. In this case, the Court of Appeal stated in passing that, as far as duty solicitors were concerned, since they were well known to the police, it would be very difficult to justify delaying access to any of them if another solicitor was denied access to the suspect. In other words, denial of access to a *particular* solicitor may be justified, but denial of access to all solicitors is another matter. This is emphasised in note for guidance B4 to Code C, which states:

> The effect of para 1, above, is that the officer may authorise delaying access to a specific solicitor only if he has reasonable grounds to believe that a specific solicitor will, inadvertently or otherwise, pass on a message from the detained person or act in some other way which will lead to any of the three results in para 1 coming about. In these circumstances, the officer should offer the detained person access to a solicitor (who is not the specific solicitor referred to above) on the Duty Solicitor Scheme.

However, in *R v Alladice* (1988), the Court of Appeal, whilst supporting the decision in *R v Samuel*, dismissed an appeal against the defendant's conviction for robbery where a confession was obtained whilst access to legal advice was denied by a police officer of the rank of chief inspector. First, the court held that, since the chief inspector was acting under the authority of an acting chief superintendent, he was to be treated as if he were the holder of the substantive rank, 'unless the appointment to the acting rank was a colourable pretence, which was not suggested in the present case'. Secondly, whilst acknowledging that there had been a breach of the defendant's right to legal advice under s 58, the court held that there was no suggestion of oppression or that the confession was given because of the absence of a solicitor and that the confession was unreliable. Subsequently, the breach did not require the court to render the confession inadmissible. The provisions of s 107 of PACE as follows should be noted at this stage:

Police officers performing duties of higher rank

(1) For the purpose of any provision of this Act or any other Act under which a power in respect of the investigation of offences or the treatment of persons in police custody is exercisable only by or with the authority of a police officer of at least the rank of superintendent, an officer of the rank of chief inspector shall be treated as holding the rank of superintendent if:

(a) he has been authorised by an officer holding a rank above the rank of superintendent to exercise the power or, as the case may be, to give his authority for its exercise; or

(b) he is acting during the absence of an officer holding the rank of superintendent who has authorised him, for the duration of that absence, to exercise the power or, as the case may be, to give his authority for its exercise.

(2) For the purpose of any provision of this Act or any other Act under which such a power is exercisable only by or with the authority of an officer of at least the rank of inspector, an officer of the rank of sergeant shall be treated as holding the rank of inspector if he has been authorised by an officer of at least the rank of superintendent to exercise the power or, as the case may be, to give his authority for its exercise.

The *general* provisions regarding access to legal advice, and the right to have a person informed of a suspect's arrest and subsequent detention, were discussed above, p 130. It should be noted that Pt B of Annex B contains special provisions regarding the delay of access to legal advice and notification of arrest in respect of persons detained under the Prevention of Terrorism (Temporary Provisions) Act 1989. Also, as discussed below, p 149, the provisions under Annex B are modified in the case of juveniles and the mentally disordered or handicapped.

Warrants for further detention by magistrates

Under s 43 of PACE, further detention without charge beyond the 36 hour maximum may be authorised by magistrates. Unless a stipendiary magistrate is in court, who may make the authorisation sitting alone, the authority to extend the 36 hour period must be made by at least two lay magistrates, although three is the usual number. Where further detention is being sought, a constable may apply on oath for their authority to keep the suspect in detention beyond 36 hours. This must be supported by 'an information', a copy of which the suspect should already have in his or her possession when attending court at the time the application is being made. The 'information', in this context, means the nature of the offence and the evidence which justified the suspect's arrest, as well as inquiries made to date and anticipated further inquiries in addition to the grounds for applying for further detention. An application for further detention will only be justified where the offence is a serious arrestable offence and the investigation is proceeding diligently and expeditiously, and this is necessary to secure or preserve evidence or to obtain it by questioning the suspect.

Where a suspect has been denied legal access under s 58 of PACE and is due to be taken before magistrates under an application for further detention, reasonable time should be allowed for the detained person to consult with a solicitor before the hearing. In any event, the detainee is entitled to legal representation during the application and an adjournment may be granted, if necessary, in order for such representation to be obtained. The legal representative may cross-examine the police applicant on oath and the application may be challenged accordingly. Particular care has to be taken in anticipating whether further detention may be necessary as, unlike many police stations, magistrates' courts are not operational 24 hours a day and seven days a week. It is therefore permissible for an application for further detention to be made prior to the expiry of the 36 hour period, in order to ensure that the court is sitting. However, where the court is not sitting at the end of the first 36 hours (and it was not reasonably practicable to have made the application before then), but the court is due to sit during the following six hours, the application for further detention may be made within that six hour period. The suspect may be kept in police detention during this time and these facts must be recorded in the custody record accordingly.

Where the application is made in court beyond the expiry of the first 36 hours and it appears to the court that it was unreasonable for the police not to have done so before, it is a mandatory requirement that the court dismiss the application. In *R v Slough Justices ex p Stirling* (1987), it was held that, in failing to bring an application in good time when the police officer was in a position to do so (in this case, the application was made just eight minutes before the expiry of the first 36 hours), that officer did not act reasonably within s 43(7) of PACE. It was also confirmed that the application for further detention occurs when the police officer makes the application in court and gives evidence.

The application to magistrates for further detention is by no means a rubber stamp process. Under s 43 of PACE, magistrates may refuse the application if they feel that further detention is not justified and a further application against a refusal may only be considered by the court if new evidence is discovered. Where appropriate, the court may adjourn the hearing, but only if the 36 hour maximum period of police detention has not expired. Where there has been a refusal, the police may continue to detain the suspect without charge, but only up until the normal maximum of 24 hours, or up to 36 hours if continued authorisation was made by a police superintendent. But, if during the application for further detention the court rules that the offence is not a serious arrestable offence, the custody officer must ensure the release of the suspect once the first 24 hour period has elapsed, regardless of whether a superintendent has authorised continued detention. The suspect must either be charged or released (unconditionally or on bail) where the court rejects an application for any reason or where the appropriate 24 or 36 hour detention period expires.

If the court agrees to issue a warrant of further detention, it may do so for a maximum period of 36 hours, having regard to all the circumstances of the case. At the end of this maximum period (which can be less than 36 hours), the suspect must be either be charged or released unconditionally or on bail, and may not be subject to further arrest for the offence without warrant, unless new evidence has been discovered.

Extended powers of detention by magistrates

Under s 44 of PACE, the warrant of further detention may be extended (repeatedly if necessary) if the court is satisfied that there are reasonable grounds for believing that this is justified. In such cases, the same procedures apply as those governing initial applications for warrants of further detention, and include an application being made on oath by a police officer – supported by an information, a copy of the latter being given to the detained suspect – and the entitlement to legal representation. If an application to extend a warrant of further detention is refused by the court, the suspect must either be charged, immediately released on bail or released unconditionally, or any of these may be done at the end of the previous detention period authorised by magistrates. Where the court agrees to extend a warrant of further detention (or even one or more extensions since then), it may be for any period the court thinks fit, but the extension period must not exceed 36 hours. No extension may result in a total period of 96 hours' detention being exceeded from the relevant time. Also, due account should be taken of any time spent in waiting for the court to sit when the first 36 hours of police detention has expired. At the end of the period specified in an extension or further extension of a warrant of further detention, the suspect must either be charged, released on bail or released unconditionally, and may not be subject to further arrest for the offence without warrant, unless new evidence is discovered. The suspect need not be charged or released at that stage, of course, if a further extension is granted by the court.

Police detention under prevention of terrorism legislation

The time limits described above in respect of the detention of suspects without charge do not apply to certain offences under prevention of terrorism legislation. Section 14 of the Prevention of Terrorism (Temporary Provisions) Act 1989 provides that a person arrested for, *inter alia*, being concerned in the commission, preparation or instigation of certain acts of terrorism may be detained by the police without charge for up to 48 hours (sub-s (4)). Under sub-s (5), this may, in turn, be extended by the Home Secretary for a period or periods totalling up to five days. The complete detention period without charge may, therefore, be up to seven days in all. Note earlier comments regarding the 1989 Act, which has been repealed by the Terrorism Act 2000. Many of the provisions of the 1989 Act have been recast in it and this is due to take effect in 2001, once it comes into force.

SAFEGUARDS REGARDING VULNERABLE PERSONS

Whilst PACE and the Codes of Practice contain many provisions designed to protect the rights of persons in police custody, further measures are available to ensure that particularly vulnerable suspects are subject to additional safeguards. These are juveniles, persons who are mentally disordered or mentally handicapped, deaf persons, blind persons, foreign suspects and those unable to understand English. It should be mentioned that, in the case of juveniles, the child or young person should be of a minimum age of 10 and no older than 17 years. The most important provisions either originate or are largely echoed in Code C, the relevant parts of which are summarised as follows.

General

Section 1 of Code C makes the following general provisions regarding vulnerable persons held in police custody. Where a police officer suspects or is informed in good faith that a person of any age may be mentally disordered or mentally handicapped, or is mentally incapable of understanding questions put to him or her or understanding any replies, that person will fall under the scope of this Code in protecting such persons. Note for guidance 1G endeavours to define mental disorder and mental handicap for the purposes of this Code of Practice. For the sake of brevity, both terms collectively mean mental illness (such as schizophrenia and manic depression, to name but two), psychopathic disorder and various states of mental impairment caused as a result of brain damage or an undeveloped brain (arrested or retarded development). In any event, the presence of an appropriate adult should be sought where the custody officer has any doubt regarding the mental state or capacity of a detained person.

Section 1 goes on to state that, for the purposes of this Code and in the absence of clear evidence to the contrary, persons appearing to be under the age of 17 shall be treated as juveniles, and persons appearing to be blind or seriously visually handicapped, deaf, unable to read, speak or who have difficulty orally because of a speech impediment, also fall under the provisions of this Code.

With regard to juveniles and those who are mentally disordered or mentally handicapped, provision is made for such persons to have the support of 'the appropriate adult' when in police custody. The definition as to whom the appropriate adult may be is variable, depending on the category of vulnerable person in question. The Code of Practice therefore defines the appropriate adult in each case as follows.

In the case of juveniles, the 'appropriate adult' means the child or young person's parent or guardian and, if the juvenile is in care, this will mean the relevant local authority or voluntary organisation. The term 'in care' is defined under the Code of Practice as all cases in which a juvenile is 'looked after' by a local authority under the terms of the Children Act 1989. The appropriate adult may also be a social worker and, if any of the above are not available, the presence of another responsible adult aged 18 or over is permissible, provided that person is not a police officer or employed by the police service. In addition to these rules, the police should still be alert as to the general suitability of persons who may be asked to act as the appropriate adult. In *R v Morse and Others* (1991), it was held that the father of the suspect in this case should not have been asked to act as the appropriate adult, since he may have been unable to appreciate the seriousness of the situation due to being illiterate and of low intelligence.

With regard to the mentally disordered or mentally handicapped, the appropriate adult may be a relative, guardian or other person responsible for that person's care or custody. Alternatively, that person may be someone with experience in dealing with mentally disordered or mentally handicapped people, such as an officer of a local social services authority appointed to act as an 'approved social worker' for the purposes of the Mental Health Act 1983, or any other specialist social worker. However, the person with the relevant experience must not be a police officer or any employee within the police service. In any of these are not available, then the appropriate adult may be some other responsible person aged 18 or over, provided that the person is not a police officer or a police employee. Note for guidance 1E states that, in certain circumstances, it may be better for all concerned if the appropriate adult is someone with experience and training in the care of the mentally disordered or mentally handicapped, rather than a relative without such qualifications. But it goes on to state that the detained person's wishes should be respected, if practicable, where that person prefers a relative to a better qualified stranger. In *R v Aspinall* (1999), the defendant was arrested for a drug offence and, on his arrival at the police station, he informed the custody officer that he was a schizophrenic. Two doctors later confirmed that he was probably in a fit state to be interviewed; meanwhile, he asked for a solicitor, who was not obtained, due to a mistake by the police. The defendant was interviewed 13 hours later, without the presence of a solicitor or an appropriate adult. His conviction for conspiracy to supply heroin was quashed on the grounds that the custody officer knew that he was suffering from a mental illness and that there was a clear breach of para 11.14 of Code C, which stipulates that such persons must not be interviewed without an appropriate adult. The unfairness of the proceedings was also made worse by the absence of legal advice during the interview.

Notes for guidance 1C, 1D, 1EE and 1F provide further guidelines regarding appropriate adults. They begin by making the important point that no one, including a parent or guardian, should be an appropriate adult if he or she is suspected of involvement in the offence in question, or is the victim of it, or is a witness, or is involved in the investigation of the offence or has received admissions prior to attending the police station to act as the appropriate adult. In *DPP v Morris* (1990), it was held that a social worker probably should not have acted as the appropriate adult in this case, because that person had called the police. This would have led to the juvenile viewing the social worker as being biased towards the police.

If the parent of a juvenile is estranged from that child or young person, the parent should not be asked to act as the appropriate adult if the juvenile expressly objects to that parent's presence. The notes for guidance continue by providing that, in the interests of fairness, if a juvenile admits to an offence in the presence of a social worker, except when acting as the appropriate adult, then another social worker should act in that capacity. The guidance ends by stating that a solicitor or lay visitor, who happens to be in the police station in that capacity at the time, may not act as the appropriate adult and that, when an appropriate adult is called to a police station, a detained person should always be given an opportunity to consult privately with a solicitor in the appropriate adult's absence. Normally, only one person should be designated as the appropriate adult, although in *H and M v DPP* (1997), it was held that, in certain circumstances, it may be permissible to have more than one person performing this function during a juvenile's interview. This would apply, for instance, where both the parents were present or where one parent was present but, due to language difficulties, needed someone to assist in overcoming this problem.

Custody records

Section 2 of Code C states that, as soon as practicable after their arrival at the police station, a solicitor or appropriate adult must be allowed to consult the custody record of a detained person. When that person leaves police custody or is taken before a court, he or she, or the legal representative or the appropriate adult, must be supplied with a copy of the custody record if requested, as soon as practicable, provided the request is made within 12 months following that person's release. The original custody record may be examined by any of these three classes of person after the detained person has left police custody, if reasonable notice is given. If this inspection takes place, it shall be noted in the custody record.

Initial action

Section 3 makes a number of provisions affecting all classes of vulnerable persons together with references to the relevant notes for guidance.

Detained persons: normal procedure

Under this subheading, the Code provides that a citizen of an independent Commonwealth country or a national of a foreign state, including the Irish Republic, must be informed, as soon as practicable, of the right to communicate with his or her High Commission, Embassy or Consulate. This right is covered in detail under Section 7 of this Code.

Detained persons: special groups

The custody officer must, as soon as practicable, call an interpreter if effective communication cannot be established, because it appears that a person is deaf or there is doubt about that person's hearing or ability to speak or understand English. Detailed provisions regarding interpreters are given in Section 13 of Code C.

Where the detained person is a juvenile, the custody officer must, if practicable, ascertain the identity of a person responsible for the welfare of the child or young person, who may be a parent, guardian, or the care authority or voluntary organisation if in care, or any other person who has assumed responsibility for the juvenile's welfare. That person must be informed, as soon as practicable, that the juvenile has been arrested, the reason why and where they are detained. This right may be exercised in addition to the general right not to be held incommunicado. Even where Annex B to Code C applies, this action must be taken. Note for guidance 3C makes provision where a juvenile is in care, but living with his or her parents or other adults responsible for the juvenile's welfare. In such cases, whilst there is no legal obligation to do this, it is advised that they too should normally be informed, as well as the relevant authority or organisation, unless suspected of involvement in the offence in question. Consideration should still be given to informing a juvenile's parents, even where a juvenile in care is not living with them.

Where a juvenile is detained, or a person in police custody appears to be mentally disordered or handicapped, the custody officer must, as soon as practicable, inform the appropriate adult of the reasons for and the location of the detention and request that person's presence (see *R v Aspinall* (1999), regarding those which fall under the latter category). In the case of a juvenile, the appropriate adult may or may not be a person responsible for the welfare of that individual. Again, this action must be taken, even if the provisions under Annex B to Code C apply. If a detained child or young person is known to be under a supervision order, the police must take reasonable steps to notify the probation officer or local authority social worker who is responsible for supervising that person.

Mentally disordered or handicapped persons detained under s 136 of the Mental Health Act 1983 must be assessed as soon as possible. An approved social worker and a medical practitioner must be called without delay, in order to examine the person if that assessment is to take place at the police station. That person can no longer be detained under s 136 once this has been done and arrangements have been made for that person's care and treatment. In the meantime, that person should not be released until seen by the approved social worker and medical practitioner.

Earlier in this chapter, the normal procedures in dealing initially with arrested persons were described (see particularly p 130 *et seq*). Under Section 3 of Code C, these procedures must be conducted in the presence of the appropriate adult if already at the police station. If those procedures are not complied with in the appropriate adult's absence, then they must be repeated in that person's presence once he or she arrives. This provision is designed to protect juveniles and mentally disordered or handicapped people who may not understand the significance of the rights that are being stated at the time. The appropriate action must be taken immediately if a detained person within that category wishes to have access to legal advice and this should not be delayed, pending the arrival of the appropriate adult. The person detained by the police must be informed by the custody officer that the appropriate adult is there to assist and advise him or her, and that he or she is also entitled to consult privately with the appropriate adult at any time.

Another important aspect of Section 3 is directed towards the blind and those who are seriously visually handicapped. If such a person suffers from such a disability or is unable to read, the custody officer is under a duty to ensure that a suitable person is available to help in checking any documentation. Such persons may include the solicitor, a relative, the appropriate adult or some other person who is likely to take an interest in the detained person, but who is not involved in the investigation. That person may be asked to sign on the detained person's behalf anything which requires consent or signification. This is because blind or seriously visually handicapped people may be unwilling to sign police documents; therefore, the alternative of their representative signing on their behalf is a measure designed to protect the interests of all concerned.

Section 13 of this Code covers the use of interpreters in respect of deaf persons or those who do not understand English, and Annex E provides a summary of provisions relating to the mentally disordered and the mentally handicapped, which largely echoes provisions made in different parts of Code C. The remaining aspects of this Code of Practice which affect vulnerable suspects are covered below and also in the following chapter, especially the provisions under Annex C which override some of the above safeguards, but which are subject to several strict prerequisites. It should be noted that, with regard to juveniles, even where delay is authorised under ss 56 and 58 of PACE, the police are under a duty to take all practicable steps in order to ascertain the identity of the person responsible for the welfare of the child or young person and to inform that person of the juvenile's arrest. Also, note for guidance 11C states that arresting a juvenile at their place of education is to be avoided if possible. Where this cannot be avoided, the person in charge of that establishment must be informed.

THE CHARGING OF SUSPECTS AND SUBSEQUENT DETENTION

Introduction

Paragraph 16.1 of Code C makes the following provisions regarding the duties of investigating and custody officers, once all that can be achieved from detaining a suspect without charge has been accomplished:

> When an officer considers that there is sufficient evidence to prosecute a detained person and that there is sufficient evidence for the prosecution to succeed, and that the person has said all that he wishes to say about the offence, he shall, without delay (and, subject to the following qualification), bring him before the custody officer, who shall then be responsible for considering whether or not he should be charged. When a person is detained in respect of more than one offence, it is permissible to delay bringing him before the custody officer, until the above conditions are satisfied in respect of all the offences ...[12] Any resulting action shall be taken in the presence of the appropriate adult if the person is a juvenile or mentally disordered or mentally handicapped.

Section 37(7) of PACE states that if the custody officer determines that there is sufficient evidence to charge a suspect with the offence for which he or she was arrested, that person shall be charged or released without charge (either on bail or released unconditionally). Persons unfit to be charged or released may be kept in police detention until they are fit to be dealt with accordingly (this is commonly due to intoxication). Where a person has been released without being charged and no decision has been taken at that time as to whether that person will be prosecuted, the released suspect must be

---

12   At this stage, para 16.1 refers to para 11.4 which, *inter alia*, states that, once police questioning has ceased, this should not prevent certain other investigating officers from inviting suspects to complete a formal questions and answer record after the conclusion of the police interview. These include officers in revenue cases or those acting under the confiscation provisions of the Criminal Justice Act 1988 or the Drug Trafficking Offences Act 1986.

informed as such. This is to avoid leading the suspect into thinking that the matter is completely finished, when a prosecution may still arise.

It should be noted that, instead of charging a person with an offence, the suspect may be reported for the offence instead. This means that the police may prosecute a person and proceed by way of a summons if the offence proves to be of a minor nature. For instance, a person may be arrested on suspicion of taking a motor vehicle without consent, but further inquiries disclose that the suspect has merely failed in the duty to inform the relevant authority (the DVLA) of a change of the vehicle's ownership. In those circumstances, the custody officer may report the suspect for this offence, as would a police officer, discovering this offence whilst on street duty. Some suspects are cautioned rather than charged, depending upon the nature of the offence and the offender's background. (This subject is covered in the final part of this chapter). Within the context of the charging of suspects, it should again be mentioned when a suspect's detention time has expired, that person must either be charged, released unconditionally or on bail (see Figure 11). When a suspect is charged with an offence or is being informed that he or she may be prosecuted, that person must also be cautioned as follows:

You do not have to say anything. But it may harm your defence if you do not mention now something which you later rely on in court. Anything you do say may be given in evidence.

[Note the slight difference in wording compared to cautions given under other circumstances.]

This procedure should be followed by the suspect being given a written notice, disclosing the particulars of the offence. Where an appropriate adult has had to be present, the written notice shall be given to that person. Anything said by a detained person when charged shall be recorded.

Release or detention after charge?

Under s 38 of PACE, when a person has been arrested and subsequently charged with an offence (whether or not it is arrestable), provided that person has not been arrested under a warrant endorsed for bail, the custody officer then has to decide on one of four courses of action. The suspect may either be released on bail or without bail, or released on bail, but with conditions attached,[13] or may be detained in police custody until the suspect can be

---

13 Under the Criminal Justice and Public Order Act 1994, s 27, the police may attach almost any conditions to bail when releasing a charged suspect that a court may impose, except the conditions to reside at a bail hostel and to co-operate in the making of any report. This may only be justified in order to ensure that a charged suspect surrenders to custody at a later date, does not offend whilst on bail, does not interfere with witnesses or generally obstruct the course of justice (these conditions also govern the requirement of a surety or security being imposed). A person given conditional bail may ask the custody officer to vary the conditions. This request may be directed to another custody officer, but at the same police station, although the custody [Contd ...]

produced in court (see Figure 11). Section 38 goes on to state that the custody officer may only detain a person in police custody after charge when the following conditions are met:

(a) if the name or address of the person cannot be ascertained or the custody officer has reasonable grounds for doubting whether any name or address given by the suspect is genuine;

(b) where the custody officer has reasonable grounds for believing that the suspect will fail to answer to bail and will not appear in court (in other words, may 'jump bail'. This decision will be influenced by the nature and seriousness of the offence, the relevant background and lifestyle of the suspect, any record of previous bail-jumping and the strength of evidence. These factors must also be applied to the criteria in (c)–(e), below, inclusive;

(c) provided the suspect has been arrested for an offence which is imprisonable, the custody officer may detain that person in police custody after charge where there are reasonable grounds for believing that this is necessary to prevent the suspect from re-offending;

(d) even where a person has been arrested for an offence which is not imprisonable, detention after charge may be authorised by the custody officer where there are reasonable grounds to believe that this is necessary to prevent the suspect from causing physical injury to any other person or causing the loss of or damage to property;

(e) the custody officer may detain the suspect in police custody where there are reasonable grounds to believe that this is necessary to prevent that person from interfering with the administration of justice or with the investigation of any offence;

(f) where there are reasonable grounds for believing that it is necessary for the suspect's own protection, the custody officer may authorise that person to be detained in police custody after being charged.

An additional ground for detaining juveniles

If the person charged is an arrested juvenile, the above grounds may also be applied, although the following additional ground exists, which may justify detention after charge. Section 38(1)(b)(ii) of PACE provides that, in the case of

---

13 [Contd] officer has the power to vary the conditions, so as to make them more restrictive. Custody officers granting conditional police bail or varying such conditions must enter their reasons in the custody record and inform the person charged. The Criminal Justice and Public Order Act 1994, Sched 3, para 3, enables persons given conditional police bail to appeal to the magistrates' court, in order to have the conditions varied, although the court also has the power to make the conditions more restrictive and may even withhold bail completely. (See further commentary in Jason-Lloyd, L, *The Criminal Justice and Public Order Act 1994: A Basic Guide for Practitioners*, 1996, London: Frank Cass.)

juveniles only, the custody officer may order detention after charge where there are reasonable grounds for believing that it is in the interests of that person to be detained. Although detention in the interests of an arrested juvenile may also run very close to detention for his or her own protection, there is a difference, bearing in mind the relative youth and vulnerability of such persons:

> The concept of 'own interests' is intended to be wider than 'own protection', although the distinction will not always be easy to draw. This criterion might apply where the juvenile would otherwise be released to vagrancy, homelessness, prostitution or loneliness.[14]

Juveniles who are not released after being charged must be moved to local authority accommodation, unless it is impracticable to do so or where no secure accommodation is available in the case of arrested 12 year olds or above and that other local authority accommodation would be inadequate to protect the public from serious harm from that person. Where any of these conditions are present and such action is taken, this must be certified by the custody officer.

The exception to the above rules

Section 25 of the Criminal Justice and Public Order Act 1994 (as amended by s 56 of the Crime and Disorder Act 1998) provides that bail may only be granted to a person charged with murder, attempted murder, manslaughter, rape or attempted rape and where that person has a previous conviction for any of these offences, *if* the police officer (or the court) considering bail is satisfied that there are exceptional circumstances which justify it. The original s 25 of the 1994 Act made it a strict rule that bail in the case of those previously convicted of such offences was automatically refused. The only exception was if any previous manslaughter conviction did not result in a prison sentence or long term detention in the case of a child or young person.

How will a custody officer recognise the 'exceptional circumstances' that would justify granting bail to a person charged with any of the above offences who has a previous conviction for any of them? Some doubt has been cast on the practicality of these new measures, as follows:

> Section 56 removes the absolute ban, but it goes nowhere near reverting to the general presumption in favour of bail under the Bail Act 1976. Instead, it provides that, in the situations with which s 25 is concerned, bail is to be granted only if the court or custody officer is satisfied that there are exceptional circumstances which justify it. Section 56, in effect, introduces a strong rebuttable presumption against the grant of bail in such cases, in place of the absolute ban. This presumption can be rebutted by satisfying the court or, as

---

14 *Op cit*, Levenson, Fairweather and Cape, fn 11.

the case may be, the custody officer considering the grant of bail. *It would seem most unlikely that a custody officer would ever be so satisfied.*[15]

Police bail in general

If a person released on police bail fails to surrender to custody without reasonable cause, that person commits an offence under s 6 of the Bail Act 1976 and may be arrested without warrant. When a person who is released from police detention on bail returns to the police station as required, or is arrested and taken to the police station because of failure to surrender to bail, any unused time from the previous period whilst detained may be used to detain that person further without charge, but not exceeding the maximum period allowed. This is contingent on the custody officer having reasonable grounds for believing that this is necessary to secure or preserve evidence, or to obtain it by questioning the suspect.

Questioning after charge

Once a person has been charged, there are limitations on the extent of any questioning from that point onwards. Under paras 16.4, 16.5 and 16.8 of Code C, these rules are as follows:

16.4 If, at any time after a person has been charged with or informed that he may be prosecuted for an offence, a police officer wishes to bring to the notice of that person any written statement made by another person or the content of an interview with another person, he shall hand to that person a true copy of any such written statement or bring to his attention the content of the interview record,[16] but shall say or do nothing to invite any reply or comment, save to warn him that he does not have to say anything, but that anything he does say may be given in evidence and to remind him of his right to legal advice in accordance with para 6.5, above.[17] If the person cannot read, then the officer may read it to him. If the person is a juvenile or mentally disordered or mentally handicapped, the copy shall also be given to, or the interview record brought to the attention of, the appropriate adult.

16.5 Questions relating to an offence may not be put to a person after he has been charged with that offence or informed that he may be prosecuted for it, unless they are necessary for the purpose of preventing or minimising harm or loss to some other person or to the public, or for clearing up an

---

15 Card, R and Ward, R, *The Crime and Disorder Act 1998: A Practitioner's Guide*, 1998, Bristol: Jordans (emphasis added).

16 This means playing back any tape recording of an interview (*op cit*, Lidstone and Palmer, fn 7).

17 The essence of para 6.5 was discussed above, p 130.

ambiguity in a previous answer or statement, or where it is in the interests of justice that the person should have put to him and have an opportunity to comment on information concerning the offence which has come to light since he was charged or informed that he might be prosecuted. Before any such questions are put to him, he shall be warned that he does not have to say anything, but that anything he does say may be given in evidence and reminded of his right to legal advice in accordance with para 6.5, above ...

Paragraph 16.8 states that when any questions are put after a suspect has been charged and answers given, these shall be contemporaneously recorded on the forms provided. The record shall then be signed by the suspect. If that persons refuses to sign, then this document shall be signed by the interviewing officer and anyone else who is present. The provisions set out in Code E will apply where the questions have been tape recorded.

The duty to take a charged person before a court

Section 46 of PACE states that a person charged with an offence, who is then kept in police detention, or in local authority accommodation in the case of juveniles, must be brought before a magistrates' court as soon as is practicable and, in any event, not later than the first sitting after being charged. In most cases, both the police station and the relevant magistrates' court will be in the same petty sessions area and the person charged will therefore be produced in court either on the day when charged or the following day (this excludes Sundays, Good Friday and Christmas Day). In less straightforward situations, the custody officer must inform the court clerk of the presence of a charged person in custody, in order that a sitting may be arranged in accordance with s 46. There is no requirement for a person charged with an offence who is in hospital to be produced in court if that person is not well enough.

CAUTIONING

Cautioning in this context is different from actually administering cautions to suspects where a warning is given on arrest or prior to formal questions being asked. In many cases, where a suspect may be charged with an offence, the case may be disposed of by means of a caution. As far as children and young persons are concerned (10–17 year olds inclusive), a reprimand and warning scheme was piloted last year and implemented nationwide in April 2000. This scheme is discussed in further detail below, p 161. Older offenders are cautioned in accordance with Home Office Circular 18/94, which provides guidance as to the use of this disposal option. This document is entitled 'National Standards for Cautioning (Revised)' and consists of six main sections, which are headed as follows, together with the relevant provisions.

Aims

A caution is not a sentence; therefore, a caution is not contingent upon certain activities being performed, such as reparation or payment of compensation, which only the courts may impose. The aims of cautioning are to deal quickly and simply with less serious offenders, to divert them from unnecessary appearance in the criminal courts and to reduce the prospects of their re-offending.

Decision to caution

Although a caution does not constitute a criminal record, it is still recorded by the police and may be cited in any later court proceedings. Earlier cautions should also be considered by the police if considering whether or not to prosecute. A caution should be administered only where there is a realistic prospect of a conviction and the offender admits to the offence and is capable of understanding the significance of this admission.

Public interest considerations

The police should consider whether giving a caution would be in the public interest and, in this respect, they are referred to the guidance under the Code for Crown Prosecutors. They are also encouraged to be more favourably inclined towards cautioning certain classes of offenders, rather than prosecuting them. These include the elderly and the physically and mentally handicapped, although it is stressed that this must not constitute complete immunity in all cases. Much depends upon the offender's attitude to the offence and the degree of wilfulness in which it was committed. Also, where group offending is concerned, each offender's degree of involvement should be considered.

Views of the victim

Prior to any caution being given, the police are advised to contact the victim of the offence, in order to ascertain his or her views, as well as the effect of the crime on that person and whether the offender has made any form of voluntary reparation or compensation. Under no circumstances should the police be involved in arranging or negotiating any such recompense.

Administration of a caution

A caution should be administered by a uniformed police officer and at a police station if practicable. The officer should normally be of the rank of inspector or above, although designated 'cautioning officers' may be appointed where appropriate and this may include using a sergeant instead of an inspector or community or home beat officers.

Recording cautions

Every caution should be recorded as directed by the Home Secretary and their usage should be monitored on a force-wide basis. Cautions should be cited in court where they are relevant to the offence in question, although care must be taken not to confuse cautions with criminal convictions when presenting the offender's antecedents.

The reprimand and warning scheme for juveniles

As mentioned above, a system of reprimands and warnings for juveniles has been in force nationally since April 2000. The main reason for a separate cautioning regime for children and young persons can perhaps be best summarised in the following comment:

> The system of police cautions is replaced by s 65 of the Crime and Disorder Act 1998, which introduces a system of reprimands and warnings for young offenders. Although police cautions are considered useful, they are not seen as sufficient without other support structures. The system of cautioning is also believed to be too haphazard; there is no consistency across police forces and repeated ineffective cautioning has a minimal effect on re-offending.[18]

This statement is reinforced by the Home Office publication, entitled *Tackling Youth Crime: Reforming Youth Justice*,[19] as follows:

> While cautioning works well with most first time offenders (about 80% of whom do not re-offend within two years), it becomes progressively less effective once a pattern of offending sets in. If cautioning is used inconsistently or repeated without positive intervention to reverse offending habits, it will not be effective.

The consultation paper then points out that approximately one in five offenders do not respond to police cautioning and, subsequently, they become involved in a pattern of offending. There was an obvious need to replace the

---

18 Hutton, G and Johnston, D, *Blackstone's Police Manual: Evidence and Procedure*, 2000, London: Blackstone.

19 Home Office, Consultation Paper, September 1997, London: HMSO.

cautioning system affecting juveniles with something more positive, hence ss 65 and 66 of the Crime and Disorder Act 1998, which make the following provisions.

If the police decide not to prosecute a young offender nor take informal action by giving firm advice to the youngster and his or her parents, they may either issue a reprimand, if the offence is of a minor nature, or they may issue a warning, if the offence is more serious. If the offender re-offends after receiving a reprimand, the police must then issue a warning, assuming they do not prosecute on that occasion. No more than one reprimand may be given and no more than one warning may be issued, unless more than two years have lapsed between the first warning and the latest offence and the latter is not serious enough to require a charge to be brought. Only then may a second warning be given, but under no circumstances will a further warning be issued afterwards.

Final warnings are not intended to be a mere indication that young offenders have reached the final stage before prosecution. Whenever the police issue a juvenile with a final warning, they are under a duty to refer that person to a youth offending team. Where appropriate, it is intended that final warnings should then be accompanied by a programme of intervention to prevent re-offending in conjunction with local youth offending teams, which may also actively involve the offender's parents. The police may also request that the relevant youth offending team makes a prior assessment of the young offender in order to assist in making the decision as to whether a final warning should be given.

If a person is convicted of an offence committed within two years of being given a warning by the police, the courts may not impose a conditional discharge on the offender, unless the court is of the opinion that there are exceptional circumstances relating to the offence or the offender which justify this sentence. Where this applies, the court must state the reasons for its opinion. Any record of a police reprimand, warning or failure to participate in a rehabilitation programme under a warning may be cited in criminal proceedings in the same circumstances as previous convictions.[20]

The drug arrest referral scheme

Before departing from the issue of police powers of detention, it should be mentioned that a new innovation called the 'drug arrest referral scheme' has recently been piloted in a number of police forces and is due to be implemented nationally by the end of 2000. This scheme constitutes an

---

20 This commentary on the reprimand and warning scheme has been taken from Jason-Lloyd, L, *The Crime and Disorder Act 1998: A Concise Guide*, 2nd edn, 1999, Cambridgeshire: Elm.

appendage to the detention process regarding suspects arrested for drug related crimes.

It is now widely known that the funding of drug taking is a major motivation behind certain criminal activities. Research in selected areas has shown that over 80% of all persons arrested for shoplifting, domestic burglaries and car theft tested positive for at least one drug.[71] In an endeavour to try and break the 'revolving door' pattern of offending on the part of drug users, the police have developed an interventionist approach to drug related crime, rather than adopt purely an enforcement role. The essence of the scheme can be found in three main types of referral. First, the 'information' method, where the arrested person is simply given a leaflet or other document containing the details of a drug agency; secondly, there is the 'proactive' method, involving drug workers actually performing their work in police stations and having direct access to persons detained; and, thirdly, there is the 'incentive' method, where persons who come into contact with the police are motivated to seek help in order to deal with their drug problem. The arrest referral scheme does not alter the suspect's status or treatment whilst being held by the police, such as the granting of bail or decisions regarding detention or charging.[22]

---

21 Bennett, T, *Drugs and Crime: The Results of Research on Drug Testing and Interviewing Arrestees*, Home Office Research Study No 183, 1998, London: HMSO.

22 See, also, the proposed new police power to test for drugs under cl 52 of the Criminal Justice and Court Services Bill (below, p 202).

CHAPTER 7

THE QUESTIONING AND GENERAL TREATMENT OF DETAINED PERSONS

INTRODUCTION

The line of demarcation between Chapter 6 and the present chapter can be difficult to draw sometimes. This is because, among other things, many of the procedures discussed in the previous chapter may be applied to detained persons under a wide variety of circumstances, including the alleged offences involved and the period that they are detained for. The topics that will now be discussed include the general conditions of detention and the treatment of detained persons, the administering of cautions, the conduct of interviews including access to legal advice, the tape recording of interviews, confessions, fingerprinting and other identification procedures, including the taking of body samples.

GENERAL CONDITIONS OF DETENTION

The general conditions under which detained persons may be held in police custody are contained in the provisions under Section 8 of Code C, as follows. Wherever possible, no more than one person shall occupy a cell. A juvenile must not be placed in a police cell unless no other secure accommodation is available or a cell would be more comfortable than another secure place in the police station. Whenever a juvenile is placed in a cell, this must be recorded and, in any event, a juvenile may not be placed in a cell with a detained adult. Cells must be adequately heated, cleaned, ventilated and lit, although the latter includes such dimming as to allow people to sleep at night time, but without compromising safety and security. Bedding must be of a clean and generally reasonable standard and access to toilet and washing facilities must be available.[1] If practicable, brief outdoor exercise shall be offered daily.

In any 24 hour period, a minimum of two light meals and one main meal shall be offered, together with drinks, and a record must be kept of meals offered. Further drinks should be provided between meals where reasonable. As far as practicable, the meals should be offered at recognised meal times, be of a varied diet and meet any special dietary needs or religious beliefs;

---

1   In *Hague v Deputy Governor of Parkhurst Prison* (1991), it was held that, whilst a claim in negligence could be made where a person was detained in extremely poor conditions, this would not render the detention unlawful.

whenever necessary, advice shall be sought on medical and dietary matters from the police surgeon. A detained person may have meals supplied by friends or relatives, but not at public expense.

Where it is necessary to remove a detained person's clothes for investigation purposes, for hygiene or health reasons or for cleaning, that person is to be issued with replacement clothing of a reasonable standard and only when adequate clothing has been offered to the suspect may that person be interviewed. Any replacement clothing issued to the suspect must be recorded.

Where restraint in a locked cell is absolutely necessary, only suitable handcuffs may be used. Particular care must be taken when considering the use of handcuffs in the case of those who are mentally handicapped or disordered. Detained persons shall be visited every hour, unless they are drunk, in which case they must be visited at least every 30 minutes and, during the visit, they must be roused and spoken to. Appropriate medical assistance must be sought if there is any concern regarding that person's condition. Whenever possible, juveniles and others at risk should be visited more frequently.[2]

Reasonable force may be used if necessary in order to secure compliance with reasonable instructions regarding a person's detention or to prevent escape, injury, damage to property or the destruction of evidence.

THE TREATMENT OF DETAINED PERSONS

The provisions in respect of the treatment of detained persons are covered under Section 9 of Code C which is concerned with general issues, medical treatment and documentation. First, there is the general provision that, where a complaint or concern arises regarding a person's treatment after being arrested, a report must be made, as soon as practicable, to an inspector or above who is not connected with the investigation. Where the matter concerns the possibility of unlawful force being used, the police surgeon must be called as soon as practicable. Under the Code of Practice dealing with documentation, it is stated that a record must be made of any such complaint and subsequent arrangements for an examination by a police surgeon, together with any relevant remarks by the custody officer.

Secondly, there are fairly detailed provisions regarding medical matters affecting persons held in police custody. Where a person appears to be

---

2   See *Kirkham v Chief Constable of Greater Manchester Police* (1990), where it was held that the police are under a duty of care to prevent a prisoner committing suicide where they are aware that the person has suicidal tendencies.

suffering from physical or mental illness, is injured, fails to respond to questions or conversation other than because of drunkenness alone or appears to need medical attention for other reasons, the custody officer must call the police surgeon immediately. In urgent cases, the person must be sent to hospital or the nearest available medical practitioner should be called. The Code of Practice goes on to state that the above action should be taken whether or not the person requests medical attention or has already had treatment elsewhere, unless brought to the police station direct from hospital.

Where a person has been arrested and taken to a police station under s 136 of the Mental Health Act 1983,[3] the above provisions should not delay the transfer of a person to a place of safety in order to be assessed by a medical practitioner. If such an assessment is due to take place at the police station, the custody officer has a discretion not to call the police surgeon, provided that officer believes that the assessment can be made without undue delay.

Any detained person may request a medical examination, in which case the police surgeon must be called as soon as practicable or be examined by a medical practitioner of his or her own choice, although this will not be at public expense. The provisions under the Code of Practice regarding documentation provide that, where this occurs, a record must be kept of any such request, together with the arrangements made for any examination and any medical directions subsequently given to the police. In the notes for guidance, it is stated that there is no need to call a police surgeon for minor ailments or injuries which do not need attention, although they must be recorded in the custody record, but, if in doubt, the police surgeon must be called. They also go on to remind custody officers that persons who behave in an intoxicated manner may be ill, under the influence of drugs or may have sustained head or other injury, all of which may not be easily discernible. This also includes withdrawal symptoms experienced by those needing or addicted to drugs. Therefore, when in doubt, the police should always call the police surgeon with due speed.

Where a person detained in police custody possesses medication relating to a serious condition such as heart disease, diabetes or epilepsy, or claims to need such medication, the police surgeon's advice must be sought, even if the person does not appear to need such assistance. If a person has to take or apply any medication which was prescribed before his or her detention, the police surgeon should be consulted by the custody officer before it is administered. If this is approved, the custody officer is responsible for ensuring that the medication is available for administration and for its

---

3   'Under s 136 of the 1983 Act, if a police officer finds in a place to which the public have access a person who appears to him to be suffering from mental disorder and to be in immediate need of care or control, he may, if he thinks it necessary in the interests of that person or for the protection of other persons, remove the person to a "place of safety" ... this includes (among other places) both a hospital and a police station.' (Hoggett, B, *Mental Health Law*, 4th edn, 1996, London: Sweet & Maxwell.)

safekeeping in the meantime. However, these provisions do not apply in the case of medication which is in the form of controlled drugs as defined under the Misuse of Drugs Act 1971.[4] No police officer may administer such medication, but the detained person may administer the medication to him or herself, but only under the supervision of the police surgeon. The requirement for personal supervision does not necessarily mean that the police surgeon has to be personally present each time this medication is administered. The detained person may administer the drugs to him or herself if the custody officer and the police surgeon agree that, in all the circumstances, self-administration of the controlled drug will not expose the detained person, police officers or anyone else to risk of any harm. This consultation may take place on the telephone although, if there is any doubt, the police surgeon should be asked to attend. Any such consultation should be noted in the custody record. The provisions governing documentation under this Code of Practice state that the custody officer is under a duty to record all medication in the possession of a person on arrival at the police station and, where applicable, any medication that the detained person claims to need, but does not have at the time.

Where a detained person appears to be suffering from an infectious disease of any significance or the custody officer is given this information, such persons and their property must be isolated until medical directions have been obtained as to where the person should be taken, if fumigation should take place and any precautions that police officers should take who have been, or will be, in contact with that person.

The administering of cautions to suspects

Section 10 of Code C is divided into two main Parts. Part (a) deals with when a caution must be given and Pt (b) deals with general action that has to be taken during this process. With regard to Pt (a), a caution must be given to a person suspected of an offence before any questions can be put to that person, or where further questions are put arising from answers which have given grounds for suspicion. This rule applies where that person's answers or failure or refusal to answer a question satisfactorily may be given as evidence to a court in a prosecution. Cautions are therefore not necessary when other questions are put, such as establishing the suspect's identity or in the course of routine searches. Cautions must be administered to suspects prior to

---

4   For further reading on controlled drugs and their definition, see Jason-Lloyd, L, *Drugs, Addiction and the Law*, 5th edn, 1999, Cambridgeshire: Elm. It should be noted that not all controlled drugs are prescribable (for example, hallucinogenics and cannabis resin are not prescribable), hence, reference in the Code of Practice to 'medicines which are also controlled drugs'. Also, not all controlled substances fall under the heading of 'hard drugs' like heroin and cocaine. Many are mild soporific drugs, such as valium, librium and mogadon.

questioning, even when they have not been arrested, such as those voluntarily attending police stations. At the same time, that person must be informed that he or she is not under arrest and may leave at will. If that person is subsequently arrested or where a suspect is arrested away from a police station, that person must be cautioned on being arrested, unless it is impracticable to do so because of the suspect's condition or behaviour at the time, or where a caution has been administered prior to being arrested.

With regard to Pt (b) under Section 10, where there is a break in the course of questioning, the interviewing officer must make the suspect aware that he or she is still under caution and, if there is any doubt, the caution should be given again before the resumption of the interview. The exact wording of the caution is as follows:

> You do not have to say anything. But it may harm your defence if you do not mention when questioned something which you later rely on in court. Anything you do say may be given in evidence.

Provided the sense of the caution is unaffected, minor deviations from the exact wording are acceptable. Where a person cannot understand the meaning of the caution, the police officer should explain its meaning in his or her own words.

If an arrested suspect who is subsequently interviewed does not answer certain questions, or answers them unsatisfactorily, then, after due warning, a court or jury may draw inferences under ss 36 and 37 of the Criminal Justice and Public Order Act 1994. These questions relate to any marks, objects or substances that may be found on or otherwise in the possession of the arrested person, including clothing or footwear or in the place where the arrest took place. The questions may also relate to the suspect's presence in the place where the offence was committed. However, in order for inferences to be drawn, the interviewing officer must first inform the suspect of the following in ordinary language: what offence is being investigated; what the suspect is specifically being asked to account for and that this may be due to the suspect's believed participation in the offence; that a court may draw inferences from failure or refusal to account for that fact; that a record is being made of the interview and may be given in evidence (this procedure is replicated where a suspect's interview is being tape recorded. See below, p 177).

In some cases, a detained person's failure to co-operate may have consequences regarding his or her immediate treatment even if cautioned. For instance, the suspect may commit an offence under the Road Traffic Act 1988 for failing to provide certain particulars, or may be detained in police custody after being charged with failing to provide a correct name and address. In such circumstances, the suspect should be informed of the relevant consequences and that they are not affected by the caution.

Where a juvenile or a mentally disordered or mentally handicapped person is cautioned in the absence of the appropriate adult, the caution must be administered again in the appropriate adult's presence. Any caution given under Section 10 shall be recorded either in the police officer's pocket book or in the interview record.

THE GENERAL CONDUCT OF POLICE INTERVIEWS

The overall conduct of police interviews is governed under Section 11 of Code C. In summary, these provisions are as follows. First, what is the definition of a police interview? Paragraph 11.1A states: 'An interview is the questioning of a person regarding his involvement or suspected involvement in a criminal offence or offences which ... is required to be carried out under caution ...' Once it has been decided to arrest a suspect, that person should not be interviewed about the offence in question, except at a police station or other authorised place of detention, although this rule is subject to three exceptions. The first is where the subsequent delay would be likely to lead to evidence or persons being at risk of harm or interference. The second is where delay would lead to alerting accomplices; and the third will apply where delay would hinder the recovery of property obtained in the course of committing an offence. Even so, once the relevant risk no longer exists or the necessary questions have been put in order to avoid that risk, interviewing must cease.

Subject to five main exceptions, which will be explained below, the interviewing officer has a duty to remind the suspect of entitlement to free legal advice and, subject to the exceptions just mentioned, that the interview may be delayed in order that legal advice can be obtained. These reminders should be given immediately before the commencement of any interview or series of interviews, and should be noted in the interview record. An interview may not be delayed for the purposes of obtaining and receiving legal advice under the following circumstances:

(a) where Annex B to Code C applies. This has been discussed above in Chapter 6, namely where a superintendent or above may delay access to legal advice for up to 36 hours in the case of serious arrestable offences, but subject to certain conditions;

(b) where an officer of the rank of superintendent or above has reasonable grounds for believing that delay will involve an immediate risk of harm to persons or serious loss or damage to property,[5] or where a solicitor has agreed to attend, but awaiting his or her arrival would cause unreasonable delay in the investigation;

---

5 Code C, para 6.7 provides that questioning must cease until the suspect receives legal advice, once sufficient information to avert the risk has been obtained.

(c) where the solicitor selected by the suspect cannot be contacted, has declined to attend or has previously indicated the wish not to be contacted and the suspect has refused the services of a duty solicitor or the duty solicitor is unavailable. In such circumstances, an inspector or above may authorise that the interview takes place without further delay;

(d) where the suspect initially requested legal advice, but has since had a change of mind. In such cases, the interview may be started or continued, but only if the suspect has agreed in writing or on tape to be interviewed without legal advice. Also, an inspector or above must give authority for the interview to proceed in this manner, having first ascertained the suspect's reasons for the change of mind. All these facts, including the name of the authorising officer, must be recorded, either on tape or in the written interview record at the beginning or recommencement of the interview;

(e) where Annex C to Code C applies. This is entitled 'Vulnerable suspects: urgent interviews at police stations' and states that a police superintendent or above may authorise the following if that officer considers that delay will lead to interference with evidence or interference or physical harm to persons, alert accomplices or hinder the recovery of property obtained as a result of a criminal offence:

- the interview of a person heavily under the influence of drink or drugs; or

- the interview of a juvenile or mentally disordered or handicapped person without the presence of the appropriate adult; or

- the interview of a person who has difficulty understanding English or has a hearing disability without an interpreter.

Where questioning has been authorised under these circumstances, the interview should be discontinued as soon as information necessary to avert any of the immediate risks mentioned above has been obtained. Also, a record must be made of the grounds for justifying the decision to interview a vulnerable suspect under the above conditions. Note for guidance C1 makes the important point that, since the special groups referred to are particularly vulnerable, the above measures should be applied only in exceptional cases.

At the commencement of an interview at a police station, once the caution has been administered, the suspect should have put to him or her any significant statement or silence which occurred prior to arrival at the police station. The suspect should then be asked to confirm or deny any earlier statement or silence and to make any other comments. Paragraph 11.2A states that: 'A "significant" statement or silence is one which appears capable of being used in evidence against the suspect, in particular, a direct admission of guilt or failure or refusal to answer a question or to answer it satisfactorily, which might give rise to an inference under Pt III of the Criminal Justice and Public Order Act 1994.'

Under para 11.3, no police officer may try to obtain answers to questions or obtain a statement by the use of oppression. Neither may the police indicate, unless directly asked, what action they will take if the suspect answers or refuses to answer questions or makes a statement or refuses to do so. The exception to this rule has already been mentioned above where, in specific cases, a suspect's failure to co-operate could have an immediate effect on that person's immediate treatment. Where a direct question is asked by the suspect, the police may inform that person of the action the police propose to take in such an event, 'provided that action is itself proper and warranted'.

In the course of a criminal investigation, once the police believe that there is sufficient evidence to justify a prosecution being brought against a detained suspect, that person should be asked if he or she has anything further to say. Any further questioning must then cease once the person indicates that they wish to say nothing more. However, this does not prevent investigating officers, pursuing matters under revenue cases or confiscation proceedings, from inviting that same person to complete a formal question and answer record, following the conclusion of the interview.

Paragraphs 11.5 to 11.13 and note for guidance 11D contain detailed provisions regarding interview records. The main points arising from these are as follows. An accurate record must be made of each interview which, in turn, must include the location where it took place, the time it began and ended, the time the record is made (if different) and any breaks in the interview, together with the names of all those present (except in cases involving terrorism, where the officers need to state their warrant or other identification numbers and duty station, but not their names). Written interview records must be both timed and signed by the maker. The record of the interview must be made on the forms provided for this purpose, in the officer's pocket book or tape recorded in accordance with Code E (see below, p 178). The record must be contemporaneous with the interview, unless this is impracticable or would interfere with the conduct of the interview. If either of these exceptions apply, the reasons must be noted in the officer's pocket book and the interview record must be made as soon as practicable after the interview. In any event, it must constitute either a verbatim record of what was stated or an account of the interview which summarises it adequately and accurately.

The suspect should be given the opportunity to read the interview record and sign it, if in agreement with its contents, or indicate any alleged inaccuracies, unless it is impracticable (different arrangements apply where the interview is tape recorded). If the suspect cannot read or refuses to read the record or sign it, the senior officer present must read it to the suspect and invite that person to sign it (or make their mark) or indicate any alleged inaccuracies. That police officer should then certify on the interview record what has occurred. Where an interview has been contemporaneously recorded and signed by the person questioned (or tape recorded), a written statement is not normally necessary. Although a suspect may be asked if he or she wishes to make a statement, it is usually only when the suspect expressly wishes to make a statement under caution that one is taken. Note for guidance 11D states that a suspect, having read and agreed the contents of the interview record, should then be asked to endorse the record with words to the effect, 'I agree that this is a correct record of what was said' and then sign the document. If the suspect disagrees with the record, the police officer should record details of that disagreement and then ask the suspect to sign accordingly. Any refusal to sign this document or any record of interview must be recorded. This also applies where a suspect refuses to sign a written record of any comment made by him or her which, although outside the context of the interview, may be relevant to the offence (see para 11.13 of Code C).

Paragraphs 11.14 to 11.16 and note for guidance 11B provide additional safeguards regarding juveniles and mentally disordered or mentally handicapped persons. Any person falling within these categories must not be interviewed or asked to provide or sign a written statement unless the appropriate adult is present, even if that person is not suspected of a crime. The exceptions to this rule apply where any delay would be likely to lead to interference with evidence or interference with or physical harm to other people, or to the alerting of accomplices, or where it might hinder the recovery of property obtained in connection with an offence. During the presence of the appropriate adult at an interview, that person shall be informed that he or she is not expected to be a passive observer only. The appropriate adult should then be informed that their role is to advise the person being questioned and to observe whether the interview is being conducted properly and fairly, and also to promote communication with the person being interviewed. Note for guidance 11B augments these provisions by stating the following:

> It is important to bear in mind that, although juveniles or people who are mentally disordered or mentally handicapped are often capable of providing reliable evidence, they may, without knowing or wishing to do so, be particularly prone in certain circumstances to provide information which is unreliable, misleading or self-incriminating. Special care should therefore always be exercised in questioning such a person and the appropriate adult should be involved if there is any doubt about a person's age, mental state or capacity. Because of the risk of unreliable evidence, it is also important to obtain corroboration of any facts admitted whenever possible.

Juveniles may be interviewed at their places of education only in exceptional circumstances and with the agreement of the person in charge of that establishment.[6] Where the police want to interview a juvenile, every effort should be made to inform the parents or other person responsible for the juvenile's welfare and, if a different person, the appropriate adult. Reasonable

---

6   This is basically the same as the restriction on arresting juveniles in their places of education, as mentioned in Chapter 6.

time should be allowed for the appropriate adult to be present at the interview. If unreasonable delay would be caused by waiting for the arrival of the appropriate adult, the person in charge of the educational establishment may act in this capacity, unless the suspected offence was committed against that establishment.

Interviews at police stations

The rules governing the general conduct of interviews in police stations are contained in Section 12 of Code C. This begins by stating that the custody officer is responsible for deciding whether to deliver a suspect into the custody of a police officer who wishes to interview or conduct inquiries which require the presence of that detained person. A record must be made, covering the period when the suspect is not in the custody of the custody officer and the reason why and, where applicable, the reason for any refusal to deliver the suspect out of that custody. Bearing in mind the strict rules regarding maximum periods of detention (see Chapter 6), a suspect must be allowed a continuous period of at least eight hours rest in any 24 hour period. This should normally be at night and must be free from questioning, travel or any interruption by the police regarding the investigation. This rest period may be interrupted or delayed if there are reasonable grounds for believing that there is risk of harm to persons or of serious damage to or loss of property, or the outcome of the investigation would be prejudiced or that it would delay the suspect's release from custody. Also, the rest period may be interrupted at the request of the detained person, the appropriate adult or the legal representative. Where a person initially attends a police station voluntarily and is later arrested there, the 24 hour period starts from the time of the arrest and not the time of arriving at the police station. The starting of a fresh 24 hour period will not be justified where any action is required under the general conditions of detention (see Section 8 and p 165, above) or regarding medical advice, or at the request of the detained person, the appropriate adult or the legal representative.

No detained person may be supplied with intoxicating liquor, except on medical directions and a record must be made accordingly. Where a person is unable to appreciate the significance of questions or answers due to being intoxicated through drink or drugs, that person shall not be questioned about an offence whilst in that condition. An exception to this rule is where Annex C applies (as discussed above, p 171). Where appropriate, a police surgeon's advice may be sought in order to ascertain whether a person is fit to be interviewed under these circumstances.

Before any interview commences, each interviewing officer must identify him or herself and any other officers present to the suspect. This will normally be their name and rank, except in cases involving terrorist investigations, where their rank and warrant or other identification number, rather than their names, shall be given. Interviews should, as far as practicable, be held in interview rooms, which must be provided with adequate heating, lighting and ventilation. During questioning and the making of statements, suspects must not be required to stand. There must be breaks from interviewing at recognised meal times, lasting at least 45 minutes and, at intervals of approximately two hours, there shall be short refreshment breaks, lasting at least 15 minutes, although this is subject to the discretion of the interviewing officer to delay a break if there are reasonable grounds for believing that this would involve a risk of harm to people or serious loss of or damage to property, unnecessary delay in the suspect's release or otherwise prejudice the investigation. Any prolonged interview should be compensated for by providing a longer break afterwards. Where there is a short interview and it is contemplated that this will be followed by another short period of questioning, the length of the break may be reduced if there are reasonable grounds to believe that to do otherwise would involve the risk of harm to persons or serious loss of or damage to property, unnecessary delay to the suspect's release or otherwise prejudice the investigation. Any decision to delay a break, together with the reasons, must be recorded in the interview record.

With regard to written statements made under caution at police stations, these must be written on the forms provided for this purpose and all such statements must conform to the rules under Annex D, as follows:

(a) Written by a person under caution

1 A person shall always be invited to write down himself what he wants to say.

2 Where the person wishes to write it himself, he shall be asked to write out and sign, before writing what he wants to say, the following:

> I make this statement of my own free will. I understand that I do not have to say anything, but that it may harm my defence if I do not mention when questioned something which I later rely on in court. This statement may be given in evidence.

3 Any person writing his own statement shall be allowed to do so without any prompting, except that a police officer may indicate to him which matters are material or question any ambiguity in the statement.

(b) Written by a police officer

4 If a person says that he would like someone to write it for him, a police officer shall write the statement but, before starting, he must ask him to sign or make his mark to the following:

> I ... wish to make a statement. I want someone to write down what I say. I understand that I do not have to say anything, but that it may harm my defence if I do not mention when questioned something which I later rely on in court. This statement may be given in evidence.

5   Where a police officer writes the statement, he must take down the exact words spoken by the person making it and he must not edit or paraphrase it. Any questions that are necessary (for example, to make it more intelligible) and the answers given must be recorded contemporaneously on the statement form.

6   When the writing of a statement by a police officer is finished, the person making it shall be asked to read it and make any corrections, alterations or additions he wishes. When he has finished reading it, he shall be asked to write and sign or make his mark on the following certificate at the end of the statement:

> I have read the above statement and I have been able to correct, alter or add anything I wish. This statement is true. I have made it of my own free will.

7   If the person making the statement cannot read, or refuses to read it, or to write the above mentioned certificate at the end of it or to sign it, the senior police officer present shall read it to him and ask him whether he would like to correct, alter or add anything and to put his signature or make his mark at the end. The police officer shall then certify on the statement itself what has occurred.

Where a complaint is made by the suspect in the course of an interview, or where a complaint is made on that person's behalf, the interviewing officer must record it in the interview record and inform the custody officer, who will be responsible for dealing with the complaint in accordance with Section 9 under Code C (see p 166, above).

The role of the solicitor during interviews

The rights and restrictions on access to legal advice have been covered earlier under different contexts. The general role and conduct of solicitors during interviews fall under the latter half of Section 6 and the notes for guidance, which will now be discussed.

A solicitor must be allowed to be present while a suspect is being interviewed if that person is permitted to consult a legal adviser. This is contingent on the solicitor being available. A solicitor may be required to leave an interview only if his or her conduct prevents the interviewing officer from properly putting questions to the suspect.[7] In such cases, the interviewing officer should stop the interview and consult an officer not below the rank of superintendent. If such an officer is not readily available, an officer of at least the rank of inspector may be consulted instead, provided that officer is not connected with the investigation. The officer who has been consulted should

---

7   Note for guidance 6D gives two examples of unacceptable conduct in this context. First, answering questions on the behalf of a suspect and, secondly, providing written answers to questions for the suspect to quote.

speak to the solicitor and will then decide if the interview should continue with that same solicitor present. If it is decided that it should not, the suspect may consult another solicitor before the interview continues, who will be given the opportunity to be present. A record must be made on the interview record if an interview has been commenced in the absence of a solicitor where one has been requested, or where the solicitor has been required to leave. In view of the serious implications in removing a solicitor from an interview, consideration should be given by the police as to whether the incident should be reported to the Law Society. The superintendent or above who took the decision to remove the solicitor will consider whether such steps should be taken and, if an officer below that rank removed the solicitor, the facts of the incident should be reported to a superintendent or above who, in turn, will consider whether to report the matter to the Law Society. This should also be reported to the Legal Aid Board if it was a duty solicitor who was removed from the interview.

Whether or not a detained person is being interviewed, that person must be informed of a solicitor's arrival at the police station and asked if he or she wishes to see the legal adviser. The exception to this rule is where Annex B applies (see above, p 170). Apart from this exception, the detained person has the right to be informed of a solicitor's arrival, even if there was an initial refusal of legal advice or an agreement to be interviewed without it. A note should be made in the custody record regarding the solicitor's attendance and the decision of the detained person. In *R v Franklin* (1994), it was held that failure to inform a suspect that a solicitor has arrived at the police station could result in any subsequent interview being excluded as evidence where the solicitor is absent (see *Rixon and Others v Chief Constable of Kent* (2000), regarding the right of solicitors to see their clients at police stations).

Tape recorded interviews

Section 60 of PACE states the following with regard to the interviewing of suspects:

(1) It shall be the duty of the Secretary of State:

    (a) to issue a Code of Practice in connection with the tape recording of interviews of persons suspected of the commission of criminal offences, which are held by police officers at police stations; and

    (b) to make an order requiring the tape recording of interviews of persons suspected of the commission of criminal offences, or of such descriptions of criminal offences as may be specified in the order, which are so held in accordance with the Code as it has effect for the time being.

(2) An order under sub-s (1) above shall be made by statutory instrument and shall be subject to annulment in pursuance of a resolution of either House of Parliament.

The provisions governing the tape recording of interviews with suspects are to be found in the whole of Code E, which is divided into six sections, each accompanied by their own notes for guidance. A summary of these will now be given in turn.

General

Apart from confirming that the terms 'appropriate adult', 'solicitor' and 'custody officer' mean the same in Code E as they do elsewhere in the Codes of Practice, and the requirement for these Codes to be available for inspection at police stations, the main aspect of this section is the statement that it does not apply to the following groups of people: persons arrested in Scotland under cross-border arrest powers (see Chapter 3); people arrested under s 3(5) of the Asylum and Immigration Appeals Act 1993 in order to be fingerprinted (although this is due to be replaced by s 141 of the Immigration and Asylum Act 1999 when put into force); persons served notice, advising them of their detention under the Immigration Act 1971; and convicted or remanded prisoners held in police cells on behalf of the Prison Service.

Recording and the sealing of master tapes

Whilst it is stated that the tape recording of interviews should be conducted openly, in order to instil confidence in its general integrity, the notes for guidance also mention the desirability for tape recording arrangements to be unobtrusive. There should always be a master tape, which must be sealed before it leaves the presence of the suspect, and a second tape should be used as a working copy. Where a twin deck machine is used, both tapes will record simultaneously, but the use of a single deck machine will necessitate a working copy being made from the master tape in the presence of the suspect.

Interviews to be tape recorded

This section provides the following list of circumstances under which interviews must be tape recorded; however, this is now the way in which all police interviews are usually conducted, since the police have a discretion to conduct other interviews in this manner (note for guidance 3A):

(a) where a person has been cautioned in respect of an indictable only offence or one which is triable either way;

(b) in exceptional circumstances, where the police put further questions to a suspect about an offence falling within (a), above, after that person has been charged or informed of a possible prosecution;

(c) where the police bring to a suspect's attention any written statement or content of an interview with another person where the suspect has already been charged or told he or she may be prosecuted.

There is no mandatory requirement to tape record interviews for certain offences under the Prevention of Terrorism (Temporary Provisions) Act 1989 or for an offence under s 1 of the Official Secrets Act 1911.

An interview must be recorded in writing where the custody officer authorises the interviewing officer not to make a tape recording, because of equipment failure or unavailability of a recording room, or where it becomes obvious that no prosecution will ensue and where the interview should not be delayed. The reason should be duly noted by the custody officer and in specific terms because, under note for guidance 3K, a decision not to tape record an interview may be the subject of comment in court; therefore, the authorising officer should be prepared to justify the decision. This section ends by stating that each interview shall be tape recorded in its entirety, which will include the taking of any statement and the reading back of it to the suspect.

The interview

This section under Code E provides that, as soon as the suspect enters the interview room, clean tapes should be unwrapped and then loaded in the machine in full view of that person, and the machine then set to record. The interviewing officer must then tell the suspect that the interview is being tape recorded and the police officer must state his or her name and rank, together with the names and ranks of other police officers present (there is always an exception to this rule with regard to inquiries linked to terrorist investigations, as mentioned above; in such cases, the officer need only state his or her number). The interviewing officer must then go on to announce the suspect's name and any other person who may be present, such as the solicitor, although it is advised that it will be helpful if each of those present actually identify themselves. The date, time of commencement and location of the interview must also be given and, finally, it should be announced that the suspect will be given a notice describing what will happen to the tapes. This explains how the tape recording will be used and how access to it may be gained, and that, if the suspect is charged or prosecuted, a copy will be supplied as soon as practicable. The police officer must then administer the caution as follows, although minor deviations are acceptable, provided the meaning is preserved:

> You do not have to say anything. But it may harm your defence if you do not mention when questioned something which you later rely on in court. Anything you do say may be given in evidence.

The suspect should then be reminded of the right to free and independent legal advice in accordance with the provisions of Code C described earlier (subject to the special rules regarding delaying access to legal advice). The police officer should then put any significant statement to the suspect which occurred before the commencement of the tape recorded interview or any failure or refusal to answer a question or to answer it satisfactorily. The suspect should then be asked whether he or she wishes to confirm or deny the earlier statement or unanswered question, or whether he or she wishes to add anything. If the suspect is deaf or there is any doubt about the suspect's hearing ability, the interview shall be both tape recorded and written contemporaneously.

As mentioned on p 169, above, special warnings may be given under ss 36 and 37 of the Criminal Justice and Public Order Act 1994. This applies to suspects who refuse or fail to answer questions relating to their being in certain places or to account for marks or substances on their person or clothing, etc. In order that a court may draw inferences of guilt from such refusals, the same procedure as outlined above also applies where the interview is being tape recorded.

If a suspect objects to the interview being tape recorded at any stage during the process (including during breaks), it should be explained that there is the requirement for these objections to be recorded on tape. The tape recorder may then be turned off by the police officer once the suspect has recorded any objections on tape or has refused to do so, having first explained to the suspect that the recorder is being stopped and the reasons for doing so. The exception to this rule is where the police officer reasonably considers that questions may continue to be put to the suspect and be tape recorded; otherwise, the interview must be recorded in written form. However, it should be borne in mind that to tape record an interview against the suspect's wishes may be the subject of comment in court.

Where a complaint is received in the course of the tape recording regarding the interview or the suspect's general treatment in custody, the interviewing officer has a duty to record it in the interview record and then inform the custody officer, who must then deal with the matter in accordance with Section 9 of Code C (see p 166, above). Notes for guidance 4H and 4J to Code E state further that, wherever possible, the tape recorder should be left running until the custody officer enters the room and speaks to the complainant, provided the custody officer is called immediately. The interview may be continued or terminated at the discretion of the interviewing officer whilst awaiting action by the inspector to whom the complaint must be reported (see para 9.1 of Code C). The interviewing officer also has a discretion to continue with the interview if the complaint is not connected with the interview or the suspect's general treatment in custody. Where this occurs, the suspect should be told that the custody officer will be informed as soon as possible about the complaint on completion of the interview, and this must be complied with accordingly.

This section under Code E then goes on to provide details regarding suspects who wish to discuss matters outside the criminal investigation and the procedures concerning the changing of interview tapes. This is followed by provisions in respect of breaks during interviews. If the break is of short duration and the suspect and the police officer remain in the room, it should be announced on tape that a break is being taken, together with the reasons and the time. When the break is over, the time of the recommencement of the interview should be recorded. Although the machine may be switched off during the break, there is no need to remove the tapes. Where a break is taken and the suspect is due to vacate the room, this should be recorded, together with the reasons and the time. In such cases, the tape must then be removed from the machine after the suspect has been asked if he or she wishes to clarify or add anything. The interviewing officer is under a duty to ensure that the suspect is aware of the right to legal advice and that he or she is under caution whenever there is a break in questioning. The caution must be given again in full when the interview continues if there is any doubt.

At the conclusion of the tape recorded interview, the suspect must be offered the opportunity to clarify anything already stated or include anything further. Where applicable, the taking and reading back of any written statement will be part of the concluding procedure and, once all this has been completed, the tape recorder should then be switched off. The master tape should be sealed in the prescribed manner and the labelling procedure complied with accordingly.

After the interview

The police officer should make a notebook entry that a tape recorded interview has taken place, its date, time and duration, together with the identification number of the master tape. Even where no legal proceedings are taken against the suspect, the interview tapes must still be kept securely, in accordance with the rules under Section 6 of Code E, the main provisions of which now follow.

Tape security

The responsibility for making the necessary arrangements for the security of interview tapes falls upon the officer in charge of each police station where interviews with suspects are recorded. This applies not only to their safe storage, but also accounting for their movements on the same basis as other evidence. No police officer may break the seal on a master tape which is required for criminal proceedings. Where this is necessary, the seal must be broken in the presence of a representative of the Crown Prosecution Service and the defendant, or the defendant's legal adviser shall be given a reasonable opportunity to be present. Either of these two, if present, shall be invited to reseal the master tape and sign it. In the event of refusal or non-attendance, the Crown Prosecution Service representative shall perform this task. It is the responsibility of the chief officer of police to establish arrangements for breaking the seal of a master tape, if necessary, where no criminal proceedings result from the matter which was connected with the tape recorded interview.

CONFESSIONS

Section 82(1) of PACE defines a confession as 'any statement wholly or partly adverse to the person who made it, whether made to a person in authority or not and whether made in words or otherwise'. This can include not only verbal or written communication, but also conduct, such as the re-enactment of an offence recorded on video tape (see *Li Shu-Ling v R* (1989)). Also, an admission need not be confined to the police. Apart from the discretionary power available to the courts under s 78 of PACE to exclude any evidence which, *inter alia*, has been obtained improperly (see *R v Fennelley* (1989) in Chapter 3), s 76(2)(a) and (b) of PACE places a duty on the courts to exclude any confession which has been obtained by oppression or which might have been rendered unreliable 'as a result of anything said or done'.

What is 'oppression'? In *R v Fulling* (1987), the meaning of this term was considered by the Court of Appeal in a case where the defendant had made a bogus insurance claim and was subsequently convicted of obtaining property by deception. When interviewed by the police, she remained silent until she was told that a woman in the next cell was having an affair with her lover. She then confessed to the charge because, as she stated under cross-examination during the trial, 'I agreed to the statement being taken, it was the only way I was going to be released from the cells' (although not suggesting that bail was offered as an inducement). The defence sought to have the confession excluded at the trial, but the judge ruled that it was admissible, since the word 'oppression' implied some impropriety and he was satisfied that this had not been made out. In dismissing the appeal against conviction, the Court of Appeal held that the word 'oppression' should be given its ordinary dictionary meaning, that is to say: '... the exercise of authority or power in a burdensome, harsh or wrongful manner, unjust or cruel treatment of subjects, inferiors, or the imposition of unreasonable or unjust burdens.' The court ruled that the trial judge had correctly concluded that the police had not acted oppressively in this case. However, in *R v Paris, Abdullahi and Miller* (1993), one of defendants, Miller, who had a low mental age, was held to have been subjected to hectoring and bullying during questioning which amounted to oppression. The Court of Appeal commented on the extremely hostile and intimidating method used to obtain a confession in this case and severely criticised the solicitor present during the interviews, who did nothing to prevent this treatment. There is a difference between discourteous and even rude or aggressive questioning and actual hectoring or bullying of a suspect. This case clearly exemplified the dividing line between the two. It should be noted that s 76(8) of PACE provides that, 'In this section, "oppression" includes torture, inhuman or degrading treatment and the use or threat of violence (whether or not amounting to torture)', although this can include a much broader definition of such conduct, as shown in *R v Davison* (1988). In this case, the court regarded a confession as being obtained by oppression where it was obtained in the course of a three hour interview and in the absence of a solicitor, which had started six hours after the suspect had initially been unlawfully detained. In *R v Grieve* (1996), oppressive conduct included, *inter alia*, the unlawful re-interviewing of the co-accused and the subsequent unjustified re-arrest of the defendant, and the police should have ensured the presence of a solicitor during the defendant's second interview. The evidence of the latter was therefore excluded.

A confession may be judged 'unreliable' depending on a number of factors surrounding the making of it. In *R v Barry* (1991), it was held that the offer of bail as an inducement to making a confession clearly fell within s 76(2)(b) of PACE and, in *R v Jasper* (1994), this also applies where a suspect is told by the police that he or she will have to remain in custody pending further inquiries unless that he or she talks to the police in order that they may conclude the matter. In this case, the defendant was convicted of theft, despite a submission by the defence that, during the interview, the police had impliedly said: 'Unless and until you tell us something about this affair, you will remain in custody whilst further inquiries are carried out.' The Court of Appeal held that the evidence obtained in consequence of such comments should have been excluded and subsequently ordered a retrial. But, contrast *R v Weeks* (1995), where an appeal against conviction for drug offences was dismissed where the defendant made a confession shortly after being told that he would remain in custody unless he told the police what they wanted to hear. In this case, the Court of Appeal held that the nature of the admissions was limited and that the defendant was a very astute young man with previous experience of being questioned by the police.

Under s 78 of PACE, mentioned above, p 182, the courts have a discretion to exclude any evidence on which the prosecution proposes to rely which, by virtue of the way it has been obtained, *inter alia*, would have such an unfair effect on the fairness of the trial that the court ought not to admit it. This discretionary power can be used to exclude confessions in criminal proceedings in cases which fall short of oppression or unreliability, as in *R v Mason* (1987). In this case, a confession obtained by deceit was excluded under s 78, even though the defendant was legally represented at the time. The confession was made following an interview where the police falsely told both him and his solicitor that his fingerprints had been discovered on a bottle of inflammable liquid near the scene of an arson attack.

Special protection for the mentally handicapped

Section 77 of PACE makes provision regarding confessions made by mentally handicapped persons. Oddly, it is only the mentally handicapped who are expressly provided for in this section and not also the mentally disordered, who are both covered under the same safeguards under the Codes of Practice. Where a case against a mentally handicapped person depends wholly or mainly on his or her confession, and that this was not made in the presence of an 'independent person' (a person other than someone in or employed by the police service), the courts must exercise special caution before convicting such a person in reliance on that confession. As far as Crown Court trials are concerned, the judge must give a warning to the jury to this effect and, in summary trials, magistrates must take this into account. In *R v Lamont* (1989), the trial judge failed to give the relevant warning to the jury in a case of attempted murder where little other evidence existed apart from the confession. The Court of Appeal subsequently quashed the conviction and substituted a lesser verdict. The rules under s 77 do not apply where there is other evidence to the extent that the prosecution's case does not depend wholly or mainly on such a confession.

There is some uncertainty as to whom precisely the term 'independent person' applies, especially in view of *R v Bailey* (1995), where a retrial was ordered in a case of murder and arson, on the ground that the trial judge had not given a warning under s 77 where the mentally handicapped defendant confessed to friends and then to the police. A friend was held not to constitute an 'independent person' in this instance, as such a person was not independent of the suspect. Section 77(3) of PACE merely states: '... "independent person" does not include a police officer or a person employed for, or engaged on, police purposes ...' This clearly excludes serving police officers, cadets, special constables and police civilian employees, but it appears there remains the need for clarification as to whom the term specifically applies; although, in *R v Lewis* (1995), it was held that an 'independent person' would include a solicitor instructed on behalf of the defendant and that the issue of an 'independent person' only arises where a confession was not made in the presence of such a person; therefore, only a small number of cases will involve s 77. However, even where an appropriate adult is not present when a mentally handicapped person makes an admission, this will not necessarily justify the exclusion of this evidence under s 76(2) of PACE. In *DPP v Cornish* (1997), it was held that, in coming to such a decision, a court should also examine the content of the interview, as well as considering those present, in order to ascertain the effect on the interview of the absence of the appropriate adult.

Section 77(3) also goes on to provide a definition of 'mentally handicapped' as follows: '... "mentally handicapped", in relation to a person, means that he is in a state of arrested or incomplete development of mind, which includes significant impairment of intelligence and social functioning ...' The issue as to whether the defendant is mentally handicapped within this definition is important in view of the decision in *R v Ham* (1995), where it was held that a finding as to whether the defendant was mentally handicapped had to be based on medical evidence and that it was wrong for a judge to place reliance on the evidence of a police officer in this respect. In *R v Everett* (1988) and in *R v Silcott, Braithwaite and Raghip* (1991), it was held that the question of mental handicap is tested objectively; therefore, it is a question of what the defendant's mental condition actually is, rather than the opinion of the police officers.

IDENTIFICATION PROCEDURES

General safeguards

Section 1 of Code D ('Code of Practice for the identification of persons by police officers') makes a number of general provisions regarding identification by witnesses, identification by fingerprints and photographs, as well as identification by body samples and impressions. Many of these echo similar provisions in Code C; for instance, para 1.1 states that this Code of Practice must be readily available at all police stations, and para 1.6 provides that the terms 'appropriate adult' and 'solicitor' will have the same meaning as defined in Code C. Section 1 relates many of the safeguards concerning vulnerable persons stated under Code C to police powers and duties in respect of the identification of persons. Also, notes for guidance 1A–1F similarly repeat key safeguards previously stated in Code C in respect of appropriate adults and others who may represent vulnerable persons.

With regard to all suspects, whether or not they fall under the vulnerable category, para 2.0 of Code D states that a record must be made of the suspect's description as first given by a potential witness. This must be done before the witness participates in an identification parade, a group identification, identification using a video film, a confrontation or by the showing of photographs. This must be recorded in a manner which can be accurately reproduced in written form, for presentation to the suspect or the suspect's solicitor prior to any of the aforementioned identification procedures being carried out. Under para 2.2, the arrangements and conduct of these identification procedures are the responsibility of the 'identification officer', who must be a uniformed police officer of at least the rank of inspector and who is not involved with the investigation. Furthermore, no officer connected with the relevant investigation should participate in any of those identification procedures.

Paragraphs 2.15 and 2.16 provide that, before an identification parade or group or video identification, the identification officer must explain 12 relevant points to the suspect, which should be contained in a written notice and then handed to him or her for signature. Some of these main points include the purposes of the identification procedure due to take place, the entitlement to free legal advice, any special arrangements if the suspect is a juvenile or is mentally disordered or handicapped, the suspect's right to refuse to consent or co-operate in the identification procedures and the consequences of doing so, as well as the consequences of significantly altering his or her appearance and the right of the suspect or the solicitor to be given details of the first description given by any witness attending the relevant identification procedure. The identification officer should make a record on the forms provided of any identification parade, group or video identification procedure carried out, as well as a person's refusal to co-operate with any of these procedures.

It is now quite common for the police to use the media in order to show video films or photographs of incidents to the public, so as to trace and facilitate the recognition of suspects. Any such material released by the police should be preserved and the suspect or the solicitor should be allowed to view it before an identification parade, a group identification, a video identification or a confrontation occurs. This is subject to the proviso that it is practicable to do so and would not unreasonably delay the investigation. Every witness involved in the relevant identification procedure must be asked afterwards whether they have seen any such media coverage and their replies must then be recorded.

Identification parades

Paragraph 2.3 of Code D provides that, where there is a dispute regarding a suspect's involvement in a crime, because that person either alleges that he or she was not present at the scene or was present, but did not take part, then an identification parade must be held if the suspect consents. However, there are several exceptions to this rule. The first is where the identification officer considers that it would not be a fair parade, because it would be impracticable to assemble enough people who resembled the suspect. Among other things, this will occur where the suspect is of unusual appearance. Secondly, the *investigating* officer in the case may consider it better to arrange a group identification, rather than a parade, if the witness is fearful or if, for some other reason, this method may be more satisfactory. Thirdly, the *investigating* officer may consider that it would be better for the identification officer to show a witness a video film of the suspect. This may be due to the suspect's refusal to co-operate with an identification parade or group identification, or for other reasons that would make this course of action more satisfactory. Fourthly, if the suspect significantly changes his or her appearance before the parade, the identification officer may consider other methods of identification. Where it is considered that it is not practicable to hold a parade, the identification officer is under a duty to convey the reason to the suspect and to place this on record accordingly.

In *R v Popat (No 2)* (1999), it was held that para 2.3 of Code D did not apply where a full and satisfactory informal (street) identification of the suspect was made by a witness, and that para 2.3 should not be subject to a 'literalist interpretation'. The Court of Appeal stated that the decision in the original case of *Popat* (1998) was to be preferred to *R v Forbes* (1999), which was relied upon by the Criminal Cases Review Commission when referring this case to the Court of Appeal. In *Forbes*, it was held that para 2.3 was mandatory. The decision in *Popat (No 2)* has been criticised and a contrary view expressed.[8] No doubt, this issue may be clarified in the proposed new Codes of Practice due to be published in 2001 but, in the meantime, it is submitted that the police may wish to consider *Parry v DPP* (1998), where it was stated that, even if an identification is not required, it may be of assistance to hold one. In this case, the Divisional Court held that the saving by not having a parade was probably illusory.

It should be noted that an identification parade may also be held if the investigating officer considers that it would be useful and the suspect consents, and that a parade may possibly be conducted after a suspect has been charged, as well as before charge.[9] Paragraph 2.5 provides that an identification parade must be conducted in accordance with Annex A and a video recording or colour photograph must be taken of the proceedings. The main provisions of Annex A regarding the general conduct and conditions of a parade include the following in summary.

No less than eight persons, in addition to the suspect, shall comprise an identification parade and they must, as far as possible, resemble the suspect in overall appearance. Normally, only one suspect should be present in a parade, but two may be paraded together if they broadly resemble each other, although at least 12 other people must also be present on the parade when this occurs. However, no more than two suspects may be included in a parade at the same time and, where separate parades are held, they must be comprised of different persons. No unauthorised persons may be present in a place where a parade is to be conducted (which can be a normal room or one containing a screen, so that witnesses can view members of the parade without themselves being seen). Prior to the parade being held, the suspect

---

8   See Birch, D [2000] Crim LR 55, pp 55–56.
9   Levenson, H, Fairweather, F and Cape, E, *Police Powers. A Practitioner's Guide*, 3rd edn, 1996, London: Legal Action Group (citing *R v Joseph* (1994)).

must be given a reasonable opportunity to have a solicitor or friend present and either the suspect or the solicitor should be provided with the first description of the suspect. The suspect should be asked to indicate his or her desire to have a solicitor or friend present on a second copy of the notice, containing the 12 points mentioned above, under paras 2.15 and 2.16 (p 186).

The suspect must be given the opportunity to raise any objections regarding the general arrangements and the participants in the parade, and these objections should be acceded to where possible. Where this is not practicable, the identification officer should give the reasons to the suspect. Each place in the line must be clearly numbered and the suspect may not only select his or her position in the line, but may also change it if more than one witness is involved. The identification officer must ensure that, prior to attending a parade, witnesses are prevented from communicating with each other about the case or overhearing a witness who has already seen the parade. Witnesses must also be prevented from seeing any member of the parade beforehand or being given any indication or reminder about the suspect's identity, or from seeing the suspect before or after the parade.

Just before a witness inspects the parade, that person should be informed by the identification officer that the suspect may or may not be in the line up and if the witness cannot positively identify the suspect, then he or she should state this, but not until each person in the parade has been looked at no less than twice by the witness. The identification officer should then go on to inform the witness that he or she should carefully look at each member of the parade at least twice and, once the officer is satisfied that this has been done, the witness shall be asked to state the relevant number if the suspect is on the parade. Identification should be based on the suspect's physical features, instead of clothing. In *R v Hutton* (1998), the Court of Appeal held that it was inappropriate for everyone in an identification parade to wear baseball hats and scarves, masking the lower half of their faces. Although the parade were masked only to a limited extent, this, coupled with the limited opportunity for the witness to have seen the suspect, amounted to insufficient evidence for the case to have continued (see, also, *D v DPP* (1998) and *Parry v DPP* (1998)).

Provision is made whereby a witness may hear any parade member speak or see them move or adopt a specific posture, but not until the witness has been asked if identification can be made on the basis of physical appearance only and, where speech is requested, reminded that the members of the parade have been chosen exclusively on the basis of physical appearance. With regard to voice identification, in *R v Gummerson and Steadman* (1998), it was held that, whilst Code D did not create a duty to consider a voice identification parade, if one were held, then, in principle, it would be admissible, although it may be helpful to note the earlier case of *R v Hersey* (1997), where some guidance on this issue was given by the Court of Appeal. In this instance, H was one of two people who robbed a shop whilst wearing balaclava helmets. During the robbery, both of them conversed extensively for a period of about 15 minutes and the shopkeeper was certain that one of them was a customer of long standing. A voice identification parade, consisting of 12 persons, including H, was arranged, during which the shopkeeper identified the voice of H, although two other witnesses failed to pick him out. An expert witness wanted to give evidence that too many voices were used on the parade, that, with one exception, they were of significantly higher pitch and that the only person on the parade who read out the required text in a manner which made sense was H. The trial judge ruled that this expert evidence was not admissible before the jury and allowed in evidence of the voice identification. In upholding this decision, the Court of Appeal held that, whilst there may be a danger of the jury placing undue weight on the parade identification, the effect of the shopkeeper's previous association with H on the subsequent identification would be obvious to them. This could be dealt with in the closing speech of defence counsel and also by the trial judge during the summing up. The court stated that the parade provided the witness with the opportunity to test his identification and this, even more importantly, gave the defendant the opportunity to be excluded in the event of an erroneous original identification. In addressing the criticism of the technical aspects of the parade, the court stated that 'the police must do the best they can in such circumstances' and added that 'a judge will undoubtedly rule out the evidence of an identification parade he considers unfair'. However, according to the court, 'There was not a great deal of authority on how a judge should direct a jury in respect of voice identification' (see, also, *R v Deenik* (1992)).

The conduct of a parade must be fully documented and recorded not only on the relevant forms, but also photographed in colour or video recorded, as mentioned above, p 185. A copy of the photograph or recording must be supplied on request and in reasonable time to the suspect or the solicitor. These must be destroyed or wiped clean if the person is not convicted of the offence or is not cautioned for it.

Paragraph 2.20 provides that if a suspect's identity is known[10] to the police and that person is immediately or will shortly be available for an identification parade, no witness should be shown any photographs, photofit, identikit or similar pictures. Under para 2.6, if a suspect agrees to an identification parade, but fails to attend, or the holding of one is impracticable or the suspect simply refuses, arrangements must be made, if possible, so as to allow witnesses an opportunity of seeing the suspect in a group identification, a video identification or a confrontation. These will be covered in turn below.

---

10 Being 'known' in this context means that the police have sufficient information to justify the arrest of a specific person for the offence (note for guidance 2E).

Group identification

This aspect of identification procedure is governed largely by Section 2 of Code D, together with Annex E, which concentrates on the conduct of group identification in which a witness views a suspect amongst an informal group of people. This may occur with the suspect's consent and co-operation, although, if a suspect has refused to co-operate with an identification parade or a group identification, which includes failing to attend, this may take place covertly. Group identification may also be arranged where the officer in charge of the criminal investigation considers that this would be more satisfactory than a parade because of, *inter alia*, fear on the part of a witness.

The suspect's consent to a group identification should be sought and the 12 points mentioned above (p 186), under paras 2.15 and 2.16, should be conveyed to the suspect accordingly. If it is practicable, the identification officer has a discretion to proceed with a group identification where consent is refused. The general conduct of this procedure is governed by Annex E, some of the main points of which are summarised as follows.

The location of a group identification should be a place where people congregate informally or generally pass through, so that the suspect can join them and be seen as part of a group. Examples given under Annex E include people leaving an escalator, persons walking through a shopping arcade, people waiting on railway stations and even the foyer of a magistrates' court.[11] In any event, it is up to the identification officer as to the choice of venue, although account must be taken of any representations made by the suspect, the appropriate adult where applicable or the suspect's solicitor or friend. Police stations should only be used for group identifications where this is necessary by virtue of safety or security reasons, or because it may be impracticable to hold them somewhere else. Where this is the case, the procedure may involve the use of screens or one way mirrors.[12] If the procedure is to be conducted covertly, then the choice of venue must, of course, include places which the suspect frequents and where sufficient numbers of other people will also be present. This will include regular travel routes used by the suspect.

Many of the safeguards applicable to identification parades are echoed in Annex E. These include details of the first description by witnesses being given to the suspect or the solicitor and reasonable opportunity for the suspect to also have a friend present, as well as the taking of a colour photograph of the procedure whilst in progress, although, in the case of group identifications, a video recording may only be made contemporaneously if this is practicable; otherwise, a colour photograph or video recording should

---

11   *R v Tiplady* (1994), cited in Zander, M, *The Police and Criminal Evidence Act 1984*, 3rd edn, 1995, London; Sweet & Maxwell.

12   *Ibid*, Zander.

be made of the general scene after the event, whether or not the suspect consents. If any photograph or video film includes the suspect, all copies must be destroyed or wiped clean if the suspect is not convicted of the offence or is not cautioned for it. There is also another modification of the general rules where a group setting is involved: this is that the identification officer does not have to be in uniform at the time. Where the suspect does not consent, covert identifications should, as far as possible, comply with the rules where consent has been given. However, such persons will automatically deny themselves the right to legal advice by virtue of being unaware of the identification procedure at the time.

Any undue impediment of the group identification procedure on the part of the suspect, such as unreasonable delays in joining the group or deliberately concealing him or herself from the view of the witnesses, shall be regarded as a refusal to co-operate. Where a person in the group is singled out by a witness and that person is not a suspect, a police officer should approach that person and request his or her name and address, although that person is under no legal obligation to provide these details.

A distinction is drawn under Annex E between moving and stationary groups. Where moving groups are concerned, one important provision is that the identification officer must tell a witness to point out the suspect and then, if practicable, arrange for that witness to take a closer look at the person indicated and ask if they can make a positive identification. Where this is not possible, the witness should be asked how sure he or she is that the person singled out is the suspect. This same procedure also applies to stationary groups, although a major distinction between this procedure and the one applicable to moving groups is that, where the suspect is in a static situation, such as in a queue, the witness should pass along or amongst the group and look at each person at least twice.

Video film identification

A witness may be shown a video film of a suspect by the identification officer where the investigating officer considers that this would be the most appropriate course of action. Factors which would influence such a decision include, *inter alia*, the suspect's refusal to participate in an identification parade or a group identification. The consent of the suspect should be sought although, where this is not given, the identification officer has the discretion to proceed with a video identification where this is practicable. Where consent has been obtained, the suspect should be informed of the 12 points mentioned above, under paras 2.15 and 2.16. The general conduct and detailed procedures governing video identification are contained under Annex B and a summary of its main features now follows.

Annex B begins by referring to video identification as a 'video parade' and goes on to provide that the overall arrangements for making and subsequent showing of a video film are the responsibility of one or more identification officers who have no direct involvement in the case. The film must include at least eight people plus the suspect and the requirements where more than one suspect is involved also follow the same provisions as those governing 'live' identification parades. Several other provisions in Annex B follow the same pattern as those applicable to identification parades as in Annex A, such as the measures designed to prevent communication between witnesses at the crucial times and avoiding 'leading' witnesses by drawing attention to any person being viewed. The important distinction is that witnesses are seeing a visual recording and not a live identification parade. Witnesses would, therefore, be unable to request that certain body postures are adopted at the time of the viewing, although para 4 under Annex B provides that all those being filmed shall, as far as possible, be in the same positions or carrying out the same activity. This seems to imply that the video recording might include the participants making certain movements where this was requested in advance. Another consequence of seeing a film, rather than participating in an identification parade, is that the witness does not have to walk along or among the participants and this is particularly beneficial where nervous witnesses are involved. Witnesses should view the film at least twice and may request as many other replays as necessary or may ask for a particular picture to be frozen. The Code of Practice emphasises that there is no limit to the number of times that the tape can be viewed in whole or part.

The suspect, a friend, the solicitor or the appropriate adult, where applicable, must be given a reasonable opportunity to see the film prior to it being shown to witnesses. If there is any reasonable objection to it, then all practicable steps should be taken to accommodate these objections. Where this is not possible, the identification officer must explain the reasons and record this on the relevant forms accordingly. The suspect's solicitor shall, where practicable, be given reasonable notice of the time and venue that a video identification is due to occur, so that a representative may attend on the suspect's behalf. If no solicitor is instructed, then the suspect must be informed, but the suspect should not be present at the showing of the video. Where the suspect's representative does not attend, the entire viewing procedure must also be recorded on video. The identification officer must, *inter alia*, preserve the overall security of the tapes and ensure that no officer involved in the investigation is allowed to see the contents of the video film before it is shown to witnesses. A video film must be destroyed where the suspect is cleared of the offence or is not officially cautioned. The suspect may witness this destruction, provided a request is made within five days of being cleared or informed that no prosecution is to take place.

The overall flexibility and other advantages of using video film in the identification of suspects seems likely to increase its usage as time progresses.

It seems highly probable that the use of video film will eventually replace other forms of identification to a large extent, as the technology becomes more widespread.[13]

Confrontation

Paragraph 2.13 provides that a suspect may be confronted by a witness if neither an identification parade, a group identification nor a video identification is arranged or is practicable. A confrontation does not require the consent of the suspect, although, in *R v Jones and Nelson* (1999), it was held that it was a breach of the relevant Code of Practice to threaten the use of force in order to effect a confrontation. If a suspect insists on this method of identification in the presence of his or her solicitor, then there is no need to hold any other form of identification procedure.[14] The provisions governing the procedures for a confrontation are to be found under Annex C to Code D, which are summarised as follows.

Most of the procedures stated under Annex C largely echo the provisions applicable to the other methods of identification mentioned above. These include the measures that have to be taken where the police release photographs or video films to the media and the suspect or the solicitor being provided with a first description given by witnesses prior to the identification taking place. However, there is no provision here which requires the suspect to be informed of the 12 points applicable to the other identification procedures covered under paras 2.15 and 2.16, above. The procedure governing the actual confrontation of a suspect by a witness is the responsibility of the identification officer and no officer may take part in the proceedings who is involved in the investigation. In *R v Ryan* (1992),[15] it was held that there had been a major breach of para 2.2 of Code D where the investigating officer accompanied a witness to a confrontation, although, in this case, the evidence was allowed in, because the interests of the defendant had been sufficiently protected by his solicitor.

A confrontation should normally take place in a police station either in an ordinary room or one equipped with a one-way screen in order to prevent witnesses being seen. Where a screen is used, either the suspect's solicitor, friend or appropriate adult must be present or the confrontation video recorded. Unless it would cause unreasonable delay, confrontation must take place in the presence of the suspect's solicitor, interpreter or friend, during which the suspect should be confronted independently by each witness, who

---

13 *Op cit*, Levenson, Fairweather and Cape, fn 9.
14 See *R v Miller* (1991), cited in *op cit*, Levenson, Fairweather and Cape, fn 9.
15 Cited in *op cit*, Zander, fn 11 and, also, *op cit*, Levenson, Fairweather, and Cape, fn 9.

shall be asked: 'Is this the person?' It has been asserted that confrontation is the least satisfactory method in identifying suspects.[16]

Fingerprinting

The issue of fingerprinting in its entirety is covered under ss 27, 61, 63A and 64 of PACE, together with Section 3 of Code D. Normally, consent is required before a person can be fingerprinted. If this is done at a police station, the consent must be in writing, whereas it can be given orally if performed elsewhere. The latter will include victims of crime, who provide their fingerprints in order that these may be eliminated from others found at the scene of the crime, although these must be destroyed once they are no longer needed. Fingerprints may be taken without consent under the circumstances discussed below and the taking of fingerprints may also include taking a palm print where appropriate.[17]

Before the police take a person's fingerprints, they have a duty to inform that person of the reasons for taking them, whether or not they are taken with consent. They must also inform the person that those prints will be destroyed as soon as practicable if that person is not prosecuted for the offence[18] or if there is a prosecution, but he or she is cleared. If an application is received from the person within five days of being cleared of the alleged offence or being informed that he or she will not be prosecuted, there will be the opportunity to witness the destruction of the fingerprints. This does not apply to fingerprints taken under the Prevention of Terrorism (Temporary Provisions) Act 1989 or the Immigration Act 1971. Once the fingerprints are destroyed, access to relevant computer data will be rendered impossible as soon as practicable[19] and the reasons for the destruction of fingerprints must be recorded as soon as possible. Whether or not consent is given, the person whose fingerprints are to be taken must be informed that those prints may be the subject of a speculative search against other fingerprints. This means that a check may be made against other fingerprints held in records to which the police have access, although this only applies to arrested suspects. Whenever a person has been informed of the possibility of a speculative search, a record shall be made accordingly. All the police duties to inform persons of the relevant rights and procedures must be given in the presence of the appropriate adult where applicable.

---

16 Lidstone, K and Palmer, C, *Bevan and Lidstone's The Investigation of Crime: A Guide to Police Powers*, 2nd edn, 1996, London: Butterworths.

17 Code D, para 3.6. See, also, *R v Tottenham Justices ex p L (A Minor)* (1985) for a definition of a palm print.

18 Unless that person admits committing the offence and is subsequently cautioned for it.

19 Code D, para 3.5. A person has the entitlement to a certificate confirming that this has been done within three months of applying.

Sections 27 and 61 of PACE provide that fingerprints may be taken without consent from anyone over the age of 10 under the circumstances listed below. Reasonable force may be used if necessary under s 117 of PACE in order to obtain fingerprints and a record must be made of the circumstances under which this occurred, including those present. Where fingerprints are taken without consent, a record must be made as soon as possible, containing the reasons, which must include any of the following:

(a) where a police superintendent or above authorises such action as a result of having reasonable grounds to suspect that the fingerprints will tend to confirm or disprove the suspect's involvement in a criminal offence;[20]

(b) where a person is detained at a police station and has either been charged or reported for a 'recordable offence'.[21] This will only apply where that person's fingerprints have not already been taken in connection with that offence;

---

20 'The offence for which the fingerprints are taken need not be the offence for which the suspect is detained ... If no fingerprints were found during the investigation, there could be no grounds for fingerprinting under this provision.' *Op cit*, Levenson, Fairweather and Cape, fn 9. They also state that the offence in question here need not necessarily be a 'recordable offence'.

21 'Recordable offences' are those offences which may be held on national police records and include all offences which can attract a term of imprisonment, whether or not this is the sentence actually passed on conviction, as well as a number of other offences which are not imprisonable. These miscellaneous offences which do not attract a prison sentence are as follows: loitering/soliciting for prostitution; improper use of public telecommunications system; tampering with motor vehicles; sending letters, etc, with intent to cause distress or anxiety; giving intoxicating liquor to child under five; exposing children under 12 to risk of burning; failing to provide for safety of children at entertainments; drunkenness in public; failing to deliver up authority to possess prohibited weapon or ammunition; possession of an assembled shotgun by unsupervised person under 15; possession of an air weapon or ammunition for an air weapon by unsupervised person under 14; possession of an air weapon in public by an unsupervised person under 17; trespassing on land during daytime in search of game; refusal by such a trespasser to provide name and address; five or more persons found armed in daytime in search of game and using violence or refusing to provide name and address; being drunk in the highway or in public; obstructing a constable or local authority officer inspecting premises for use as registered club; permitting drunkenness on licensed premises; failing to leave licensed premises when requested; allowing prostitutes to assemble on licensed premises; permitting licensed premises to be used as a brothel; allowing a constable to remain on licensed premises when on duty; supplying intoxicants or refreshments to a constable or bribing a constable; making a false statement when applying for a sex establishment license; falsely claiming a professional qualification; taking or destroying game or rabbits by night; wearing a police uniform with intent to deceive; unlawful possession of a police uniform; causing harassment, alarm or distress; failing to give notice of a public procession; failing to comply with condition imposed on a public procession; taking part in a prohibited public procession; failing to comply with a condition imposed on a public assembly; taking part in a prohibited assembly; failing to comply with directions; failing to provide a roadside specimen of breath; kerb-crawling, persistently soliciting women; in connection with sporting events; allowing alcohol to be carried on public vehicles; allowing alcohol to be drunk on such vehicles; allowing alcohol to be carried in some other vehicles; trying to enter a designated sports ground while drunk; the unauthorised drinking or supplying alcohol at a designated sports ground; and taking/riding pedal cycle without consent (English, J and Card, R, *Butterworths Police Law*, 6th edn, 1999, London: Butterworths).

(c) where a person has been convicted[22] of a recordable offence, but has not, as yet, been in police detention for that offence, nor had his or her fingerprints taken. This situation can occur where, for instance, a person has been reported for an offence away from a police station and has later attended court by way of a summons and subsequently been convicted of a recordable offence. In those circumstances, s 27 of PACE empowers the police to require that person to attend a police station in order to be fingerprinted within one month of conviction. At least seven days' notice must be given and a constable may arrest without warrant any person who fails to comply with this requirement (see Chapter 3).

Photographs

The provisions regarding the photographing of suspects are to be found under Section 4 of Code D. An arrested person detained at a police station may have their photograph taken with written consent only, unless any of the exceptions to this rule apply (see below). Where this applies, force may not be used to make a photograph. Whether or not consent is given, the suspect must be told why it is being taken and that it will be destroyed (including negatives and all copies) if he or she is prosecuted and later cleared or the person is not prosecuted, unless the offence is admitted and the person cautioned, or where the suspect has a previous conviction for a recordable offence. These provisions do not require that copies of a photograph in a police gazette be destroyed where pictures of persons wanted by the police are circulated. The reason for the destruction of any photographs must be recorded as soon as possible. The suspect must be informed of the right to witness the destruction of the photograph or be provided with a certificate confirming that this has been done if an application is made within five days of being cleared or informed that there will be no prosecution. Furthermore, the suspect must be informed that if he or she significantly alters his or her appearance between the photograph being taken and any attempt to hold an identification procedure, this may be given in evidence at any trial.

Photographs may be taken without consent under the following circumstances and the reason recorded as soon as possible:

(a) if the suspect is arrested at the same time as other people or at a time when it is likely that other people will be arrested, and a photograph is necessary, in order to ascertain who was arrested and the location and time this occurred; or

---

22 PACE, s 27(4A) extends the term 'conviction' to include the following:

    (a) a caution within the meaning of the Police Act 1997, Pt V; and

    (b) a reprimand and warning given under the Crime and Disorder Act 1998, s 65.

(b) where a person has been charged for a recordable offence or has been reported for such an offence and is in police custody, but has not been brought before a court;

(c) where a person is convicted of a recordable offence and his or her photograph is not already on record as a result of (a) or (b), above. The police have no power of arrest in order to take a person's photograph under these circumstances, but this may be done where the person is in custody as a result of the exercise of another power (para 4.2(iii) of Code D suggests that this may be done if the person has been arrested under s 27 of PACE in order to be fingerprinted); or

(d) where a police superintendent or above authorises the taking of a photograph if that officer has reasonable grounds for suspecting that the person may have been involved in a criminal offence and where there is identification evidence regarding that offence.

The actual showing of photographs to witnesses of crime must conform to the procedures under Annex D to Code D, which are summarised as follows. Whilst the actual showing of photographs may be done by a police officer of any rank or even a civilian employee within the police service, a police officer of at least the rank of sergeant must supervise and direct the showing of photographs. The first description of the suspect given by the witness must be recorded and this has to be confirmed before the photographs can be shown. If there is any doubt, the showing must be postponed. Only one witness at a time should be shown the photographs and that person must be given as much privacy as practicable; during this process, each witness shall not be allowed to communicate with any other witnesses in the case. The witness must be told that the person seen may or may not be among the photographs shown and he or she should be left to make any selection without any help; therefore, there must be no prompting or guidance. No less than 12 photographs at a time may be shown, which should all be of a similar type as far as possible, and a record of the showing must be kept, including comments made by the witness, whether or not an identification is made.

If a witness makes a positive identification from photographs (or a photofit, identikit or similar picture), then, unless the person identified has been cleared of suspicion by the police, any other witnesses involved shall not be shown the photograph or other picture. Where this occurs, all witnesses, including the one who identified the alleged suspect, should be asked to attend an identification parade or take part in group or video identification if possible, unless there is no dispute about the suspect's identification. The suspect and that person's solicitor must be informed prior to an identification parade if a witness has already been shown any pictures beforehand. Any photographs used must not be destroyed, regardless of whether or not an identification has been made, as they may be required by the court.

TAKING FORENSIC SAMPLES FROM SUSPECTS

Introduction

The taking of forensic samples from suspects is an important aspect of police duties in the detection of crime. One of the most well known is the police power under the Road Traffic Act 1988 to require a person to provide a specimen of breath, urine or blood in cases of suspected drink-driving. The power to take samples from suspects under the common law was significantly extended by PACE; as a result of amendments under the Criminal Justice and Public Order Act 1994, arising from the development of DNA profiling in particular, the legal rules regarding the taking and retention of samples are contained under the amended provisions of ss 62–65 of PACE (augmented by Section 5 of Code D). Forensic samples are either classed as intimate or non-intimate. Those which are non-intimate may be taken by force if necessary, whereas intimate samples cannot, although any refusal to provide the latter may result in the court drawing inferences which may corroborate any evidence against that person.[23]

Intimate samples

The definition of an intimate sample means blood, semen or other tissue fluid, urine, pubic hair, a dental impression and a swab taken from the body orifice except the mouth.[24] An intimate sample can only be taken from a suspect in police detention (which may include taking the sample at a hospital) where a police superintendent or above has authorised it and has reasonable grounds for suspecting that the person has been involved in a recordable offence, has reasonable grounds for believing that the sample will either confirm or disprove the suspect's involvement in that offence and that person has given the appropriate written consent.[25] The authorisation may be given orally initially (including over the telephone), but, in any event, this must be put into writing as soon as possible. Where the required consent is given, the suspect must be informed that the authorisation to take the sample has been given, together with the grounds and the nature of the offence, which must be duly

---

23 *Op cit*, Lidstone and Palmer, fn 16.

24 The exclusion of swabs and saliva samples, etc, taken from the mouths of suspects from the ambit of intimate samples was effected through the Criminal Justice and Public Order Act 1994, ss 58(2) and 59.

25 'Appropriate written consent' is defined under PACE, s 65, as:

    (a) in relation to a person who has attained the age of 17 years, the consent of that person;

    (b) in relation to a person who has not attained that age, but has attained the age of 14 years, the consent of that person and his parent or guardian;

    (c) in relation to a person who has not attained the age of 14 years, the consent of his parent or guardian.

confirmed in the custody record. The authorisation, the grounds and confirmation of the consent must be recorded as soon as practicable in the custody record after the sample has been taken. A suspect who is mentally disordered or mentally handicapped or a juvenile may request the presence of an adult of the opposite sex. Where a juvenile is concerned, unless he or she objects, an appropriate adult must be present if any clothing is removed and the appropriate adult must agree to being absent if this is requested.

Under the original s 62 of PACE, the taking of intimate samples applied only to serious arrestable offences. The downgrading to recordable offences (see above, fn 21) significantly increases the size and scope of the use of this power:

> This means that offences such as assault and most burglaries, which had previously been excluded from the power, will now be subject to it and the range of offences in which samples can be taken is equivalent to that for taking fingerprints, the difference being, at least in respect of intimate samples, that written consent must be obtained. Indeed, the objective is to create a data bank of DNA profiles of all those convicted of recordable offences, similar to that which exists for fingerprints.[26]

An intimate sample, with the appropriate authority and consent, may be taken from a person who is not in police custody, but from whom at least two non-intimate samples have been taken, but have proved insufficient. This power may be used on persons on remand, in prison or on bail, and this removes the need for the police to request an intimate sample where a non-intimate sample will be sufficient. Since they will be able to request intimate samples when the person is no longer in police detention, there is no need to request them unnecessarily as a safe measure whilst detained by the police.[27] Note for guidance 5E under Code D states that these provisions do not prevent the taking of intimate samples in order to enable persons to be eliminated from suspicion of having committed certain crimes. Where a person attends a police station voluntarily in order for this to be done, that person should be advised of the entitlement to free legal advice and the safeguards regarding the role of the appropriate adult should be observed where applicable. All samples taken from persons not suspected of a crime must usually be destroyed at the conclusion of the proceedings.

Prior to the police requesting an intimate sample, the suspect must be warned that refusal without good cause[28] may harm that person's defence. Note for guidance 5A provides that the following form of words may be used:

26 *Op cit*, Lidstone and Palmer, fn 16.

27 Wasik, M and Taylor, R, *Blackstone's Guide to the Criminal Justice and Public Order Act 1994*, 1995, London: Blackstone.

28 According to Lidstone and Palmer (*op cit*, fn 16), the term 'good cause' may include religious objections, a parent's belligerence at the prospect of having one's child treated in this manner, drunkenness or general indignation.

> You do not have to [provide this sample]/[allow this swab or impression to be taken], but I must warn you that if you refuse without good cause, your refusal may harm your case if it comes to trial.

A record of the above warning must be made after it is administered. If the suspect is in police detention and not legally represented, that person must be reminded of the entitlement to free legal advice, which should, in turn, be entered in the custody record. The suspect should also be told that any sample taken may be the subject of a speculative search and this fact must be duly recorded as soon as practicable in the custody record. Only urine samples may be obtained by the police. Dental impressions may only be obtained by dental practitioners and all other samples must be taken by medical practitioners.

Non-intimate samples

The definition of non-intimate samples includes non-pubic hair, a sample taken from a nail or under it, a swab taken from any part of the body including the mouth (but excluding any other body orifice), saliva, a footprint or any similar impression of part of a person's body, except part of the hand (because this will usually be a finger or palm print). It should be noted that dental impressions, whilst technically falling under an impression of part of a person's body, are expressly classed as intimate samples.

Non-intimate samples can be taken with or without the appropriate written consent (see fn 25, above, for what constitutes 'appropriate written consent'). Whether or not consent is given, the police should tell the suspect that the sample may be the subject of a speculative search, which must then be written in the custody record after the sample has been taken. If the appropriate consent is not given, a non-intimate sample may be taken using reasonable force if necessary.[29] This will apply where the suspect is in police detention or is being held in police custody on the authority of a court, and where an officer of the rank of superintendent or above authorises the taking of a sample without the suspect's consent. This will occur where that officer has reasonable grounds for suspecting the suspect's involvement in a recordable offence and has reasonable grounds to believe that the sample will tend to confirm or disprove his or her involvement in the offence. The authorisation may be given orally initially, but must be confirmed in writing.

A non-intimate sample may also be taken without consent, whether or not the person is in police detention or custody, if that person has been charged or reported for a recordable offence and either a non-intimate sample has not been taken during the investigation or one has been taken, but is unsuitable or

---

29 PACE, s 117. Where force is used to obtain a non-intimate sample, a record must be made of the circumstances which must also include a record of all those present.

insufficient. A non-intimate sample may also be taken without consent where a person has been convicted of a recordable offence. Where applicable, depending on whether or not such action was taken during police detention or custody, the suspect must be informed of the authorisation and the grounds or reasons for it which, in turn, should be recorded in the custody record as soon as practicable.

Any non-pubic hair required as non-intimate samples may be plucked or cut. Where it is necessary to pluck hair for DNA purposes, the suspect should be given a choice as to which part of the body it should be taken from and, normally, hairs should be removed individually, unless the suspect expresses a contrary wish. In any event, no more should be taken than the police consider to be reasonably necessary.

Any constable may require a person not in police detention or custody to attend a police station to have a non-intimate sample taken where that person has been charged or reported for a recordable offence and where either no sample was taken during the investigation or one was taken, but has proved to be unsuitable or insufficient. The same provision also applies where a person has been convicted of a recordable offence and either no sample has been taken since conviction or one was taken before or after conviction, but is insufficient or unsuitable. This requirement must be exercised within one month, where applicable, from either the date the suspect was charged or reported, or from the date of the appropriate officer[30] being informed of the unsuitability or insufficiency of the sample for analysis or from the date of conviction. The actual period of notice under which the person may be required to attend a police station for this purpose is at least seven days and anyone who fails to meet this requirement may be arrested without warrant.

It has been submitted that the above power to require the attendance of a suspect also applies to the taking of intimate samples:

> Although the procedure seems primarily to be directed at the new powers to take non-intimate samples without consent, there is nothing in the sub-section to limit it to non-intimate samples, so it would seem also that a person can be required to attend for the purposes of an intimate sample being taken under the new s 62(1A) of PACE (where two or more non-intimate samples have proved insufficient). However, this power is exercisable only if the suspect gives consent and this cannot be overridden by s 63A, but the power to require attendance may still be useful to the police, since the suspect may, in fact,

---

30 The 'appropriate officer' can have one of two meanings, depending upon which provisions apply in each case. Where a person has been either charged or reported for a recordable offence and has not had a sample taken in the course of the investigation or did have one taken, but it was insufficient or unsuitable for analysis, the appropriate officer will be the investigating officer in the case. Where a person has been convicted of a recordable offence and either a sample has not been taken since the conviction or he has had one taken before or after conviction, but the sample has proved to be unsuitable or insufficient for analysis, the appropriate officer will be the police officer in charge of the police station where the criminal investigation was conducted.

consent, either because he hopes the sample will clear him or because his refusal permits inferences to be drawn against him under s 62(10).[31]

Provisions regarding both intimate and non-intimate samples

Paragraph 5.11B of Code D provides that before an intimate or non-intimate sample is taken, the suspect must be informed of the grounds on which the relevant authority has been given and, where appropriate, the nature of the offence in question. Paragraph 5.8 states that a sample or impression must be destroyed as soon as possible where the suspect, having been prosecuted for the offence, is subsequently cleared or where the suspect is not prosecuted, unless the person admits to the offence and is cautioned.[32] The exception to this rule can be found under the amended s 64 of PACE, which provides that samples need not be destroyed if they were taken for the purpose of a criminal investigation for which someone has been convicted and from whom a sample was taken. This is augmented by note for guidance 5F, which provides that the retention of samples under this provision is designed to allow all samples in a case to be available for any later miscarriage of justice investigation. It then goes on to state that the samples and any information derived from them may not be used against any person who would otherwise be entitled to have his or her sample destroyed. In *R v Nathaniel* (1995), it was held that the police should not use a blood sample in a further criminal investigation where they failed to destroy an earlier sample and the defendant had been told that it would be destroyed if he was cleared of the offence.[33]

Proposed new power to take samples

Clause 52 of the current Criminal Justice and Court Services Bill proposes to insert new ss 63B and 63C into PACE. Once enacted, the police will be given the power to test persons in police detention for the presence of certain drugs. The main purposes behind this intended power are to assist in the monitoring of drug misuse and to provide assistance to the courts when making bail decisions. This power is initially intended to apply only to heroin, cocaine and 'crack' cocaine, although there is provision for the Home Secretary to include other controlled drugs.

---

31 *Op cit*, Wasik and Taylor, fn 27.

32 It has already been noted above that, at the conclusion of the proceedings, samples taken from non-suspects must usually be destroyed.

33 See, also, *Attorney General's Reference (No 3 of 1999)* and *R v Weir* (2000), where this principle was upheld regarding the use of illegally retained DNA samples in an endeavour to link the defendants with an earlier rape and a subsequent burglary and murder respectively.

A sample of urine or a non-intimate sample may be taken from a person in police detention in order to ascertain whether that person has any of these 'specified' Class A controlled drugs in his or her body. However, there are several conditions that must be fulfilled. The detained person must be *charged* with any of the following offences under the Theft Act 1968: theft; robbery; burglary; aggravated burglary; taking a conveyance without consent; aggravated vehicle taking; obtaining property by deception; and going equipped for stealing, or any of the following offences under the Misuse of Drugs Act 1971: the production or supply of controlled drugs; simple possession; or possession with intent to supply them. Alternatively, the detained person may be charged with another offence, but may still fall within the scope of this power. This will apply if an inspector or above has reasonable grounds for suspecting that the misuse of any of the specified Class A drugs caused or contributed to the offence, and subsequently authorises the drug test accordingly. The detained person must be at least 18 years old and will only be obliged to provide a body sample where this is requested by the police, including where an authorisation has been made by an inspector or above. A warning must then be given that a failure to provide a sample without good cause is an offence punishable on summary conviction, to a maximum of three months' imprisonment and/or a level 4 fine on the standard scale (currently £2,500).

Clause 52 also contains a proposed amendment to s 38 of PACE ('duties of custody officer after charge'). As discussed in Chapter 6, the custody officer is under a duty to release a suspect once charged, unless certain conditions are present (see above, pp 155–57). Clause 52 inserts an additional ground for detaining suspects after charge where a drug test is required, although this is restricted to a time limit of no more than six hours from the time that the charge was made.

This power is due to be piloted in three areas from the spring of 2001 for a period of two years. The Home Secretary will be empowered to change a number of these provisions, once enacted. These include extending, where necessary, the range of specified Class A drugs as mentioned above, and he may extend the drug testing provisions to persons arrested, but not charged, with a relevant offence. The Home Secretary will also be under a duty to make regulations regarding the taking of samples from detained persons, including provisions as to who may perform this procedure.

CHAPTER 8

COMPLAINTS AGAINST THE POLICE

INTRODUCTION

All the foregoing chapters have endeavoured to provide an introductory guide to the key issues affecting the exercise of police powers. Inevitably, a book of this nature tends to present the subject in a rather sanitised manner, without much reference to the stark realities of the overall environment in which such powers are exercised, both from the public, as well as the police, standpoint. However high the standards of the police service may be, there must be appropriate mechanisms of accountability at all levels in order to maintain credibility. The latter is most important, for it is upon this that the concept of policing by consent depends. One of the ways in which any modern police service in a democratic society can preserve public support is by having a fair and efficient police complaints system.

THE DEVELOPMENT OF THE COMPLAINTS SYSTEM

Prior to the enactment of the Police and Criminal Evidence Act 1984 (PACE), which significantly reformed this process, the police complaints system in this country had become the subject of increasing criticism. The earlier system inspired little public confidence because, *inter alia*, the complaints procedure was the same regardless of whether a complaint was serious or trivial, and this often wasted the time of senior police officers where the matter could be dealt with less formally. Also, there were doubts about the independence of the body responsible for investigating complaints enacted under the Police Act 1976, namely, the Police Complaints Board, especially in view of reports that investigating officers had sometimes tried to persuade complainants to withdraw their allegations.[1] Therefore, Pt IX of PACE, headed 'police complaints and discipline', contained measures which constituted an overhaul of the earlier system. One of its principle reforms was the forming of an independent Police Complaints Authority (PCA), which replaced the Police Complaints Board (see the coverage of the PCA, below, p 209).

In response to pressure for further reforms, the provisions of PACE were replaced initially by the relevant measures under the Police and Magistrates' Courts Act 1994, but are now to be found under the Police Act 1996, together

---

1   Zander, M, *The Police and Criminal Evidence Act 1984*, 3rd edn, 1995, London: Sweet & Maxwell.

with accompanying regulations. Since April 1999, a new system of police complaints and discipline has been in force, which will now be described below.

THE SCOPE OF COMPLAINTS

First, what is a complaint against the police? Section 65 of the 1996 Act defines this as a complaint by or on behalf of a member of the public about a police officer's conduct. Complaints made on behalf of a member of the public must be with the written consent of the complainant and this will probably include e-mails and other messages using the new technology.[2] Third parties acting on behalf of a complainant include law centres, Citizens Advice Bureaux, MPs, friends, associates, relatives or the person's own legal adviser. The complaints system only applies to the alleged conduct of regular (full time) police officers. Therefore, this does not apply to special constables, police cadets or civilian employees working for the police service. However, a complaint may be made where the police officer in question was off duty at the time. Complaints must apply to police officers in respect of their actions or omissions in specific events. This does not apply to matters of a more generalised or widespread nature, such as a lack of police patrols in certain areas. Such matters fall under a chief police officer's 'direction and control' regarding his or her police force. There are many routes through which this form of complaint may be made. These include letters to MPs or other public representatives, such as local councillors. Also, meetings of local groups, including neighbourhood watch committees, may provide an effective medium through which complaints of this nature may be addressed. Under s 77 of the 1996 Act, every police authority and Her Majesty's Inspectorate of Constabulary are under a duty to keep themselves informed in respect of the recording and investigation of complaints against the police; furthermore, under s 78, the Home Secretary may make regulations regarding police complaints in respect of non-Home Office police forces (for example, the British Transport Police) or voluntary agreements may be entered into between such police forces and the Home Secretary regarding the handling of complaints.

A complaint may be withdrawn at any stage, although this must be confirmed in writing by the complainant or the person acting on his or her behalf.[3] Dispensation may be sought from the PCA in order to absolve the

---

2   Sampson, F, *Blackstone's Police Manual: General Police Duties*, 2000, London: Blackstone.

3   'Approximately 40% of complaints are withdrawn and there is evidence that, while some withdrawals are justified, others result from improper pressure from the police.' Cape, E and Jawaid, L, *Defending Suspects at Police Stations: The Practitioner's Guide to Advice and Representation*, 3rd edn, 1999, London: Legal Action Group.

requirement to investigate complaints which cannot or should not be investigated. These include undue delay in the complainant making the allegations (usually, a gap of more than one year), anonymous complaints where the person cannot be contacted, repetitious complaints from the same person on a matter already dealt with and where there is no fresh evidence, or where the complaint is generally maliciously motivated or the conduct of the complainant makes an investigation impracticable.[4] It should be noted that it is not uncommon for complaints to be used as a means to 'get back' at police officers and, where false allegations have been made, the investigating officer may adopt the course of action just described. Even if the complaint is not supervised by the PCA, the investigating officer may report his or her misgivings to the relevant department within the police force concerned.

PRELIMINARY ACTION AND THE 'APPROPRIATE AUTHORITY'

Section 67 of the Police Act 1996 makes the following provisions regarding preliminary measures to be taken on receipt of a complaint. Where a complaint is submitted to a chief police officer, he or she is under a duty to obtain or preserve any evidence relating to the conduct complained of. In practice, this responsibility is usually delegated to an assistant chief constable who has been designated this task. On completion of this procedure, the chief officer then has to determine whether or not this is a matter which he or she must personally deal with or whether the complaint must be dealt with by some other person or body. Section 65 of the 1996 Act calls such persons or bodies the 'appropriate authority'. This means that if the complaint concerns a police officer in the Metropolitan Police Service, the 'appropriate authority', namely, the person to whom the complaint should be referred, will be the commissioner. In the case of complaints against 'senior officers' (these include chief constables and assistant chief constables; in other words, officers above the rank of (chief)[5] superintendent), the 'appropriate authority' in dealing with this matter will be the relevant police authority. Where a complaint is made regarding ranks from constable up to and including superintendent, the 'appropriate authority' will be the chief officer of police for that area. Where a chief officer of police determines that the matter falls within the responsibility of another such person or body, that officer must then refer the complaint to the 'appropriate authority' and inform the complainant or that person's

4   *Op cit*, Sampson, fn 2.

5   In view of the rather fluid situation regarding the rank of chief superintendent and the possible reinstatement of this substantive rank, the word 'chief' has been placed in parentheses, even though it does not accord with the precise wording of the relevant statutory provisions.

representative accordingly. Section 67 ends by stating that none of these or any of the following measures apply where the conduct complained of is wholly or partly related to criminal or disciplinary proceedings. Regulation 5 of both the Police (Conduct) Regulations 1999 and the Police (Conduct) (Senior Officers) Regulations 1999 makes provision whereby senior officers or lower ranking police officers may be suspended from duty where they do not meet the 'appropriate standard' (see below for the definition of this term). This may apply, *inter alia*, where any such officer is the subject of a complaint.

COMPLAINTS AGAINST SENIOR OFFICERS

Section 68 makes provisions where a complaint is made against a senior police officer and the matter is subsequently referred to the relevant police authority (or to the commissioner if the officer is from the Metropolis of London). Where the matter is not very serious, the police authority may deal with the complaint by the process known as 'informal resolution', which will be discussed below. This may occur where the police authority concludes that, even if proved, the conduct would not justify criminal or disciplinary proceedings being taken and therefore exercises its discretion accordingly. However, before this or any other action is taken, the matter must first be recorded. Where the complaint is more serious, the police authority should appoint a police officer of at least the rank of the officer complained of in order to investigate the allegations. The investigating officer may be from the same police force or from another police area.

COMPLAINTS AGAINST OTHER RANKS: STANDARD PROCEDURE

The standard procedure for investigating complaints is covered under s 69, which applies to all ranks up to and including (chief) superintendent. In cases where a complaint is made against a police officer within this category, the relevant chief officer of police, having first recorded the matter, should consider whether this is an appropriate case for informal resolution. If so, a police officer may then be appointed to try to resolve the matter informally. If this does not succeed, or the complaint is unsuitable for informal resolution, the chief officer must appoint a police officer from the same or another force to investigate the matter. In the case of the more serious complaints, it is usual to adopt the latter course of action. The investigating officer should report to the chief officer, unless the PCA are supervising the investigation under a reference in accordance with s 70, mentioned below, in which case the investigating officer will report to them both.

REFERENCES TO THE POLICE COMPLAINTS AUTHORITY

Any 'appropriate authority' mentioned above may either be required to refer certain complaints to the PCA or may do so of their own volition. Under s 70, an appropriate authority has a duty to refer any complaint to the PCA where death or serious injury has resulted from the alleged conduct or where the complaint is of a description specified in regulations made by the Home Secretary[6] or, where a complaint has come to the notice of the PCA, it may require this to be referred to them. An appropriate authority has the discretion to refer any complaint to the PCA, even when not required to do so. Under s 71, an appropriate authority may refer any matter to the PCA where no complaint has been forthcoming but where a police officer may have committed a criminal or disciplinary offence of sufficient gravity or under exceptional circumstances.

THE POLICE COMPLAINTS AUTHORITY

Section 66 of the 1996 Act preserves the existence of the PCA as an independent body corporate, originally instituted under PACE, and the structure, membership and funding of this body are subject to Sched 5. Members of the PCA should consist of a minimum of eight members plus a chairperson. Whilst the latter is appointed by the Queen, the other members are appointed by the Home Secretary. Members may either be on the PCA full or part time, but for no more than three years at a time and no one will be appointed if they are or have been a constable in any part of the UK. Section 79 of the 1996 Act requires the PCA to submit annual reports to the Home Secretary, who may also require them to report on any matter relating to their functions. The PCA may, in turn, report on any grave or exceptional matter that should be brought to the attention of the Home Secretary.

INFORMAL RESOLUTION

Informal resolutions are restricted under s 69(3) (and also s 68(2)) to cases where the complainant consents to it and the chief officer of police is satisfied that, even if proved, the complaint would not justify criminal or disciplinary proceedings being taken. It therefore follows that this method of dealing with complaints should not be used where the matter is under the supervision of the PCA. The rules regarding this procedure exist largely under the Police

---

6   These include complaints where the allegations involve corruption, actual bodily harm or any serious arrestable offence (see Chapter 3 for a description of the latter).

(Complaints) (Informal Resolution) Regulations 1985 and the main reason for its existence is that it avoids the need for full investigations into very minor complaints and provides a flexible and relatively quick way to resolve the matter in question. The latter can be very apparent in the case of early resolutions, where a supervisory officer of any rank can take steps to deal with a complaint virtually at the time it is made. If the officer who is the subject of the complaint is available and willing to deal with the matter in this way, he or she can render an explanation or an apology as appropriate. A satisfactory outcome may then be achieved if the complainant is willing to accept either or both. The police officer complained of is under no compulsion to make an apology, although that officer's supervisor may make a general apology or may do so on that officer's behalf if it is considered that his or her conduct justified this and that the conduct has been admitted by that officer. Where the outcome is satisfactory, the supervisor should then inform the relevant officer, who will then record the matter and write to the complainant accordingly. Provided there are no representations by the complainant, the matter may then be noted as resolved informally.

The 1985 Regulations enable the appointment of an officer to deal with an informal resolution. It is the duty of that officer to seek the views of the complainant and the officer concerned as soon as practicable, and to take any other appropriate steps in resolving the matter. This includes arranging a meeting between the complainant and the officer complained of, together with any other person, although the police officer concerned is not obliged to attend. Where an informal resolution cannot be achieved or evidence emerges in the course of this procedure indicating a more serious matter, the complaint must then be formally investigated.

COMPLAINTS SUPERVISED BY THE PCA

Under s 72 of the 1996 Act, the PCA must supervise any complaint connected with a person's death or serious injury, or any complaint specified under regulations made by the Home Secretary and any complaint referred to it under s 71 by an appropriate authority, as well as any other complaint where it is desirable in the public interest to do so. The PCA cannot act on its own volition. Any matter which the PCA deals with must stem from an appropriate authority's referral, whether it be mandatory or discretionary.

Where the investigation is supervised by the PCA, they may exercise their right to approve or disapprove the appropriate person's appointment of the investigator, or to direct the appropriate person to select another investigator if they are not satisfied with the person selected. The PCA may also require that the investigation is directed in a certain manner, although there must be some consultation between the PCA and the relevant chief officer of police with regard to the resource implications involved in an investigation.

REPORTS ON INVESTIGATIONS

If the complaint is not investigated under the supervision of the PCA, the investigating officer will work independently and compile a report at the end of the investigation to the appropriate authority. Under s 73 of the 1996 Act, where the PCA are involved, the investigating officer has a duty to submit a report to them on completion of the investigation and to send a copy to the appropriate authority. The PCA will then consider the report before them and submit an 'appropriate statement' to the appropriate authority, and also send a copy of this statement to the officer complained of and to the complainant, or his or her representative, where it is practicable to do so. The 'appropriate statement' by the PCA will include whether the investigation was conducted to the PCA's satisfaction, specifying any aspect of it which was not and any other matters which regulations made by the Home Secretary may provide for. A separate statement may be issued regarding any criminal or disciplinary aspects of the investigation, but no disciplinary proceedings may be brought until the appropriate statement is submitted to the appropriate authority and, likewise, no criminal proceedings may be brought by the appropriate authority or the Director of Public Prosecutions (DPP) until this statement has been submitted. The only exception regarding the latter is where it appears to the DPP that there are exceptional circumstances which would make it undesirable to wait for the submission of the statement.

STEPS TO BE TAKEN AFTER INVESTIGATION

Senior officers

Under s 74 of the 1996 Act, where a complaint has been investigated in the case of a senior police officer, the appropriate authority in receipt of the relevant report (if the complaint was not supervised by the PCA) or a copy of it (if it was supervised) should then send a copy to the DPP. The exception to this rule is where the appropriate authority is satisfied that no criminal offence has been committed. If this applies, or the DPP has dealt with the question of criminal proceedings, the senior officer may be subject to the Police (Conduct) (Senior Officers) Regulations 1999. This may entail being dealt with by a disciplinary tribunal and could lead to the following sanctions being taken where appropriate: dismissal from the force; requirement to resign as an alternative to dismissal; a reprimand; or no further action (notwithstanding a finding that the senior officer failed to meet the 'appropriate standard').[7]

---

7   The 'appropriate standard' refers to the standards stipulated under the Code of Conduct, which is reproduced below, p 215.

However, where there is not a hearing, even if the senior officer admits failure to reach the appropriate standard, the appropriate authority may exercise its discretion to deal with the matter other than imposing any of the aforementioned sanctions. The senior officer may appeal against any decision to the newly formed Police Appeals Tribunal under the Police Appeals Tribunals Rules 1999.

Standard procedure (non-senior officers)

Section 75 of the 1996 Act provides that, in the case of police officers complained of who rank no higher than (chief) superintendent, once an investigation has been completed and the relevant report (or copy) has been sent to the appropriate authority, if that report discloses any criminal offence, the following course of action must be adopted. The chief officer of police must send a copy of the report to the DPP. If no criminal offence is disclosed in the report, or it has been sent to the DPP who subsequently deals with the question of criminal proceedings, the chief officer of police may either take no further action or initiate disciplinary proceedings under the Police (Conduct) Regulations 1999. Whatever the decision, the chief officer must send to the PCA a memorandum, stating what disciplinary proceedings have been or are intended to be brought, or why such proceedings have not been initiated. In the case of the latter, the PCA have powers to go against the chief officer's decision. This will now be discussed below.

POWERS OF THE POLICE COMPLAINTS AUTHORITY REGARDING DISCIPLINARY PROCEEDINGS

Section 76 of the 1996 Act enables the PCA to recommend to the relevant chief officer of police that disciplinary proceedings be brought against an officer who is the subject of a memorandum as discussed above and where it was proposed that no such action be taken. If the chief officer remains unwilling to take such action, the PCA may direct that officer to bring disciplinary action and this must be complied with accordingly. Unless the direction is subsequently withdrawn, the chief officer must advise the PCA as to what action has been taken and supply them with any such information reasonably required in order to enable the discharge of their functions under s 76.

THE POLICE APPEALS TRIBUNAL

As a result of a complaint, a police officer may be subject to dismissal from the force, be required to resign or be reduced in rank. These (and other sanctions) may also apply in consequence of other misconduct where this is identified by a person within the police service or where the officer's performance of his or her duties is unsatisfactory. In either case, such sanctions are made as a result of a conduct or inefficiency hearing, followed by a review on the part of the relevant chief officer. A police officer may then appeal against any of the three specific sanctions listed above to the new Police Appeals Tribunal, which replaces the earlier system whereby police officers could appeal to the Home Secretary. This body has a slightly different composition depending upon whether the appellant is a senior officer or not. The common ground is that there must always be a legally qualified chairperson and a member of a police authority. On the conclusion of the proceedings, the Police Appeals Tribunal will either uphold the original decision or make an order which is less severe than the original decision. The rules governing the overall structure of the Police Appeals Tribunal are to be found under s 85 and Sched 6 to the 1996 Act and detailed provisions in respect of the procedures involved are contained in the Police Appeals Tribunals Rules 1999.

The essence of the new measures in dealing with not only misconduct within the police service, but also general inefficiency can be found in the Home Office News Release dated 31 March 1999, which is reproduced immediately below. This is followed by the Code of Conduct under the Police (Conduct) Regulations 1999, which exemplifies the standards expected of police officers, which, if not reached, can lead to disciplinary action being taken, whether or not a complaint is involved.

Home Office News Release (115/99, 31 March 1999)

New police discipline procedures come into force

New procedures for dealing with unsatisfactory performance or misconduct by police officers will come into effect tomorrow. These measure take forward proposals set out in the Government's response to the Home Affairs Select Committee report on police complaints and discipline last year. They also implement the Stephen Lawrence Inquiry Report's recommendation on police discipline. Key changes to modernise and reform police discipline include:

- introducing the civil standard of proof at disciplinary hearings;[8]

---

8   The civil standard of proof (based on the balance of probabilities) applies to all disciplinary offences, although the Police Complaints Authority requested the reduction from the criminal standard of proof (beyond reasonable doubt) only in minor cases. See English, J, 'The "police at the sharp end" and the investigation of complaints' (2000) 101 The Criminal Lawyer 6.

- allowing an officer acquitted in a criminal court to be disciplined for a like offence;
- a fast track procedure, with full rights of appeal, to deal swiftly with officers caught committing serious criminal offences – cases will be heard within six weeks of being identified, in advance of criminal proceedings;
- formal procedures for dealing with unsatisfactory performance – chief constables will be able to require an officer to resign where efficiency cannot be brought up to standard;
- racist language or behaviour would be a breach of the new Code of Conduct and, in many cases, would result in dismissal.

Home Secretary Jack Straw said:

> The vast majority of police officers in this country deserve our praise for their honesty, integrity and professional competence.
>
> The reputation of the Service is put at risk, however, by a very small minority of officers whose behaviour falls below the standards which the public expects. Their actions undermine the work of honest officers and shake public confidence in the service as a whole.
>
> The changes I have made to police disciplinary procedures aim to give the Service the powers they need to deal effectively with this corrosive minority of bad officers.
>
> I have also introduced, for the first time, separate formal procedures for dealing with poor performance by individual officers.
>
> Building a police service in which all sections of the community can have trust and confidence is central to policing by consent. These changes to police disciplinary procedures will contribute towards restoring this core relationship.

Other changes include:

- greater powers to hold a hearing in the absence of an accused officer, so that, where accused officers claim that they are unable, through ill health, to appear at disciplinary hearings, matters can be decided in their absence, with appropriate safeguards;
- a new system for disciplinary cases not covered by the new fast track procedure where cases will be tried by an assistant chief constable (ACC) with two superintendents – or two more ACC's if the accused is a superintendent – instead of a hearing by the chief constable or deputy chief for less serious matters;
- a two stage appeal process:
  (1) a review by the chief constable available to all officers, followed by;
  (2) an appeal to a Police Appeals Tribunal (replacing the present appellate authority, the Home Secretary), set up by the police authority for those officers who are dismissed, required to resign or have their rank reduced.

Other police disciplinary matters requiring further consideration include:

- the availability of disciplinary sanctions after retirement;
- whether legislation should be introduced to enable police pensions to be forfeited for serious disciplinary offences, in addition to the current application to criminal offences;
- ending the 'right of silence' of officers in disciplinary hearings and applying the same modified caution as laid down in the Criminal Justice and Public Order Act 1994.

SCHEDULE 1

Code of Conduct

The Police (Conduct) Regulations 1999 (SI 1999/730)

Honesty and integrity

1   It is of paramount importance that the public has faith in the honesty and integrity of police officers. Officers should therefore be open and truthful in their dealings, avoid being improperly beholden to any person or institution and discharge their duties with integrity.

Fairness and impartiality

2   Police officers have a particular responsibility to act with fairness and impartiality in all their dealings with the public and their colleagues.

Politeness and tolerance

3   Officers should treat members of the public and colleagues with courtesy and respect, avoiding abusive or deriding attitudes or behaviour. In particular, officers must avoid: favouritism of an individual or group; all forms of harassment, victimisation or unreasonable discrimination; and overbearing conduct to a colleague, particularly to one junior in rank or service.

Use of force and abuse of authority

4   Officers must never knowingly use more force than is reasonable, nor should they abuse their authority.

Performance of duties

5   Officers should be conscientious and diligent in the performance of their duties. Officers should attend work promptly when rostered for duty. If absent through sickness or injury, they should avoid activities likely to retard their return to duty.

Lawful orders

6   The police service is a disciplined body. Unless there is good and sufficient cause to do otherwise, officers must obey all lawful orders and abide by the provisions of Police Regulations. Officers should support their colleagues in the execution of their lawful duties and oppose any improper behaviour, reporting it where appropriate.

Confidentiality

7 Information which comes into the possession of the police should be treated as confidential. It should not be used for personal benefit and nor should it be divulged to other parties, except in the proper course of police duty. Similarly, officers should respect as confidential, information about force policy and operations, unless authorised to disclose it in the course of their duties.

Criminal offences

8 Officers must report any proceedings for a criminal offence taken against them. Conviction of a criminal offence may, of itself, result in further action being taken.

Property

9 Officers must exercise reasonable care to prevent loss or damage to property (excluding their own personal property, but including police property).

Sobriety

10 Whilst on duty, officers must be sober. Officers should not consume alcohol when on duty, unless specifically authorised to do so or it becomes necessary for the proper discharge of police duty.

Appearance

11 Unless on duties which dictate otherwise, officers should always be well turned out, clean and tidy whilst on duty in uniform or in plain clothes.

General conduct

12 Whether on or off duty, police officers should not behave in a way which is likely to bring discredit upon the police service.

Notes

(a) The primary duties of those who hold the office of constable are the protection of life and property, the preservation of the Queen's peace and the prevention and detection of criminal offences. To fulfil these duties, they are granted extraordinary powers; the public and the police service therefore have the right to expect the highest standards of conduct from them.

(b) This Code sets out the principles which guide police officers' conduct. It does not seek to restrict officers' discretion; rather, it aims to define the parameters of conduct within which that discretion should be exercised. However, it is important to note that any breach of the principles in this Code may result in action being taken by the organisation, which, in serious cases, could involve dismissal.

(c) This Code applies to the conduct of police officers in all ranks whilst on duty or whilst off duty if the conduct is serious enough to indicate that an officer is not fit to be a police officer. It will be applied in a reasonable and objective manner. Due regard will be paid to the degree of negligence or deliberate fault and to the nature and circumstances of an officer's conduct. Where off duty conduct is in question, this will be measured against the generally accepted standards of the day.

OTHER FORMS OF REDRESS

'Probably the strongest means of enforcement of good conduct by the police is the exclusion of improperly obtained evidence under ss 76 and 78 of PACE.'[9] Apart from this potent sanction (discussed in previous chapters), there are other ways in which misconduct by the police may be dealt with. In the more extreme cases where, for instance, property may have been damaged unnecessarily by officers during a search or where excessive or unnecessary force was used in the exercise of their powers, a criminal prosecution could ensue, especially where the damage or any injury was severe or, in the latter instance, even fatal. With regard to fatalities, it is mandatory for a coroner to empanel a jury for an inquest where a person has died as a result of injuries inflicted by the police or where a person has died in police custody. In more recent years, a small number of police officers have faced homicide charges arising from such proceedings. However, such cases are comparatively rare, and include the situation where non-fatal harm is inflicted; it is, therefore, more common for civil action to be taken against the police in appropriate cases. Whilst breaches of the provisions of PACE or the Codes of Practice do not necessarily give rise to criminal or civil liability, a breach may be relevant in other actions and taken into account by the courts.[10]

A fairly common civil action taken against the police is the tort[11] of trespass to the person, the two main forms of which are an assault and battery, and false imprisonment. An assault and battery constitutes the unlawful application of force against another person, no matter how slight. Therefore, no injury need be inflicted, although the case will attract greater damages if personal injury resulted from the conduct in question. The court will also take into account any actions by the plaintiff which may have contributed to the incident. An assault and battery would apply in instances where excessive force was used by the police in exercising their powers or where a person was unlawfully searched or detained, even if very little restraint was applied against that person. False imprisonment will apply in cases where a person has been unlawfully deprived of his or her liberty, even if this was for a short time. This does not only mean unlawful detention in a police station, but will apply if a person was unlawfully detained elsewhere. Although there is no single tort of wrongful arrest or detention, this conduct usually falls under the heading of false imprisonment and, if any measure of force was used, an assault and battery as well.

---

9   *Op cit*, Cape and Jawaid, fn 3. See, also, *R v Fennelley* (1989).

10 *Op cit*, Cape and Jawaid, fn 3.

11 Meaning a civil wrong.

The police may also be subject to an action under trespass to land where, for instance, they have entered property without lawful authority. If damage has been done to the property or anything in it, then they could also be liable for an action under trespass to goods. Other civil actions may include negligence and malicious prosecution. However, many cases are settled out of court – a common feature of the civil law process.[12]

Before departing from the issue of police misconduct, it is submitted that a very candid and realistic view of this subject can be found in the following extract from a comparatively little known publication:[13]

In its various ugly forms, violence is all too prevalent a part of the hurly burly of the police officer's daily life in some areas. Many assaults take place. Every day, police officers are injured in London. All these incidents are hurtful and unpleasant and, occasionally, some are very serious indeed, leading to grave incapacity and, tragically, even to death. Rightly, there is always public concern about these assaults; much is said, and many new initiatives are proposed, in the quest to reduce the level of violence in our society though, alas, progress seems painfully slow to those of us who have to face it daily. And when things go badly awry, on an individual or on a Force basis, and police are accused of assault or brutality, the spotlight rightly falls on us. Out of even relatively simple cases, great debates arise. Accusation and counter-accusation abound.

The actions of individual officers are probed again and again. Explanations, though they be true or false, are hoisted up to the light and penetrated and shaken, sometimes with scant regard to the fact that, at the time, the officer had not the facility of this fine hindsight and was obliged to judge things in an instant, to react immediately. But that is the way of police life, of course, and it is proper and right that there should be careful public invigilation of our use of force. And the more so since, on a number of occasions, we have been found wanting; incidents ranging from careless over-reaction and burly excess to deliberate and wicked assault have been levelled, and proved, against individual officers. All the more important, then, that we should develop our ability to remain calm and restrained, and to apply force economically and humanely.

You should regard it as a matter of personal pride to be able to arrest a violent offender, quell a breach of the peace or deal expeditiously with a disturbed or drunken man quietly, skilfully and with the minimum of fuss. Your training has just that in view and it is important that police officers should develop the expertise and maintain their physical fitness to do these things well. Your experience will show you that, as your skills improve, so your confidence grows and the chances of your receiving an injury diminish ... You should

---

12 See Harrison, J and Cragg, S, *Police Misconduct: Legal Remedies*, 3rd edn, 1995, London: Legal Action Group, for complete coverage of these issues.

13 Metropolitan Police, *The Principles of Policing and Guidance for Professional Behaviour*, 1985, London: Metropolitan Police.

strive to exhibit those attitudes, whatever the pressures and the provocation. The more often you succeed in doing this, the greater will be your resolution when next faced with violence, and the more impressive your example to other officers.

It may be appropriate at this point to briefly mention some specific offences which can be committed against the police. Two of the most well known are those of assault and obstructing police under s 89(1) and (2) of the Police Act 1996. Assault on police under sub-s (1) is triable summarily and is usually confined to cases which fall within the ambit of a common assault, although it has been known for the prosecution to downgrade rather more serious cases to this level. As noted in previous chapters,[14] it is essential that the police officer in question is acting in the execution of his or her duty for this offence to be committed, and this offence extends to persons who are assisting police officers. The maximum sentence on conviction for assault on police is six months' imprisonment and/or a fine not exceeding £5,000. The offence under sub-s (2) of wilfully obstructing police includes resisting a constable in the execution of his or her duty. Whilst resisting may involve such acts as tearing away from a police officer's hold, obstructing police may not always necessitate physical contact. It has been held that any act which makes it more difficult for the police to perform their duty can amount to obstruction. This includes providing deliberately misleading information and warning persons committing offences of approaching police officers. Persons assisting the police also fall within the ambit of these offences, which are triable summarily and punishable by a maximum of one month's imprisonment and/or a fine not exceeding £1,000.

---

14   See, eg, *Collins v Wilcock* (1984) and *D'Souza v DPP* (1992).

CHAPTER 9

POLICING AND THE HUMAN RIGHTS ACT 1998

INTRODUCTION

On 2 October 2000, the Human Rights Act 1998 comes into force. In effect, this Act incorporates the European Convention on Human Rights[1] into our own domestic law and, for the first time, will enable those rights to be directly enforceable in the courts of the UK. It is not the purpose of this chapter to provide a complete coverage of the entire issue of the Convention, nor every aspect of the 1998 Act. Instead, the possible effects of the Human Rights Act on some of the key policing issues covered in this book will be focused on. Comprehensive reading is already available on the broader aspects of the Convention and the 1998 Act, and some of these are referred to in the relevant footnotes where appropriate. It must be stressed that the contents of this chapter are largely speculative. Only time will disclose the exact path that the 1998 Act will take policing and, indeed, other criminal justice institutions into in the future. In this context, it has been rightly stated that: '... the effect of the Convention in domestic law after the Human Rights Act 1998 will depend on the inventiveness of lawyers and the attitude of the judiciary.'[2]

THE HUMAN RIGHTS ACT 1998

This statute was enacted on 9 November 1998 and its long title states that it is:

An Act to give further effect to rights and freedoms guaranteed under the European Convention on Human Rights; to make provision with respect to holders of certain judicial offices who become judges of the European Court of Human Rights and for connected purposes.

The main effects of the 1998 Act are threefold. First, when deciding cases before them, all courts and tribunals are required to take into account the Convention, as well as the decisions made by its institutions. These include the European Court of Human Rights, the European Council of Ministers and, when it existed, the European Commission on Human Rights. Secondly, our national courts should read, if at all possible, both primary and secondary

---

1   The full title is 'The European Convention on Human Rights and Fundamental Freedoms' but, for the sake of brevity, it will be referred to as 'the Convention'.

2   Wadham, J and Mountfield, H, *Blackstone's Guide to the Human Rights Act 1998*, 1999, London: Blackstone.

legislation in a manner which is compatible with the Convention. This may enable our national courts in certain instances to even override secondary legislation or binding decisions of higher courts for the purposes of protecting human rights under the Convention (although the High Court and above cannot override primary legislation but, under the 1998 Act, may notify the Government of any incompatibility with the view to the relevant statute being amended). Thirdly, public authorities are under a duty to act in accordance with the Convention and failure to do so could lead to civil action being taken against them. The mechanisms within the 1998 Act, however, fall short of creating a special constitutional court or human rights commission, although it has been stated that none of these possibilities have been completely ruled out.[3]

HUMAN RIGHTS UNDER THE CONVENTION

The Convention itself is a document formulated by the Council of Europe in the wake of the devastation caused by the Second World War and the atrocities arising from years of fascist tyranny in Europe. Its purpose then, as now, was to proclaim a series of universal human rights which militate against a repetition of those events which had caused such immeasurable suffering. Although the UK ratified the Convention in 1951, it was not until 1966 that this country allowed its own citizens to take action in appropriate cases. Originally, petitions were confined to challenges by States against other States regarding alleged violations under the Convention.

The statements of individual human rights under the Convention are contained within its 'Articles', augmented by a number of 'Protocols', which have been added since its formulation. Towards the end of 1998, no fewer than 40 States had signed the Convention and this necessitated substantial reforms of its institutions, including the European Court of Human Rights in Strasbourg, which now deals with all cases alleging violations of the Convention. Previously, an institution known as the European *Commission* of Human Rights played a major part in dealing with petitions originally made but, since November 1998, this body no longer exists for the purposes of considering the admissibility of applications made after that date. Under the new Protocol 11, this function is now being performed by sections of the European Court of Human Rights.

Schedule 1 to the 1998 Act contains the Articles and Protocols which have been adopted within UK law. Those relevant to the main policing issues covered in this book will now be discussed.

---

3   Ashcroft, P, Barrie, F, Bazell, C, Damazer, A, Powell, R, Tranter, G and Gibson, B, *Human Rights and the Courts: Bringing Justice Home*, 1999, Winchester: Waterside.

Article 2 of the European Convention on Human Rights covers the right to life and reads as follows:

1 Everyone's right to life shall be protected by law. No one shall be deprived of his life, save in the execution of a sentence of a court following his conviction of a crime for which the penalty is provided by law.

2 Deprivation of life shall not be regarded as inflicted in contravention of this article when it results from the use of force which is no more than absolutely necessary:

(a) in defence of any person from unlawful violence;

(b) in order to effect a lawful arrest or to prevent the escape of a person lawfully detained;

(c) in action lawfully taken for the purpose of quelling a riot or insurrection.

For general purposes, Art 2 should be read in conjunction with the Sixth Protocol, which is one of those Protocols adopted by the UK under the 1998 Act and which reads as follows:

Abolition of the death penalty

The death penalty shall be abolished. No one shall be condemned to such penalty or executed.

Death penalty in time of war

A State may make provision in its law for the death penalty in respect of acts committed in time of war or of imminent threat of war; such penalty shall be applied only in the instances laid down in the law and in accordance with its provisions. The State shall communicate to the Secretary General of the Council of Europe the relevant provisions of that law.

On 30 September 1998, s 36 of the Crime and Disorder Act 1998 abolished the two last remaining civilian offences which, technically at least, attracted the death penalty. These are treason and piracy with violence. However, certain offences committed under military law in times of war, such as mutiny and assisting the enemy, still attract capital punishment. The passing of these provisions under our domestic law has, *inter alia*, enabled the UK to ratify the Sixth Protocol to the Convention.

Whilst the Sixth Protocol has no direct relevance to the exercise of police powers, Art 2 to the Convention does have implications where the use of force falls into the realms of lethal force. Where, particularly, the deliberate use of lethal force is used, the European Court of Human Rights,[4] in *McCann v UK* (1995),[5] has stated that it will subject such actions to the 'most careful

---

4 Henceforward, this will be referred to simply as 'the Court'.

5 This case was featured in a well known investigatory TV programme entitled *Death on the Rock*, which was so named because its subject was the fatal shooting of three members of the Provisional IRA by soldiers from the Special Air Service in Gibraltar. By a majority of 10 to nine, the Court held that there had been a violation of Art 2.

scrutiny'. It stated earlier that the use of such force must be 'strictly proportionate' when defending any person from unlawful violence or in order to effect a lawful arrest or to prevent a lawfully detained person from escaping, or to quell a riot or insurrection (Art 2(2)(a), (b) and (c)).[6] The Court went on to say that it will consider 'not only the actions of the organs of the State who actually administer the force, but also the surrounding circumstances, including such matters as the planning and control of the actions under examination'.[7] However, in *Andronicou and Constantinou v Cyprus* (1997), it was held that there was no violation of Art 2(2) where the police had shot dead a gunman and his hostage, believing that the former was more heavily armed than he was. The Court paid particular attention to the issue of 'planning and control', which featured prominently in *McCann v UK* and concluded that the force used by the police was 'strictly proportionate' in relation to the situation, since they had employed actions which minimised the risk to both parties. The Court stated that they had good reason to believe that the gunman was heavily armed, notwithstanding that they were mistaken, although some concern was expressed regarding the deployment of machine guns in a confined area. Despite regrets expressed by the Court regarding the extent of the fire power used, the decision that there was no breach was carried by five votes to four. The term 'absolutely necessary', used in Art 2(2) in relation to the use of lethal force, is extremely important in testing whether or not such action falls under the three main exceptions mentioned above, which fall under the general description of: '... curbing violence or the control of prisoners or criminals – generally, maintaining law and order.'[8] In *Stewart v UK* (1984), a teenager was accidentally killed by a plastic baton round fired into a crowd of rioters by security forces. The Commission stated that the force used was 'strictly proportionate to the achievement of the permitted purpose' and therefore was 'absolutely necessary'; as such, Art 2 had not been violated. The Commission went on to state, *inter alia*, that due regard must be paid to all the relevant circumstances, which includes the risk to life and limb and the aim which is being pursued. The further point was made that these provisions also apply to lethal force where the actual killing was not intended.

In view of the increasing level of violence faced by the police in this country, and especially where firearms are used in the commission of crime, the police service may need to re-examine its procedures regarding the use of

---

6   Article 2(2)(a) does not apply to the defence of property (see Baker, C, *Human Rights Act 1998: A Practitioner's Guide*, 1998, London: Sweet & Maxwell).

7   When commenting on the possible effects of the Human Rights Act, Lord Lester stated: 'I have no doubt that if the *McCann* case could have been dealt with by our own courts, using the criteria of the Convention, it might well have led to a different outcome in Strasbourg' (cited in Cheney, D, Dickson, L, Fitzpatrick, J and Uglow, S, *Criminal Justice and the Human Rights Act 1998*, 1999, Bristol: Jordans.

8   *Op cit,* Wadham and Mountfield, fn 2.

firearms in particular, in order to be doubly sure that the 'planning and control' element, as stated in *McCann v UK*, is complied with, since it was this element that made the UK liable. At present, s 3 of the Criminal Law Act 1967 is relied upon, which allows the use of lethal force based on the honestly held belief of the person using it; in other words, the 'reasonableness' of such action is tested subjectively:

> The test in Art 2 is different and imposes a higher standard. The standard in the Convention is whether the use of the force was 'absolutely necessary'. On the basis of that test, the determination of whether the force used was reasonable must be objectively assessed by deciding whether the force used was disproportionate to the apparent threat that it was intended to prevent.[9]

According to one commentator, it has been suggested that: '... the application of Art 2 in *Andronicou* suggests that, even in respect of trained law enforcement officers, some indulgence should be granted to "heat of the moment" reactions, along the lines of *Palmer v R* (1971).'[10] Reference to the latter case is particularly important in view of the speech made by Lord Morris of Borth-Y-Gest, in which he said:

> If there has been an attack so that defence is reasonably necessary, it will be recognised that a person defending himself cannot weigh to a nicety the exact measure of his necessary defensive action. If a jury thought that, in a moment of unexpected anguish, a person attacked had only done what he honestly and instinctively thought was necessary, that would be most potent evidence that only reasonable defensive action had been taken.

Article 3 of the Convention may also be relevant regarding any future challenges to the legitimacy of certain police powers. Under the heading of 'Prohibition of torture', it goes on to provide: 'No one shall be subjected to torture or to inhuman or degrading treatment or punishment.' Although torture can be clearly disregarded from the ambit of police activities in this country,[11] inhuman and degrading treatment are matters closely linked with other relevant Articles under the Convention, particularly Art 5 (see below, p 227 *et seq*) and cover, *inter alia*, generally oppressive conduct. As discussed earlier in this book, there are many safeguards designed to prevent oppressive conduct and also to alleviate unnecessary embarrassment on the part of suspects and others whose liberty has been interfered with in the exercise of police powers and duties. The Codes of Practice, in their entirety, contain provisions which are designed to minimise these intrusions on the liberty of citizens, whether in the course of temporary detention (stop and search), making arrests or the detention of persons in police custody. In short, the Codes endeavour, as much as possible, to preserve the dignity of those whose personal liberties have been lawfully impeded for any of these purposes.

---

9   *Op cit*, Wadham and Mountfield, fn 2.

10 [1998] Crim LR 825.

11 See *Selmouni v France* (1999), where severe beatings in a police cell were held to amount to torture.

In *McFeeley v UK* (1980), it was held that intimate searches were not sufficiently humiliating so as to constitute a violation of Art 3 (neither was the wearing of a prison uniform) and, with reference to the searching of suspects in general, it has been stated that:

> The right to bodily integrity and, generally, the freedom against compulsory physical interference is protected by the right to privacy in Art 8, as well as the guarantees against degrading and inhuman treatment under Art 3 ... There is a need for a balance to be drawn between physical interference with the person by State agents for legitimate purposes, such as the gathering of evidence or prevention of crime, and the individual's interest in preserving bodily integrity. *In England, that balance is present in the legislation and probably conforms to Convention requirements.*[12]

With regard to the exercise of police stop and search powers, para 3.1 of Code of Practice A makes the point that: 'Every reasonable effort must be made to reduce to the minimum the embarrassment that a person being searched may experience.' There then follows a series of provisions, already discussed in previous chapters, which are designed to achieve this end and to avoid unnecessary inconvenience and antagonism. The latter is exemplified under notes for guidance 1F and 1G to Code A, regarding the authorisations applicable to stop and search in order to prevent serious violence and acts of terrorism. In both instances, authorising officers are urged to set the minimum time and geographical parameters in order to avoid the mistrust of the police by the community as a whole (note for guidance 1AA). PACE itself makes its own contribution to preventing treatment that may be construed as degrading by placing restrictions on the extent of removal of any clothing in public. Section 2 confines this to no more than the removal of an outer coat, jacket or gloves. The avoidance of degrading treatment is also implicit in s 30(1)(b) of PACE, which provides that an arrested person should be taken to a police station as soon as practicable after an arrest, although appearing in handcuffs in public would not constitute degrading treatment.[13] Code B also contains safeguards which, it is submitted, should fall within the minimum requirements laid down by the Convention. Note for guidance 5A, for instance, advises officers in charge of any police search operation to avoid disturbing the occupants of premises to be searched, unless to do otherwise would frustrate its purpose.

Code C contains an abundance of safeguards against inhuman and degrading treatment, some of which overlap with the provisions under Art 5 to the Convention. For instance, the requirement under para 1.1, which states that all persons held in police custody must be dealt with and released without delay. Code C also provides that detained persons are entitled to

---

12   *Op cit,* Cheney *et al,* fn 7 (emphasis added)
13   *Op cit,* Cheney *et al,* fn 7.

adequate food and drink, toilet and washing facilities, clothing and, where necessary, medical attention, as well as exercise where possible. Police cells must meet certain minimum standards of physical comfort and this includes the provision of bedding, which must also be of a reasonable standard. There is also the right not to be held incommunicado, unless the criminal investigation or persons involved could be endangered were contact to be made with persons outside the police station. In any event, this only applies to serious arrestable offences.

The many provisions under Codes C and D designed to protect special groups have also been discussed in previous chapters. The avoidance of inhuman or degrading treatment being inflicted on particularly vulnerable persons, such as those who are mentally disordered or handicapped, is made very positively under the relevant Codes of Practice. This includes provision for the appropriate adult in cases where such persons are detained by the police, which also extends to other vulnerable suspects, including juveniles.

Article 5 of the Convention, headed 'Right to liberty and security', reads as follows:

1   Everyone has the right to liberty and security of person. No one shall be deprived of his liberty, save in the following cases and in accordance with a procedure prescribed by law:

(a) the lawful detention of a person after conviction by a competent court;

(b) the lawful arrest or detention of a person for non-compliance with the lawful order of a court or in order to secure the fulfilment of any obligation prescribed by law;

(c) the lawful arrest or detention of a person effected for the purpose of bringing him before the competent legal authority on reasonable suspicion of having committed an offence or when it is reasonably considered necessary to prevent his committing an offence or fleeing after having done so;

(d) the detention of a minor by lawful order for the purpose of educational supervision or his lawful detention for the purpose of bringing him before the competent legal authority;

(e) the lawful detention of persons for the prevention of the spreading of infectious diseases, of persons of unsound mind, alcoholics or drug addicts or vagrants;

(f) the lawful arrest or detention of a person to prevent his effecting an unauthorised entry into the country or of a person against whom action is being taken with a view to deportation or extradition.

2   Everyone who is arrested shall be informed promptly, in a language which he understands, of the reasons for his arrest and of any charge against him.

3   Everyone arrested or detained in accordance with the provisions of para 1(c) of this Article shall be brought promptly before a judge or other officer authorised by law to exercise judicial power and shall be entitled to trial within reasonable time or to release pending trial. Release may be conditioned by guarantees to appear for trial.

4   Everyone who is deprived of his liberty by arrest or detention shall be entitled to take proceedings by which the lawfulness of his detention shall be decided speedily by a court and his release ordered if the detention is not lawful.

5   Everyone who has been the victim of arrest or detention in contravention of the provisions of this Article shall have an enforceable right to compensation.

Arrest procedures under PACE and other statutes appear to comply with Art 5, since they usually require reasonable suspicion, but the position is less certain in respect of the common law power to arrest for a breach of the peace. In *Steel v UK* (1998), it was held that, whilst the definition of a breach of the peace did not contravene Art 5, an arrest for this purpose may violate it if the arrest is disproportionate to the anticipated risk and affects an individual's right to freedom of expression under Art 10 (see, also, *McLeod v UK* (1997), below).

Some concern has been expressed regarding the issue of police stop and search powers, which involve the temporary detention of suspects. It has been suggested that this form of temporary detention may fall within the ambit of Art 5(1)(b), where detention is permitted: '... in order to secure the fulfilment of any obligation prescribed by law.'[14] However, further concern has been expressed as to whether s 60 of the Criminal Justice and Public Order Act 1994 (see Chapter 2) will comply with Art 5, although this argument is based on the interpretation of Art 5(1)(c), which makes the essential requirement for reasonable suspicion.[15] The relevance of Art 3 to police powers of stop and search with regard to the conduct of such procedures has already been noted above.

With regard to Art 6, its relevance to the exercise of police powers (the right to a fair trial) is largely confined to Art 6(3)(b) and (c),[16] which provides that everyone charged with a criminal offence has the right 'to have adequate time and facilities for the preparation of his defence' and 'to defend himself in person or through legal assistance of his own choosing or, if he has not sufficient means to pay for legal assistance, to be given it free when the interests of justice so require'. As discussed earlier in this book, there are many safeguards which are designed to ensure adequate provision for legal representation at police stations. A potential difficulty may lie in justifying the grounds under which this can be delayed against the decision in *Bonzi v Switzerland* (1978), where it was stated that access to legal advice is an essential part of a person's defence.

---

14   *Op cit*, Cheney *et al*, fn 7.

15   *Op cit*, Ashcroft *et al*, fn 3.

16   Although Art 6(2) may be used to challenge the modification of the right to silence under the Criminal Justice and Public Order Act 1994, due to the wording: 'Everyone charged with a criminal offence shall be presumed innocent until proved guilty according to law.'

Article 8 covers the right to respect for private and family life and states that:

1   Everyone has the right to respect for his private and family life, his home and his correspondence.

2   There shall be no interference by a public authority with the exercise of this right, except such as is in accordance with the law and is necessary in a democratic society in the interests of national security, public safety or the economic well being of the country, for the prevention of disorder or crime, for the protection of health or morals or for the protection of the rights and freedoms of others.

Whilst it has been stated that 'in England, the power to search premises under Pt II of PACE 1984 probably conforms to Convention requirements',[17] further opinion offers the following caveat in relation to search warrants:

... an obvious case where this Article may affect the work of magistrates is in relation to applications for search warrants. The relevant UK law (principally contained in the PACE 1984) contains safeguards that should comply with Art 8. However, magistrates will need to continue to be meticulous when dealing with such applications. If valid reasons do not exist or are not properly recorded, challenges under the Convention might be hard to defend.[18]

In Chapter 3, *McLeod v UK* was discussed, where the Court held that Art 8 had been violated where police officers entered the applicant's home without reasonable grounds to apprehend a breach of the peace. Other police activities may also be subject to challenge under Art 8. As discussed in Chapter 4, Pt III of the Police Act 1997 governs the procedures to be adopted regarding covert surveillance operations. Such activities could be challenged on the grounds that judicial scrutiny does not always occur prior to such action. As noted in Chapter 4 (see fn 23), the case of *Khan v UK* (1999) was heard before the full Court, alleging infringements of Arts 6, 8 and 13. Also, whilst the safeguards involving the interception of mail and telephone tapping under the Interception of Communications Act 1985 were held to be adequate[19] in *Huvig v France* (1990) and *Kruslin v France* (1990), violations against Art 8 were held to have occurred due to a number of procedural deficiencies, which constituted insufficient safeguards against possible abuse. These included failure to set a time limit on the tapping operation or to specify the offence likely to justify such action, or to specify any measures regarding the destruction of the recordings.

At the conclusion of Chapter 4, mention was made of the Regulation of Investigatory Powers Act 2000, which expands the scope of the interception of

---

17   *Op cit*, Cheney *et al*, fn 7.
18   *Op cit*, Ashcroft *et al*, fn 3.
19   See *Christie v UK* (1994).

communications. Among other caveats, one commentator had this to say regarding the Act in relation to the Human Rights Act 1998:

> Since the definition of intrusive surveillance confines it to covert surveillance of residential premises or private vehicles, the Bill is likely to fall foul of Art 8, since the ECHR has, in a number of cases, extended the notion of private life beyond the home. Furthermore, wiring up an informant or undercover officer to obtain information from a suspect in their own home is treated as directed surveillance, requiring only internal authorisation, which, again, may well not satisfy Convention requirements.[20]

CONCLUSION

The Human Rights Act 1998 promises much challenge and controversy throughout the entire panoply of the criminal justice system, and it is hoped that the reforms likely to occur in the wake of its implementation will significantly improve our quality of justice. As far as the police are concerned, any changes in their powers and duties must be commensurate with this aim, and it is hoped that future reforms will assist in maintaining their credibility in order to preserve the cherished concept of policing by consent. Whatever changes are in store for them, it is very important that these amount to positive and constructive measures, without constituting unnecessary obstacles in their increasingly difficult task in society. But, as always, much depends not only on new rules in dealing with suspects or other persons dealt with by the police, but, equally, on the manner in which individual police officers exercise their powers and duties in the future. The tasks ahead of them will be challenging indeed.

---

20 Cape, E, 'Regulating police surveillance' (2000) 150 NLJ 452.

BIBLIOGRAPHY

Archbold's Criminal Pleadings, Evidence and Practice, London: Sweet & Maxwell

Ashcroft, P, Barrie, F, Bazell, C, Damazer, A, Powell, R, Tranter, G and Gibson, B, *Human Rights and the Courts: Bringing Justice Home*, 1999, Winchester: Waterside

Baker, C, *Human Rights Act 1998: A Practitioner's Guide*, 1998, London: Sweet & Maxwell

Barron, T, *The Special Constable's Manual*, 1997, London: Police Review

Blackstone's Criminal Practice, London: Blackstone

Bradley, A and Ewing, K, *Constitutional and Administrative Law*, 12th edn, 1997, London: Longman

Bucknell, P and Ghodse, H, *Bucknell and Ghodse on Misuse of Drugs*, 3rd edn, 1996, London: Sweet & Maxwell

Cape, E and Jawaid, L, *Defending Suspects at Police Stations: The Practitioner's Guide to Advice and Representation*, 3rd edn, 1999, London: Legal Action Group

Cape, E, 'Regulating police surveillance' (2000) 150 NLJ 452

Card, R and Ward, R, *The Crime and Disorder Act 1998: A Practitioner's Guide*, 1998, Bristol: Jordans

Card, R and Ward, R, *The Criminal Justice and Public Order Act 1994*, 1994, Bristol: Jordans

Card, R and Ward, R, *The Criminal Procedure and Investigations Act 1996*, 1996, Bristol: Jordans

Cheney, D, Dickson, L, Fitzpatrick, J and Uglow, S, *Criminal Justice and the Human Rights Act 1998*, 1999, Bristol: Jordans

De Smith, S and Brazier, R, *Constitutional and Administrative Law*, 7th edn, 1994, London: Penguin

Dicey, A, *An Introduction to the Study of the Law of the Constitution*, 10th edn, 1959, London: Macmillan

Emsley, C, *The English Police: A Political and Social History*, 2nd edn, 1996, London: Longman

English, J and Card, R, *Butterworths Police Law*, 6th edn, 1999, London: Butterworths

English, J, 'The "police at the sharp end" and the investigation of complaints' (2000) 101 The Criminal Lawyer 6

Fortson, R, *The Law on the Misuse of Drugs and Drug Trafficking Offences*, 3rd edn, 1996, London: Sweet & Maxwell

Gill, M and Mawby, R, *A Special Constable: A Study of the Police Reserve*, 1990, Aldershot: Avebury

Hoggett, B, *Mental Health Law*, 4th edn, 1996, London: Sweet & Maxwell

Home Office, Police and Criminal Evidence Act 1984 (s 60(1)(a) and s 66): Codes of Practice, rev edn, 1999, London: Stationery Office

Hood-Phillips, O, *Constitutional and Administrative Law*, 7th edn, 1987, London: Sweet & Maxwell

Hutton, G and Johnston, D, *Blackstone's Police Manual: Evidence and Procedure*, 2000, London: Blackstone

Jason-Lloyd, L, 'Changes in the police service' (1994) LXVII(2) Police Journal 105, April–June

Jason-Lloyd, L, 'Changes to Code A of the Police and Criminal Evidence Act 1984' (1997) 161 JP 715

Jason-Lloyd, L, 'Section 24(2) of the Police and Criminal Evidence Act 1984 – codification or complication?' (1999) 163 JP 944

Jason-Lloyd, L, 'Some recent changes in police powers and their effect on road users' (1997) 2 Road Traffic Indicator 1, 27 May

Jason-Lloyd, L, 'The Confiscation of Alcohol (Young Persons) Act 1997 – an overview' (1997) 161 JP 871

Jason-Lloyd, L, 'The Confiscation of Alcohol (Young Persons) Act 1997: implications for the police service' (1997) LXX(4) Police Journal 287, October–December

Jason-Lloyd, L, 'The Offensive Weapons Act 1996 – an overview' (1996) 160 JP 931

Jason-Lloyd, L, 'The Prevention of Terrorism (Additional Powers) Act 1996 – a commentary' (1996) 160 JP 503

Jason-Lloyd, L, 'Who should have power to police the police?' (1993) *The Times*, 24 August

Jason-Lloyd, L, *Drugs, Addiction and the Law*, 5th edn, 1999, Cambridgeshire: Elm

Jason-Lloyd, L, *The Crime and Disorder Act 1998: A Concise Guide*, 2nd edn, 1999, Cambridgeshire: Elm

Jason-Lloyd, L, *The Criminal Justice and Public Order Act 1994: A Basic Guide for Practitioners*, 1996, London: Frank Cass

Jason-Lloyd, L, *The Law on Money-Laundering: Statutes and Commentary*, 1997, London: Frank Cass

Leng, R and Taylor, R, *Blackstone's Guide to the Criminal Procedure and Investigations Act 1996*, 1996, London: Blackstone

Leng, R, Taylor, R and Wasik, M, *Blackstone's Guide to the Crime and Disorder Act 1998*, 1998, London: Blackstone

Levenson, H, Fairweather, F and Cape, E, *Police Powers: A Practitioner's Guide*, 3rd edn, 1996, London: Legal Action Group

Lidstone, K and Palmer, C, *Bevan and Lidstone's The Investigation of Crime: A Guide to Police Powers*, 2nd edn, 1996, London: Butterworths

Metropolitan Police, *The Principles of Policing and Guidance for Professional Behaviour*, 1985, London: Metropolitan Police

Molan, M, *Constitutional Law: The Machinery of Government*, 1997, London: Old Bailey

New Scotland Yard, *The Metropolitan Special Constabulary: An Illustrated History from 1831 to Today*, 1981, London: New Scotland Yard

Sampson, F, *Blackstone's Police Manual: General Police Duties*, 2000, London: Blackstone

Stannard, J, 'The store detective's dilemma' (1994) 58 JCL 393, November

Stone, R, *Entry, Search and Seizure: A Guide to Civil and Criminal Powers of Entry*, 3rd edn, 1997, London: Sweet & Maxwell

Wadham, J and Mountfield, H, *Blackstone's Guide to the Human Rights Act 1998*, 1999, London: Blackstone

Wasik, M and Taylor, R, *Blackstone's Guide to the Criminal Justice and Public Order Act 1994*, 1995, London: Blackstone

Zander, M, *The Police and Criminal Evidence Act 1984*, 3rd edn, 1995, London: Sweet & Maxwell

INDEX